A HISTORY OF
WORKING
WATERCRAFT
OF THE WESTERN WORLD
SECOND EDITON

Thomas C. Gillmer

  INTERNATIONAL MARINE
CAMDEN, MAINE

Published by International Marine ®

10 9 8 7 6 5 4 3 2 1

Library of Congress Cataloging-in-Publication Data
Gillmer, Thomas Charles, 1911-
        Working Watercraft / Thomas C. Gillmer. — 2nd ed.
                p.   cm.
        Includes bibliographical references and index.
        ISBN 0-07-023616-X
        1. Work boats.   I. Title
     VM378.G55 1994   94-3847
     623.8'2026—dc20   CIP

Questions regarding the content of this book should be addressed to:
International Marine
P.O. Box 220
Camden, ME 04843

Questions regarding the ordering of this book should be addressed to:
TAB Books
A Division of McGraw-Hill, Inc.
Blue Ridge Summit, PA 17294
1-800-233-1128

A History of Working Watercraft of the Western World is printed on acid-free paper.

Printed by Arcata Graphics, Fairfield, PA
Design by Ann Aspell
Production and page layout by Janet Robbins
Edited by James R. Babb, Sydne S. Matus, Tom McCarthy

Cover photos: Thera ship, S. Marinatos; Oseberg ship, Universitetets Oldsaksamling, Oslo

To Themistocles, who in the fifth century BC, for better or worse, made possible the Western World as we know it.

The Thera ship.

CONTENTS

ACKNOWLEDGMENTS, *Second Edition*

The individuals and organizations to which I expressed my gratitude in the first and more limited edition of this maritime survey still remain a basic source of the study. In this revised and enlarged edition, a number of additional people have provided invaluable help, so I will add some names to those previously acknowledged. But first I would like to add a significant name that was improperly omitted from the first edition because of haste and misunderstanding. In Chapter Two of that book, the most finely drafted studies of the native Danish boats that sail among the islands and in the Oresund were drawn by Christian Neilsen, Naval Architect, of Elsinor, Denmark. I sincerely apologize for this omission.

In this new collection we have been able to include for the first time a number of vessels of which we now have new or improved photographs. For boats of England particularly, I am deeply indebted for the help of my long-time friend, Alec Tilley, of Hampshire, England. Alec is a most remarkable and talented nautical researcher, formerly of the Royal Navy and a diver on many significant underwater wrecks, including the early uncovering of the famous *Mary Rose*, King Henry VIII's great warship. We have traveled together, Alec and I, to many nautical symposiums and shared many happy discussions and boating times.

I am equally grateful to another old friend, the great marine artist Bill Gilkerson. It does not matter what maritime subject one writes about, whether archaeological, naval-historical, or small craft, Bill's art will fill spots that nothing else can. His work in Chapters One and Four of this edition has never before been shown or published. And as only Bill can, he's shown those ancient people moving about as naturally as in an old photo. This is also true of his rendering of the Greek trireme of only 2,500 years ago.

This new edition has many other contributors, also friends, particularly Dick Steffy, the singular expert on reassembly of ancient shipwrecks. Dick is a many-talented man—a model builder of exceptional skill whose first approach to the reassembly of a raised ship's separate pieces of blackened, atrophied wood is to construct a model. He is a meticulous marine draftsman. But more importantly, he is a scholar dedicated to the advancement of maritime knowledge that has been buried for millennia. I am proud to be his friend. He is largely responsible for the re-creation of the Kyrenia ship of the fourth century BC shown in Chapter Four. Furthermore, I must express my gratitude to Michael Katzev. He was the underwater archaeologist who discovered the Kyrenia ship and supervised the recovery. He was responsible for the construction of *Kyrenia II,* the ancient ship's replica, from the designs drawn by Richard Steffy. Michael provided the excellent photographs of *Kyrenia II* under sail. Looking at these photographs gives one a comfortable and warm feeling of togetherness with the ancient sailors and shipbuilders of antiquity. They were not strange and different people, and their articulation in building a wooden sailing vessel is close to ours, in many ways superior.

Tom Price's willingness and understanding in interpreting the ideas and mental images associated with boats of the past are invaluable. I wish I had more of his drawings, but he can evoke ships of the old Norse warriors, or in this case, the Norman ships under Duke William, better than many pages of description. And then he can shift back two thousand years and illustrate a Phoenician boat dragged up on an Iberian beach for repair.

I could go on thanking other helpful friends, but space is limited, so I must resort merely to citing them by name. And these are also in addition to those named in the first edition. There are Dr. Ole Crumlin Pedersen of the Roskilde Viking Ship Museum, and Arne Emil Christensen, senior curator, Institute for Archaeology, Universitetets Oldsaksamling, Oslo.

The late Spiridon Marinatos, inspector general of antiquities of Greece, archaeologist and discoverer of the lost city of Thera on Santorini, where the ancient Minoan fresco was found, kindly provided some of the first photographs of the fresco and those remarkable ships. Owen Wicksteed of Durham, England, and scholar of Scandinavian craft, gave me the photographs of the Hardangar faerings and their drawings. David Goddard, director of the Exeter Maritime Museum, provided photographs of both the Yorkshire coble and the saveiro of Portugal. Den Phillips of Essex contributed her remarkable photography of the Colchester smack, Thames spritsail barges, and the bawley. Iver Franzen, friend, draftsman, and sailor, not only drafted the profile of the Thames spritsail barge but provided the photos of the hauled-out Bahama sloops from Nassau.

Organizations were most helpful: first, the Chesapeake Bay Maritime Museum, and its curator, Pete Lesher; the Burke Museum of the University of Washington; the Museu de Marinha, of Lisbon, Portugal, and director Pedro da Gomes Lopes.

And I remain most grateful to those who helped and were noted in the acknowledgments of the first edition.

ACKNOWLEDGMENTS, *First Edition*

The preparation and writing of this survey of present-day indigenous Western boats was a most pleasant occupation. I do not really remember when it began and it is difficult to say when it ended. Along the way, there were many people and friends whose interest and help were greatly used and appreciated. For example, there is my friend Nicolas Kenyeres, a boat-builder in Barcelona, Spain, who lent his valuable time to indulge my interest in Catalonian boats by transporting me up the coast to the Costa Brava. He stopped at every little cove and fishing harbor to inspect the boats with me and interpret the fishermen's remarks. There are international experts, such as Dr. Henning Henningsen at the fine museum of Elsinor, Denmark, who has allowed the use of his line drawings of indigenous Danish craft. There was Elmer Collemer of Camden, Maine, a master boatbuilder who acquainted me with the better features of lobsterboats nearly twenty years ago. And long before that, when I was what is now called a teenager, there was my old friend and sailor George Woodside, from Prince Edward Island. He built my first boat and it was a lovely, clinker-built sailing skiff of fourteen feet, which he built by eye and instinct. There were others, many of whom helped me over the years past. I originally wanted to supply all the illustrations myself, and with the sketches and drawings, except as noted above, I have. Perhaps less than half of the photographs are mine, but there are many others that are more rare and of a quality that I could not match. These are credited individually in the back of the book. To all of these individuals who lent me photographs, many of whom are close friends and share my interest in and fascination with boats, I wish to extend my sincere thanks for their help.

In addition to these friends, I am much beholden to a number of cooperative institutions who have made their photograph collections available.

These are:

    Field Museum of Natural History, Chicago
    Norwegian Boat Export Board, Oslo
    Science Museum, London
    Universitetets Oldsaksamling, Oslo
    National Fisherman, Rockland, Maine
    Bibliothèque et Musée, Marseilles

Finally, the Peabody Museum of Salem and the *American Neptune* editors are especially to be thanked for their permission to use the sketches from Antoine Roux's original sketchbooks as well as the pen and ink sketches by myself that were originally published in 1941 in Vol. I, No. 4, and Vol. II, No. 1, of the *American Neptune* in the article "Present-Day Craft and Rigs of the Mediterranean" by Lieut. (jg) T. C. Gillmer, U.S. Navy.

PREFACE

It is not my purpose to describe all of the individual types of working boats in the Western world—that would be impossible. This book admittedly discusses and illustrates only a selection from widely dispersed localities. The selection is my own, and there may well be many readers searching with some disappointment for favorite boats of their own. It may be said that I have included a disproportionate number of Chesapeake Bay types—and I will counter that, more than any other similar-size body of water in the world, the Chesapeake Bay area has been a microcosm of working boat evolution.

Nevertheless, the boats discussed on the following pages all seem to me to have a heritage of a kind, a background of development that is relevant to some common denominator of seacraft from the beginning. It is for this reason that Chapter One is devoted to the earliest knowledge of Western watercraft and the development of ancient construction techniques that are still alive.

Since the first publication of *Working Watercraft* in 1972, many developments have greatly added to the body of historical maritime knowledge. Technical improvements in scuba diving gear and increased diving experience have enhanced the capabilities of underwater archaeologists. The archaeologists can reach deeper into the realm of dark sea bottom that heretofore had been a secure vault of the unknown. At this writing, George Bass and his associates are recovering a ship and its treasure that sank in the eastern Mediterranean during the Bronze Age. This was in a time before Hercules was conceived, and before Ulysses sailed for Troy.

The shipbuilding techniques of classic Greece had not been discovered when *Working Watercraft* was first written. The ancient Kyrenia wreck of 450 BC had not been patiently reassembled. With this work came knowledge of the shipbuilding assembly sequence, which was confirmed by the discovery of other ancient wrecks over time. These ancient builders of wooden ships and boats did not first build the frame on the keel; they began by planking the exterior shell. This system continued for three millennia, perhaps more. It has never been abandoned by builders in the Near East or the

Muslims along the shores of the Indian Ocean. Their great sailing dhows are still built that ancient way.

But is this knowledge of great importance? It is to the students of history of discovery and geopolitics of the Western world.

The size of a wooden vessel is limited in any type of construction, but to build it shell first restricts the size even more. Not until the beginning of the sixteenth century—the Age of Discovery, with its need of vessels with greater seakeeping ability—was there a great motivation for larger, stronger ships. Only with a pre-erected frame—and better, a uniformly predetermined frame—could a ship be built to cruise the world's oceans. Thus did new ships begin to grow after Columbus's first great voyage, which began a new period of commerce, exploration, and exploitation by western Europe. To have continued to build the smaller, poorly framed vessels would have slowed and distorted the history of the world as we know it now.

There have been other nautical developments since my first book on working watercraft. Before the 1970s there was little knowledge of the old Norse watercraft. There were but two or three examples of restored ships from the era of the Vikings—dating from about one millennium past. There were essentially only two large exhumed wooden Viking ships: the beautifully exhibited and well-known Oseberg ship, with its handsome carved and scrolled ends, and its neighbor, the Gokstad ship, also in the Norwegian Ship Museum in Oslo. Nearly all of our knowledge of the appearance and size of Viking ships was based on these two watercraft. Yet we knew that they were not typical of everyday Norse trading vessels. One was a personal yacht for a Viking queen unsuitable for going beyond a beautiful Norwegian fjord. The other was the burial ship of a Viking chieftain—a ship type most suited for the much publicized activities of plunder and invasion.

Since then, *five* old Norse ships have been found and reassembled in a Danish fjord near Roskilde. These vessels are of different types—for fishing, for trading, for traveling and colonization. These five ships are working watercraft, and they put an entirely new slant on northern European history. We present these ships now among others in Chapter One.

The chapters summarizing Western watercraft have been progressively reordered. Their content has been augmented, rewritten, and expanded.

While the original message is retained, it is revealed to be a larger truth. A strong thread runs through our maritime growth, where the older methods and configurations can still be seen in existing craft, but it is receding and becoming frayed. Some of the then-existing craft I wrote about only twenty years ago are now gone. Nearly all the working watercraft I viewed and photographed in southern Europe and the Mediterranean little more than a half century ago are gone.

This narrative is a record of vanishing and vanished watercraft. These working wooden boats are links to the history of civilization.

THOMAS GILLMER
Annapolis, 1994

SIGNPOSTS
TOWARD THE ORIGINS

O<small>N</small> A VOLCANIC ISLAND in the Eastern Mediterranean, where it turns to the north forming a unique archipelago, there was a sea captain's old house, one among many. This house, at the Captain's wish, had been decorated with many paintings, all images of his remembrances and his relationship to this special environment. There were paintings of the island's flora and fauna, some imaginative, but mostly identifiable in their stylized beautiful arrangement and color. Among these paintings were two of young fishermen each exhibiting a handsome catch of fish, one with two strings of fish and the other with one. The single string of fish was clearly three rather large mackerel. The other young man had two strings of slightly smaller fish, identifiable without trouble as *Coryphaena hippurus*, about a dozen altogether. The color of the skin of these two naked youths indicates they had spent much time in the sun. There was a room painted with variously decorated shipboard enclosures of the Captain's location on the afterdeck. There were further scenes of waterfront villages and landscapes, but the unique and most beautiful scene of all the paintings was a procession of seven large ships, moving together toward the harbor from left to right among leaping dolphins. The quays and harborside buildings are crowded with people, some standing near the water's edge, others on rooftops and in windows, all gazing toward the approaching flotilla.

This remarkable and detailed painting is part of a surrounding frieze that was a border on the upper walls of one of the rooms, possibly the owner Captain's favorite room. These paintings are actually frescoes, painted with prepared pigments on wet plaster, an ancient technique used first by the Egyptians in their early dynastic paintings. It was used by the Minoans and the Greeks, used during the Italian Renaissance by the great artist Michelangelo and others, and is still used today. It requires of the artist much patience, skill, and practice.

That this old fresco-decorated house on the volcanic island in the ancient

Aegean Sea still exists is remarkable. Although it was totally enveloped by ash and pumice fallout from the volcano's cataclysmic eruption sometime around the year 1700 BC, the frescoes described survived, many in fragments painstakingly pieced together after discovery.

But the most remarkable thing about the fresco is that this procession of ships is the only known graphic evidence of the ships and seacraft of the Minoan era. This is difficult to accept about a sea kingdom whose people were sophisticated, talented, and culturally advanced—the leaders of the earliest civilized outpost of a new culture, later to become known as Western.

That period is now identified as being in the Bronze Age. The Minoans, who take their name from the god-king Minos, were the inhabitants of that island kingdom. The kingdom was centered on the large island of Crete in a capital called Knossos, whose king's palace was a few miles south of the present city of Heraklion. There is archaeological evidence that the Minoans inhabited the islands (including Crete) to the north, now called the Cyclades, and to the east, called the Dodecanese. The maritime empire was held together by naval strength, which most likely developed over centuries to control piracy and marauding among the islands.

Sir Arthur Evans, British archaeologist and discoverer of the Minoan palace at Knossos, uncovered many artworks and frescoes there, but none of watercraft. Further archaeological digs at Crete and other island searches disclosed nothing but the most vague and simply decorated jewelry and primitive graffiti with ship motifs. So it is with monocular vision that we view the fresco from the West House at ancient Akrotiri on the island of Thera to refine our conclusion concerning the configuration of Minoan ships.

First, do we know how old these ship representations are? We know only that they were found among the volcanic debris that geologists have determined to have fallen some years before the mid-second millennia—about 1700 BC. The frescoes may well have been in a precataclysmic house or may have been painted as much as several hundred years earlier. Examining them closely, we find them to have many similar features, in both configuration and detail, to more accurately dated Egyptian paintings and relief decorations. These comparable Nile vessels are dated between the twelfth and seventeenth dynasties, or about 1800 to 1600 BC.

This whole question of related comparability requires more competent archaeological study. For now, we conclude that while the Minoan vessels exhibit fundamental Egyptian likenesses, there are also uniquely Minoan features. It is safe to say that these vessels are their own kind but with old roots in the East.

The ship shown here is seen in the original fresco and as archaeologically and graphically restored. The original frescoes, which include the ship procession, are presently in the National Museum in Athens. On the wall beside my desk is a full-size color photograph of the most-intact and least-damaged ship in the fresco (Figure 1-2). It is a remarkable piece of exquisite marine art.

Figure 1-1. Thera ship at quay, circa 1700 BC. (William Gilkerson)

This ship, it is worth repeating, *is the earliest known true image of seagoing watercraft in our Western world*. It predates the Norse ships of the pre-Viking era by at least two thousand years. It predates Greek triremes of Themistocles by a thousand or more years. It predates any archaeologically recovered ship from the Mediterranean by nearly a thousand years. An archaeological exploration and recovery of a Bronze Age ship is presently in process off the coast of southern Turkey. This ongoing recovery has so far yielded the knowledge that the wooden hull, of which there is little remaining, *had a keel*—the center structural beam that did not exist in any contemporary Egyptian ships. Nor is a keel evident in any of the many details visible in the Thera fresco ship.

However, the fresco shows us other things. The ships have a dominant mast and sail, a single mast with a sail spread between upper and lower yards. The vessels are of a fundamental double-ended shape with rising sterns and bows of long overhang. However, the stern of these ships rises more quickly than the bow. The bow of the Thera ships reaches forward and tapers into some undistinguishable decorations. The decorations

are obviously temporary for the processional occasion and have therefore been eliminated in the line drawings for reconstruction clarification.

The stern is of the old and primitive curved-up spoonlike shape. This basic hull form is still found in boats of primitive people—on the Caspian Sea, on African rivers, and on the Bay of Bengal in the boats called oruwas. But that is a migration to the East. *Les Marins, vois-tu, ne ressemblent pas au reste du monde.*

The well-studied intact ship of the Thera fresco has the following most-agreed-upon dimensions:

LOA *(overall length)*	24 meters (78'9")
LWL *(length on waterline)*	16.2 meters (53'6")
Draft of water	1.0 meters (3'3")
Beam *(extreme)*	5.0 meters (16'5")
Displacement	24 tons

These dimensions may produce the impression that this vessel has been examined and measured precisely. Such, of course, is not the case. The dimensions have been taken from a recon-

Figure 1-2. A section from the original fresco, excavated in Akrotiri, Santorini, 1973, circa 1700 BC. (S. Marinatos).

struction design based on the fresco illustrations. The model design had been developed over a period of a dozen years or so during which time it had been discussed by nautical historians, presented for criticism in journals of nautical history both in Europe and America, and finally presented twice in Greece in Symposia on Ship Construction in Antiquity. The reconstructed design has been received favorably in all instances; the occasional spirited attacks have been openly defeated in oral and written discourse.

The design and the model from the design are shown in the accompanying illustrations. Figure 1-5 shows the model with the strange appendage on the stern in position as a landing platform against a beach with a normal five-degree slope. This stern structure, which the fresco shows on all but one of the seven ships, has been the object of much debate and speculation. It has been identi-

fied as everything from a hydrodynamic assist board, a centerboard for sailing to windward, to the captain's head. It seems to serve a very ordinary and sensible purpose as a gangway platform for boarding and disembarking. There are other devices on the Minoan ship that are strange to today's sailors, but we should remember that these people were very early sailors without two and a half millennia of accumulated knowledge.

The vessels in the fresco with their sails furled (some with the masts stowed) are being propelled by the paddlers along their gunwales. Since there are forty-two of them, the paddlers are obviously along for the short haul—just long enough for the parade or the celebration. Some learned archaeologists who specialize in ancient Aegean cultures propose that the occasion was an annual nautical festival that celebrated the new season. One of these noted authorities, Dr. Lyvia Morgan of Cambridge University, says such a renewal ceremony is a unifying theme among all the people of Thera, the sailors, fishermen, shepherds, rural and urban dwellers. It may well be; all of them are represented in the total frieze that included the ship procession. It is the most believable of the many interpretations advanced. However, archaeologists, by the very nature of their discipline, are confined to the activities of land-bound inhabitants. They do not understand well the workings of a ship or the ways of the sea, except for the very few experienced nautical archaeologists such as George Bass and his followers. Dr. Spiridon Marinatos, the great archaeologist and director general of Greek antiquities, who discovered the buried ruins at Akrotiri that contained these now treasured Thera fresco paintings, recognized his lack of nautical expertise. He contacted several naval architects, including myself, to assist in interpreting the ship fresco.

Thus, in her recent book, *The Miniature Wall Paintings of Thera*, Dr. Morgan is overcautious when speculating on the dimensions of the Thera ships. She consulted a random selection of ship experts in particular reference to the ratio of length to beam. In her notes she says: "Gillmer (1975) conjectures that the breadth would be 7.1m (based on a 28m overall length). On a papyrus of the Middle Kingdom, the only survivor of a shipwreck recorded he had gone to sea in a ship 120 cubits in length and 40 cubits in breadth." This note continued with other arbitrary rules of thumb applied over the millennia to ratios of length to beam.

The length dimension given here is a compromise. First it was considered 28 meters, based on the crew of paddlers, "allowing for a minimum of work-

Figure 1-3. The Thera ship at sea, circa 1700 BC, a reconstruction in watercolor. (William Gilkerson)

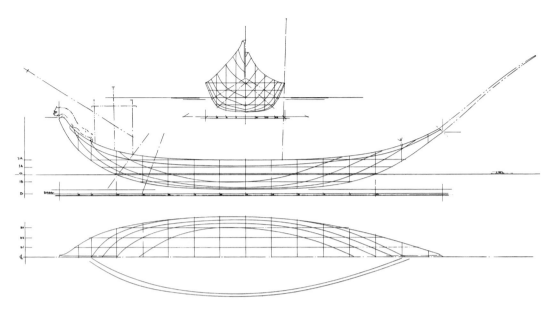

Figure 1-4. Lines draft of Thera ship.

ing space between each of the 21 men along one side." This was later modified, narrowing the distance between each man in consideration of the slightly smaller stature of humans in 1700 BC, their crowded appearance, and the temporary nature of their employment.

More importantly, the dimensions, including the hull depth and draft, sail area, etc., are based also on the scaled dimensions of the fresco image and the presumption that the boat's image as painted was accurate. The only unseen dimension is the beam, and it is an extrapolation of naval architectural acceptability.

This leaves only the presumption of the artist's ability to paint what he sees. That the artist was able to paint *accurately* what he saw is well established, not only by the ship fresco but by the multitude of other objects that our modern eyes recognize as still common in today's world. The two fishermen frescoes have readily recognizable species of fish in their catch, the leaping dolphins are identifiable as two different species, the flora are common botanical kinds, and the houses on the shoreline in the long ship's processional scene are of the same geometrical and architectural form as those Theran houses discovered buried under the volcanic ash. So why should we doubt that the fresco artist could and would also paint the watercraft as well as he painted the rest?

The oldest known seacraft as described above is a starting point for our study. We can proceed from these vessels of the Aegean Sea 3,500 years ago, when keels were something of a new idea, as were other contrivances, some to be discarded and some to be retained and perhaps improved.

Figure 1-5. A model of the Thera ship in silhouette.

As the urge persisted to discover more about their realm and the horizons beyond, the ancient mariners worked with their vessels' abilities and inabilities. I believe that the Minoans' boats could sail to windward to an extent, and that improving this ability had to be an important goal. A sailor cannot be content with a poorly performing boat. The desire to reach that farthest point of land to windward is strong enough to urge continuous refinement.

And as we examine the development of the ancient boat we must consider a few more examples from other places. We need not do this chronologically. It would be better to observe the varied maritime communities in the West that came of age, so to speak, at different times, developing their own concepts of watercraft for different uses and different environments.

NORSE SEACRAFT AND NORTHERN EUROPEAN INFLUENCE

The Norse people, for example, who were later to become the finest of seafarers, were still using frame-skin boats when the Greeks dominated the eastern Mediterranean in their great triremes. Many well-built wooden-hull merchant vessels were sailing in the early first millennium BC in ever-expanding trade, some establishing empire outposts as far west as the shores of modern Portugal.

The archaeological record shows that the boatbuilding skills of the Norse people rapidly improved. The remains of a boat found in Bjorke, Sweden, dated about AD 100, show a hull nicely planked in wood above an adzed-out log keel. It was but 24 feet long and propelled by paddles. In 1863, a peat bog in Schleswig called Nydam yielded a boat that was also obviously Scandinavian and dated at about AD 300. This boat was planked in a more sophisticated way, clinker-built and fully framed with oak. It was 75 feet long, 11 feet wide, and fitted for thirty oars. The Norse culture was then rapidly overtaking that of the languishing Mediterraneans, but Norse builders had yet to discover the techniques of handling sail and the value (and a local source) of hand-wrought iron. The Nydam boat shows in her construction an embryonic keel, which is merely a heavier bottom center plank with a heavy exterior channel.[1] But on a later boat found at Kvalsund, Norway, in 1920, dated at about AD 600, there is a distinct external, vertical

[1] It was recently verified that the Bronze Age boat (page 3) has a keel much the same—a heavier bottom plank lying flat.

keel. This boat is about 60 feet long and 10½ feet wide. It has the deeper, rounded sections with upswept ends of a boat intended for use offshore. Strangely, no mast was yet in evidence, but then it was still only AD 600 and the Norwegians were not yet inspired to travel far beyond their fjord-pierced coast, where there was always good shelter and a friendly anchorage, and the wind was light, variable, and unreliable.

But again, a boat of only two centuries later was found in Oseberg, Norway, south of Oslo. It is a formidable and beautiful example of architectural achievement. While much of Europe lay dormant in the shroud of feudalism, the Scandinavians advanced the technology of boatbuilding as far as, or farther than any culture. Judging from this Oseberg example, their boats were superbly structured with the best materials for building wooden boats to be found in any age. While the Norse boats were open, their hull configurations and sophisticated structures by the end of the first millennium AD compare favorably with any wood boat that could be built today for the function.

Figure 1-6. An unrestored fragment of the Thera fresco showing the stern platform and captain's enclosure with lion decoration. (S. Marinatos)

Figure 1-7. The Oseberg ship was restored after it was recovered from a Viking burial mound. Buried around 900 AD, this ship is a superb example of ship-building skill. (Universitetets Oldsaksamling, Oslo)

The Oseberg boat, shown in Figure 1-7, while a superb example of boatbuilding, was not itself intended for use as either a seagoing warcraft or a trading vessel. The elaborate decorative treatment of the craft together with the burial treasure it contained indicate that it was the ceremonial pleasure boat or royal yacht of the queen who has been identified with the remains. Such a boat was called a karv.

A more rugged and plainer Viking boat of the same period or a little later has been found nearby on a farm named Gokstad. This boat, which measures 76½ feet in length and 17 feet in beam, was well able to cruise offshore and move safely in a seaway. With greater freeboard, and more heavily framed with sixteen lapped and riveted oak planks per side, the Gokstad "ship" represents the

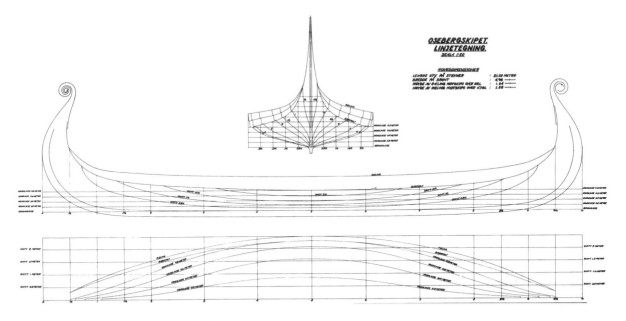

Figure 1-8. Lines draft of Oseberg ship.
(Universitetets Oldsaksamling, Oslo)

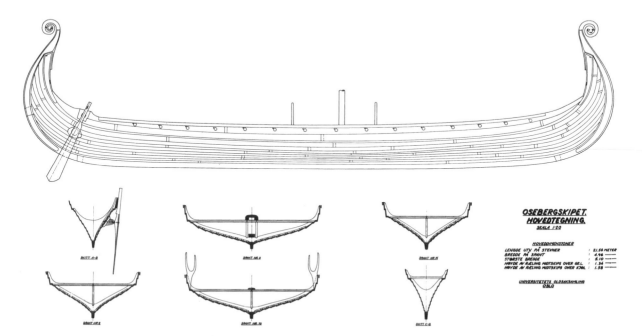

Figure 1-9. Outboard profile, Oseberg ship.
(Universitetets Oldsaksamling, Oslo)

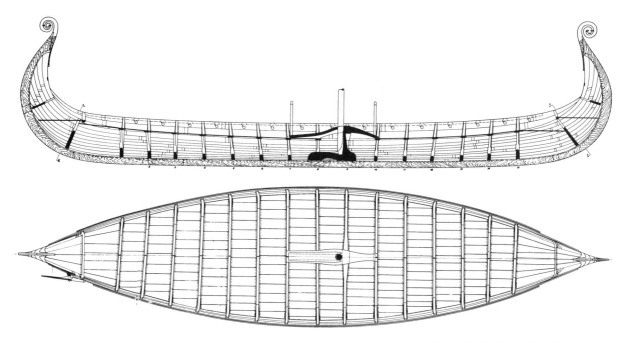

Figure 1-10. Inboard profile, Oseberg ship. (Universitetets Oldsaksamling, Oslo)

Figure 1-11. Interior, Oseberg ship (before final restoration). (Christensen)

Figure 1-12. The Gokstad ship, a Viking vessel for
sea voyages and conquest. Such boats as this were used
by the Norsemen who fought in England, Ireland,
Iceland, and elsewhere. The Norse colonists followed
later in smaller, beamier, and humbler boats. (Christensen)

best example of the early Norse seacraft. (See
Figure 1-12.)

Both the Oseberg and Gokstad boats show
the same building techniques. One such basic
technique is that used to join the frames and
planking, a method of sound engineering practice. The early Scandinavian builders seem to
have been acquainted with the need for an independent strength in the skin of their boats, unlike
the southern builders with their carvel-planked
boats. The boats of these Vikings have strong,
natural-grown frames, but throughout their curvature they are separated from the planking by
projecting integral cleats on the inner surface of
the planks that are lashed to the frames by
rawhide thongs in a secure but flexible system
(Figure 1-15). The overlapping edges of the
planking are through-riveted in the same manner
that present-day clinker-built boats are fastened
with closely spaced rivets. Such construction pro-

Figure 1-13. Interior, Gokstad ship, partially restored. (Christensen)

vides a relatively light hull with great longitudinal strength in the skin, which is firmly held in shape by a complete inner frame. Thus, with a continuous, single-piece external keel scarfed to the stem and stern posts, the hull structure of the Norse boats provided the strongest of craft with a strength-to-weight ratio that can seldom be exceeded today with any material or building technique.

While the Oseberg and Gokstad boats are clearly excellent examples of Viking construction, they are typical of only two vessels of limited employment. The Norse countries were near totally maritime-oriented. Their peoples traveled by boat in both the low country of Denmark with its many waterways, the archipelagos of Sweden, and the Norwegian fjords. The lack of roads and land trails kept Scandinavians isolated and very independent. But they had their waterborne commerce, their traveling ships, and others large and small, some similar to the Norwegian finds, some different.

From 1957 to 1962 the Danish National Museum salvaged *five* Viking ships from the bottom of Roskilde Fjord. Fishermen from the nearby harbor of Skuldelev knew that a sanded-up channel contained ships' timbers. An old legend held that Queen Margrethe, a medieval Danish ruler, had ordered five ships filled with stone and sunk across the channel to prevent attacks on the cathedral town of Roskilde by enemies from the north. Excavators organized by the Danish government began to raise these ancient Norse ship timbers in July 1957.

In the next half-dozen years the archaeologists, headed by the most capable and talented Dr. Ole Crumlin-Pedersen, had uncovered and cate-

Figure 1-14. This small Norse craft was also found in the Gokstad grave. It is a better example of the simpler boats used by the people, the fishermen, and the itinerant traders. This boat is less than 30 feet long, and her construction is the same as today's small open boats and skiffs of western Norway.

gorized five ships, each of different size and type, dating from the period of AD 1000. The ships themselves were much disassembled, having deteriorated for one millennium under the shallow water and been ravaged by souvenir hunters and fishing boats' propeller blades, among other factors. They have been, in the meantime, reassembled to differing extents of completeness, identified by type, and placed on exhibit in a new and handsome museum in the town of Roskilde.

The most interesting of the five vessels is simply labeled "No. 3." It is the most nearly complete (about 75 percent) reassembly of all and is a handsome small trading vessel or traveling ship (see Figure 1-16). The ship measures 13.8 meters (45 feet) long, 3.4 meters (11.2 feet) in beam, and about 1.3 meters (4.26) in depth from the top of gunwale to the lower edge of keel. This would make her, according to rule, 3.5 register tons—a small vessel.

The other four vessels were quite different from one another: either wider, longer, fuller,

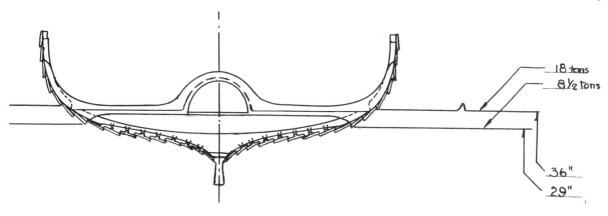

Figure 1-15. A midship's structural section of the ancient Gokstad ship discloses a most sophisticated design for strength and flexibility. The upper frame, which is molded into the sides by the integral knees on the thwartship beam, forms the crossbar of the inverted A-frame system. The lower portion of the frame, which is very carefully and skillfully fitted to the keel without the use of floor timbers, is attached with rawhide lashings to the bottom planks at their internally carved cleats. As in today's clinker-built boats, planks are fastened at their overlapped edges with copper rivets.

smaller, or all of these. Yet none was as shapely and attractive or capable of better performance under sail than Number 3. Nevertheless, they represent an excellent cross section of the shipping activity and style of a thousand years ago. The vessels found, restored when possible, and categorized are:

Wreck 1, a knorr, 16.3 × 4.5 meters, a large, full vessel for transporting cargo, livestock, etc., dated AD 1010

Wreck 2, a longship, 29.0 × 3.5 meters, a long and narrow vessel built for speed, maneuverable for rowing and sailing, dated AD 910

Wreck 3, as described above, a traveling ship, 13.8 × 3.4 meters, dated AD 1030

Wreck 4, beyond restoration.

Wreck 5, a small warship, 17.4 × 2.6 meters, dated AD 960

Wreck 6, a fishing boat, 11.6 × 2.5 meters, nicely shaped, dated AD 920

All dates given above are approximate to one hundred years, plus or minus fifty.

Wrecks numbered 1 and 3 are perhaps the most significant. According to Dr. Crumlin-Pederson, Number 1 is a vessel of the kind that carried Erik the Red and his party to Greenland. Number 3 is, if slightly enlarged, the boat that would have carried Erik's son, Leif the Lucky, on to the shores of North America in about AD 1000.

The old Norse rowing boat or skiff structure, evident in the several small boats discovered with the Gokstad ship, is remarkably similar to the present Norwegian skiffs. This is further discussed in Chapter Three. Figure 1-14 shows one of these graceful little boats, which has three lapped planks on each side, cant frames of natural crooks in the ends, and three intermediate frames. The center frame forms a shallow inverted A. This planking and framing system is identical to that of the skiffs still built in Norway (and nowhere else). The oar tholes or "kabes" on

the rail are of the same single-crook pattern also used today, but are more nicely carved and finished. Curiously, these small, ancient skiffs are fitted with proper little steering oars with tillers on the starboard side like their larger sisters.

These Norse relics, when compared with other craft, give us a very true and clear picture of the development of modern boat structures in northern Europe and much of northeastern United States and Canada. The lapstrake hull, with its light but strong system of framing, can be found in boatbuilding throughout the entire Anglo-Saxon culture. Lapstrake or "clinker-built" boats (as they came to be called) are found on the beaches and in the harbors of New England, Nova Scotia, Ireland, Scotland, England, and most of the northern European countries. Such construction allows a natural boat to form by laying one plank over the edge of the adjacent

Figure 1-16. Norse ship (Number 3), from Roskilde Fjord, Denmark. (Dr. Ole Crumlin-Pedersen)

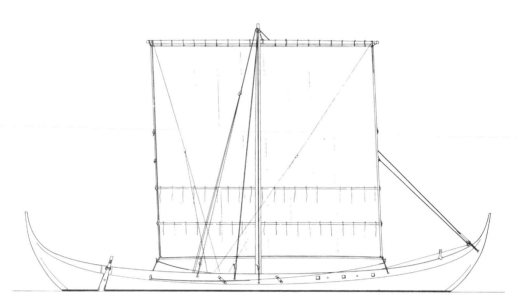

Figure 1-17. Norse Viking traveling ship, profile and sail plan from restoration of Ship Number 3.

Figure 1-18. A Yorkshire coble, a boat built by the methods used and introduced by the Norsemen more than twelve centuries ago. The vast majority of the smaller beach craft of the British Isles and northern Europe are still of this same clinker (lapstrake) construction invented by the early Norsemen. (Hull Museums)

lower one. This makes a double thickness at the plank edges that is the equivalent of a longitudinal stringer, which results in a total structure of longitudinals that needs only light, steam-bent frames to reinforce the internal form. In boats of such a nature, deck beams or continuous decks are often not necessary for added rigidity.

This ingenious system has some minor drawbacks. The exterior of the hull is one of longitudinal ridges and crevices that produce unnecessary hydrodynamic drag. Such boats, unless expertly built, tend to be a bit leaky and are difficult to caulk. Finally, in a clinker-built boat it is very difficult to repair a broken plank or a localized problem.

Compared with other methods, lapstrake construction is a relatively new boatbuilding approach. The far older method, which in the dim reaches of early civilizations improved on the primitive dug-out log, is the smooth-planked carvel hull. This method, as far as can be ascertained, was first used by the early Egyptians.

THE ANCIENT
SHELL-FIRST STRUCTURES

Sparse archaeological finds indicate that boats were becoming more refined sometime in the first or second dynasty before the Old Kingdom, approximately between 3000 and 2700 BC. They were obviously more than shaped bundles of papyrus reeds or built-up log canoe-type craft. At this time, men had acquired considerable skill in the use of metal tools. The Bronze Age was yet to come, but in Egyptian tombs of this time there have been found such tools as adzes, chisels, awls, and saw blades, all of pure hardened copper. Cedar wood was imported from Lebanon, rope was made of flax and long fibrous halfa grass, and sails were (on the better boats) of linen (flax). There is no reason why boats could not have been made of wood planks at this time. But there are no clear examples—either drawings, models, or relics—that give many clues about the structures or configurations of boats of this period and before.

Egyptologists have recently discovered a completely preserved boat that was built a little later, but still 4,600 years ago. This craft, which has been identified as the Boat of Cheops, was taken from a boat grave near the great Pyramid of Cheops in 1955. It has been painstakingly reassembled and placed on exhibit in a special hall near the pyramid. Admirers of boats are indebted to Mr. Bjorn Landstrom, Swedish boat historian and artist, for his superb description and illustrations of this ancient and beautifully built vessel in his splendid book, *Ships of the Pharaohs*.

The Boat of Cheops can serve fairly well as the original model for the emerging techniques that were to lead to the well-known methods of wood boatbuilding that would be used almost universally. This original boat lacks only a few of the basic ingredients. The cross section shown in Figure 1-19 is the elemental structural section. The boat has no keel, of course, but has three broad, heavy bottom planks. Rising from this flat

bottom with considerable flare on each side, nearly like the sides of a giant dory, are four side planks fastened edge to edge. The deck structure is supported by heavy, flat deck beams, closely spaced, which are let into holes in the upper or sheer plank. On the centerline directly under the deck beams is the early Egyptian substitute for the keel. It is a long, continuous wood girder set on edge and notched to allow the deck beams to cross over flush, and it provides longitudinal support. This girder ends just short of the bow and the stern, and is about the length of the waterline. It is supported at regular intervals by columnlike stanchions resting on transverse foundation members. This type of transverse member might be called a frame, but it does not, in my opinion, serve the same function as the conventional transverse boat frame. The Egyptian builders had something else in mind when they fitted this stretcher-foundation to the bottom and part way up the side. It is a supporting base more akin to that member in modern boats called a floor timber. It actually, and I believe

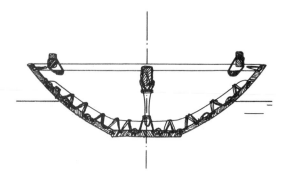

Figure 1-19. This middle structural section reveals the methods and thinking of Egyptian boatbuilders of four and one half millennia ago. This midsection of Pharaoh Cheops's boat of 2680 BC is not based on speculation. The actual boat is intact today, having been removed from a sealed tomb near the Great Pyramid of Cheops in 1955. It has been restored to its original shape.

intentionally, makes together with the vertical stanchions and the center deck girder a complete, longitudinal centerline truss. The Egyptians' knowledge and understanding of engineering were the most advanced of any civilization's for two thousand years, until the Romans borrowed and built from it.

The basic Egyptian methodology in boat construction was to use heavy, thick planking, keyed or mortised together. With heavier bottom strakes, the whole form was strengthened and held in shape by the truss system, either external, internal, or both. This complex truss system, as is evident in the reassembled Cheops boat, was absolutely necessary in the absence of the keel and transverse (or longitudinal) framing. (This boat is 138 feet long, almost 19 feet in beam, and about 12 feet in depth of hold. It would displace about 40 tons.)

Figure 1-20. *This is another existing boat of ancient Egypt, dated about 2000 BC. This boat was discovered in a boat grave with several others near Sesostris's pyramid in 1893. Notice the notched sheer plank that allows the deck beams to protrude, an Egyptian practice that later persisted for three thousand years of European boatbuilding.*

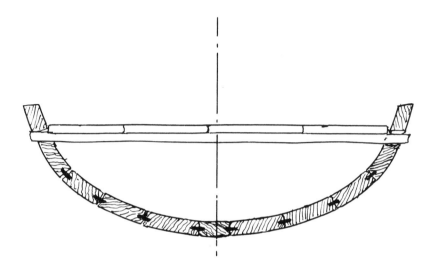

Figure 1-21. *This midsection of the Sesostris boat shows the absence of structural frames and keel. Such a boat, with heavy, hewn planks edge-fastened with tenons and keys, is structurally adequate without frames if the length is not great. This boat is about 31 feet long and 8 feet in beam. Its construction, as that of the Cheops boat, is the origin of today's carvel planking system.*

In smaller Egyptian craft (30 to 32 feet in length), of which three examples from a later dynasty exist today, there are no frames nor is there any truss system for longitudinal support. (See Figure 1-20.) The planking is joined together by "butterfly"-type keys (still used in wood joinery by Asian craftsmen). The planking is thick and so well joined by scarfs and keys that, together with deck beams, it holds the hull's shape with reasonable integrity. (See Figure 1-21.)

It is safe to say, in light of the Cheops discovery and others, that the Egyptians did *not* use transverse frames or keels until the second millennium BC. They were able, however, to build long, planked boats that held their shape, at least for a time, with considerable strength. However, the Egyptian boats needed keels and frames for serious voyages in the Mediterranean Sea, the Red Sea, or the Indian Ocean—the real seas. Their truss construction was good engineering theory, but the fastenings were not dependable. The fastenings in the Cheops boat were bindings of rope fiber or heavy twine laced through holes in the adjacent wood members. With stress and moisture, such connections become tired and move and loosen. Boats such as these long, arched Egyptian river craft surely must have been short-lived when they ventured out on the Mediterranean.

Evidence of further attempts to control the slack in Egyptian boats built a few hundred years after the Cheops boat is apparent. For example, a different truss system was used in the seagoing ships of King Sahure in 2500 BC. Reliefs on this king's tomb clearly show a row of vertical centerline stanchions supporting a long hawser-bridge attached at each end of the boat to a girdle round the bow and at the stern. The stanchions provided a much deeper web and undoubtedly rested on the framelike floors in the bottom. The hawser-bridge truss above the deck was equipped with a tourniquet rod thrust through the strands of the twisted hawser for periodic tension applications. This antihogging truss arrangement was

to continue in Egyptian vessels for at least ten dynasties, while the internal heavy deck girder under the deck beams also continued in use. It was not until well into the eighteenth dynasty (about 1500 BC) that any evidence of a keel was to be seen in Egyptian boats.

Figure 1-22. Mortise-and-tenon system of edge fastening of ancient boat planking. This system dates from at least 1500 BC in Aegean ships. It was the successful base for shell-first construction and minimum interior framing.

The use of a keel—a remarkable and fundamental milestone in the construction of boats—was probably not an Egyptian development. The Kingdom of Ancient Egypt had prospered and dominated all other civilizations for well over two thousand years, but her boats at the end of the Middle Kingdom (1800 BC) were not only stagnant in design but suffering some retrogression. The sea was no longer an unchallenged extension of the pharaoh's empire. Newer and more aggressive sea peoples living among the Aegean islands began in the early second millennium BC to roam the entire eastern Mediterranean and probe deeply into the western Mediterranean and doubtless beyond. While there is only the evidence discussed earlier of the structure of boats of the Minoans, their extensive sea trade and the home environment of their islands suggest that the boats they used must have been lighter and inherently stronger in structure than those of the Egyptians.

In retrospect, the early Egyptian boats were a most progressive step forward into a fundamental technology. The Egyptians were the first to build up a wood shell of planks into a true and often magnificent boat. Though the direction they took was the most logical to get away from the dugout log, these early boatbuilders of the Nile were always tied to the hollow-log boatbuilding syndrome. All of their boats for nearly two thousand years, basically frameless and keelless, were massively planked. These planks, really

Figure 1-23. Interior of model showing shell-first construction. When planking is completed at least to waterline level, partial floor frames are placed.

loglike timbers, were assembled and keyed together with mortises, tenons, and lashings, and then shaped and fashioned. There is the evidence of old reliefs showing the ancient builders working with adzes, literally sculpting a boat. Such reliefs may possibly be artistic impressions or they may be true renditions. Nevertheless, the ancient boats of Egypt progressed from bundles of reeds and simple hollowed logs to comparatively large vessels of planked bottoms and sides that carried lofty rigs and were capable of profitable trade on the sea. They were undoubtedly the first to lead in this inevitable direction. They unquestionably were the first to use edge-to-edge planking, which was, many centuries later, to be identified as *shell-first ship construction.*

This idea of building up the shell or the outside of a boat first is an old and fundamental approach. It is older than recorded history simply because it was the natural extension in boat evolution beyond the dugout log. The limiting size of hollowed logs and their very low profile when afloat naturally suggests adding a hewn edge plank, fastened to the log sides. This is an obvious protective barrier to keep the water out. Of course, experience quickly suggests some sort of center attachment of the sides forward and aft, leading to the idea of stem and stern posts. Some shaping with the adze makes the characteristic ends of a typical log canoe.

It is not my intent to speculate on the prehistoric course of boat development with plank upon plank added to the sides to increase its freeboard and extend its capability. We can see examples in archaeological finds and in today's watercraft of the world's water-oriented people. We can also note that in this late twentieth century, the most ubiquitous type of boat in all the world is still a dugout log canoe with a freeboard plank or two on the sides. Some are skillfully built and very shapely; others are rough and ready, useful and purposeful. (See Figures 1-24, 1-25, and 1-26.)

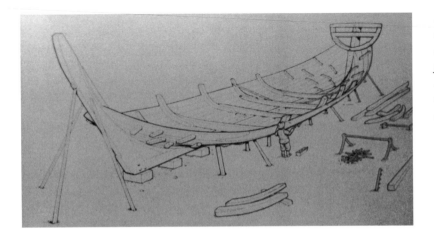

Figure 1-24. Mid-seventeenth-century ships built with modified shell-first system; note temporary wood cleats on exterior as in Figure 1-25.

Figure 1-25. An Omani (Persian Gulf) boat being built, 1975, showing clearly the shell-first construction with external cleats to hold planking in place temporarily.

Figure 1-26. Primitive boat framing following traditional procedures. These are natural-grown timbers set up for planking a West Indian sloop at Bequia, Grenadines. (Reg. A. Calvert)

As is obvious from the foregoing, two very old systems of boat planking construction have been used in boatbuilding in the Western world—the Mediterranean smooth-plank system and the Norse lapped-plank system. Boats of these two markedly different systems now coexist in both Europe and America. It is interesting, however, that in the Mediterranean, where smooth-planking began and has been so long the only method of building boats, the lapstrake system has never been accepted.

However, there is one common factor in these two systems—two basic construction styles that began separately, geographically and millennia apart. Both systems were based on the *shell-first* sequence. Both of these approaches persisted. The Mediterranean system with its heavy flush-shell planking spread throughout southern European civilization and eventually beyond and was not entirely given up until the seventeenth century. The Norse lapstrake style also shapes the shell in place, using wooden clamps to hold the planks as they are built up, plank over plank, into a graceful shell. The planks are then fastened in place by copper rivets along the lapped edges before the frames are assembled inside.

The shell-first system is characterized by the edge-to-edge fastening—the smooth carvel planking was mortised and tenoned (Figure 1-22) in place, a most tedious system, with the tenons set in sometimes as close as 6 to 8 inches apart. In this system the hull was originally planked up as far as its waterline before any interior frame was introduced. The interior frame began with the centerline floor timbers above the keel. (See Figure 1-23.) As the side planking progressed, interior framing was inserted, often randomly in the earliest boats, to fit the developing shape of the boat.

By the seventeenth century, the ships built in the Netherlands for its growing and world-renowned East India trade were still being planked from the keel outward and upward without the guidance of any preset framing structure. Some of the largest and handsomest of ships were built this way during the Netherlands' golden age—with the basic elements of planking placed before the frames.

ULTIMATE FRAME-FIRST METHOD

This sequence was so gradually overtaken by the ultimate frame-first method used today that the new system was probably resisted because of strong tradition. The old system was ultimately pushed aside by the advent of science into the shipwright's realm. It was in the late seventeenth and early eighteenth centuries that astronomers and mathematicians were startling the world with new ideas. The Age of Enlightenment had begun. The mathematics of Isaac Newton made it possible to calculate a ship's displacement and draft of water before it was built—that is, if the shape of its body had been predetermined. The shape of a hull could be established by drawing its sections transversely and cutting the frames to those shapes after "lofting" the lines to full size. Thus it was virtually required that the frames be set up on the keel before the shell was planked.

Today, smooth carvel planking is used more often than lapstrake for larger and more expensive working boats in northern Europe and America. Even in Scandinavia most of the offshore fishing craft are smooth-planked, though the builders of smaller boats and beach-operated boats continue logically to use the lighter, clinker construction.

The classic smooth-plank construction is unquestionably a preferable system today, when a hull with a smooth, clean exterior surface is the result. With proper attention to a structural frame that includes adequate bilge stringers, uniform frames—either steam-bent, sawn from grown crooks, or doubled with futtocks—sturdy keel, keelson, clamps, and shelves, and continuous deck-strengthening members, the carvel system is the ultimate in wood boat construction.

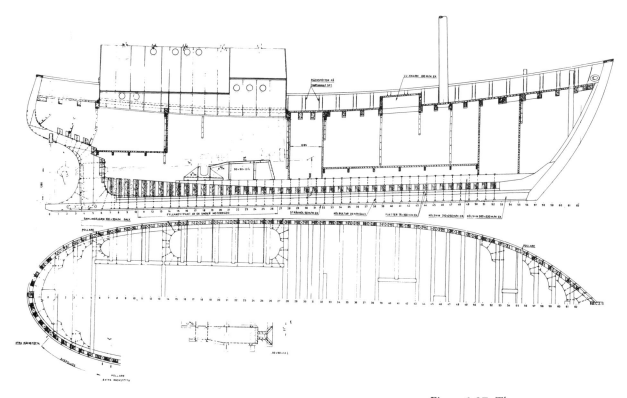

Figure 1-27. The structural profile of a Swedish trawler-seiner.

Modern carvel construction includes a certain amount of lamination in the backbone and frames, though this technique, for economy reasons, has not been adopted entirely by workboat yards. While there is much to recommend wood lamination for uniform strength and continuity, it is not economical unless the builder is building a number of boats of identical model. In the great majority of boatyards or boatbuilding localities, the techniques used are still bound by older experience and tradition. This is true in both northern and southern Europe, along the coasts of Norway, and in the Mediterranean. There are few people more conservative than the men who live by the sea.

MODERN PLANK ON FRAME

It is appropriate at this point to examine the structure of a typical and traditional small working boat of the western Mediterranean. The example chosen here might well be identified as a prototype of the small beach and harbor boats of the entire western basin of the Middle Sea from Italy to Gibraltar. They vary in size from about 14 feet to as much as 30 feet. There are local preferences and deviations in form and style as noted in Chapter Five, but in basic structure they conform to a single system. They are today

Figure 1-28. Looking down on a model of a French pointu.

Figure 1-29. Side views of a partially planked model of a pointu.

the living examples of and the primary heirs to the original Mediterranean carvel plank technology. Although in theory the carvel system is fundamentally the same as that which evolved finally during the flowering of the Roman Empire, the boat of today contains all the refinements of centuries of development and use, including the abandonment of mortise-and-tenon fastening.

This Mediterranean "original" is best shown by a model, which remains unplanked to show

her frame structure (see Figures 1-28 and 1-29). The model is of a ubiquitous double-ended Mediterranean boat with extended stem and stern posts. The keel is straight or with a very slight rocker curve, and its sectional proportion is 1:2 sided to molded dimension. It is scarfed at both ends to the curving end posts. The frames are sawn and doubled up to the turn of the bilge, where they continue singly to the railcap. The frame doubling in the bottom eliminates the necessity of the floor timbers required in the more common type of carvel framing and is far superior when the doublings are sawn from natural crooks. A longitudinal keelson or flat center plank placed on top of these double bottom frames and running out at the stem and stern posts completes a most rigid backbone. There are two or three bilge stringers per side. This particular boat is essentially an open boat, sometimes with a deck forward and aft and along the sides.

Within the Mediterranean style of boats, beyond the basic structure as illustrated, there is a variety of minor variations, aberrations, and decorations. These boats are, for example, nearly all equipped with king posts in the rail at the bow and often at the stern for snubbing mooring lines or working fishing gear. The stemheads are generally capped or carved to a distinctive profile. The sternpost is frequently cut down to accommodate the tiller adequately, but not always. Often the rudderhead rises high above an already extended sternpost as in Adriatic, Maltese, and many Spanish boats.

All in all, the boat observed here in this small model is fundamental and can serve as the prototype for Mediterranean boats. Actually, this one is a specific type used on the French coast near Marseille and Toulon, known there as a pointu or sometimes a rafiau. It is used mostly by individual fishermen or watermen and is either rowed or sailed. It is of ancient, handsome construction and is a "pure" model. A typical structural midship section of this basic example is illustrated in Figure 1-30. Mediterranean-type boats can be found in faraway places, as well. The Monterey boat of the California coast (see Figure 1-31), an American boat, is of pure Mediterranean con-

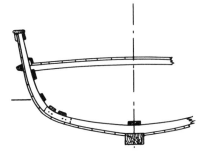

Figure 1-30. The structure of a modern carvel-planked boat is shown in this section of a Mediterranean beach boat of the coast of Spain. Notice the light planking, the sawn two-part frames, and the heavy keel.

Figure 1-31. Mediterranean influence is apparent in this Monterey boat of the U.S. West Coast. The heavy-type rubrails, dating from medieval construction, are still used here to good functional advantage.

Figure 1-32. A contemporary Aegean island fishing boat under construction; an outstanding example of frame-first construction.

struction down to its carvel wales. The plank-on-heavy-frame construction prevails today in larger boats for the offshore fisheries as well as in the inshore boats just mentioned.

MODERN ANGLO-SAXON INTERPRETATIONS

Boats have been built in the British Islands since Neolithic men first put together their skin coracles. The boats of the Celts and early Anglo-Saxons have developed into the most outstanding of boats in strength and capability.

There are few boats of any of the world's maritime regions that are able to compare in construction with the better examples of the coastal working boats of Scotland, England, or Ireland.

An example of one of the best of these, which is typical and indigenous enough to be identified as modern Irish–Anglo-Saxon, is the 52-foot motor fishing vessel whose structural profile and section are shown in Figure 1-33. This boat shows the common form of a rugged, heavy displacement hull typical of the modern inshore fishing craft working off the coasts of Ireland and England.

The hull of this boat was assembled in the latter part of 1970 in one of the best building yards in Ireland. There is nothing in her basic structure that would be unfamiliar to the better shipwrights of five hundred years ago. Her scarfed keel assembly with the inner log and her keelson over heavy floor timbers would have brought favorable comment from ancient Greek and Roman shipbuilders, though they would have expressed wonder over the uniformity of the structural members and the protective galvanized coatings of the steel fastenings. They might have been slightly skeptical of the lack of edge-fastening tenons in the planking, but their worries about plank security would surely have been quickly dispelled when they inspected the improved heavy, square-cut galvanized boat spikes and heavy bronze screws.

What would an ancient Viking boatbuilder think of this "best example" of twentieth century boatbuilding? He undoubtedly would complain that the boat was unnecessarily heavy for all its strength. He would see no excuse or purpose for through-bolting the floors to the frames, nor would he perhaps understand the heavy decks over beams connected to the frames. But

Figure 1-33. This inboard structural profile illustrates the ruggedness of a modern working boat in the Irish fisheries. She is a fine example of modern wood boat construction. Her native oak frames, many of which are natural crooks, were selected from standing trees by the builder. This is one of the rare cases where this age-old building practice was still in use only twenty years ago.

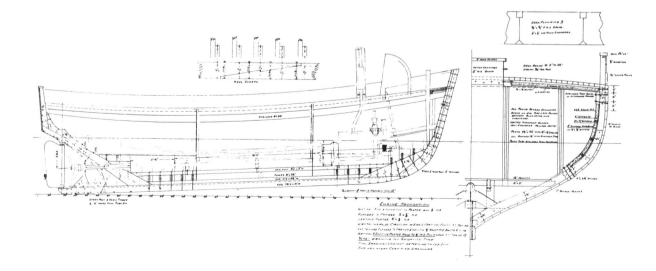

*Figure 1-34. Carvel planking is not always attached
to sawn, preset frames. This boat is being planked
over steam-bent frames set inside a cradlelike jig.
The mold is formed by setting up sectional forms that
are held in place by ribbands. The hot, steamed oak
frames are bent into this cradle. The ribbands are
removed as the planks are fitted. The boat is the*
Blue Moon, *designed by the author. (Ivor Bensen)*

this boat is not his style; it is of smooth plank,
carvel construction, for which he would probably
show contempt. Yet this same construction, even
heavier still, is found now in modern Swedish
boats (see Figure 1-27).

There is a structural framing variation in
carvel-built boats that has been long familiar to
North Americans and has found increasing use
with European builders. This system employs
the steam-bent frame rather than the sawn mul-
tifuttock frame. In this system, temporary molds
are set up on the backbone structure and temporary heavy battens or ribbands are bent around
the molds, as shown in Figure 1-34. The hot,
steamed frames are then forced into shape
against the inside surface of the ribbands and
clamped or temporarily fastened. The planking is
then attached progressively from the keel; the
ribbands are removed as the planked surface pro-

ceeds. This method can be seen in progress in the photograph. The molds are finally removed when the planking is nearly completed.

The boat in Figure 1-34 was built in Norway to the basic design of a sloop of the British Falmouth estuary, a boat type described in Chapter Three, a Falmouth quay punt, Figure 3-22. She is 23 feet long with a beam of 8½ feet and draft of 4 feet. She has an oak backbone, ash frame, fir planks, and pine deck and deck beams. Her transom and railcaps are mahogany. Her mast and spars are solid, built-up spruce. Her planking is fastened to the frames by square copper rivets that are identical to the plank fastenings used by the Norwegians since the ninth and tenth century AD.

There are newer methods of boat construction today, as is known by any who are even slightly aware of the pleasure boat explosion of the 1960–70s. Boats of molded reinforced plastic, popularly called fiberglass, are economical only when multiple units are to be built from the same mold. There are, of course, fiberglass working boats, but they are manufactured in mass quantities to be adapted to general uses in various environments. They totally lack indigenous character or style. It is true that in some cases the style and form of specific indigenous working boats have been copied in molded fiberglass boats. In such cases where this has been done for pleasure craft, the results are invariably disappointing. However, new and improved working boat forms have been developed for fiberglass construction, and this rugged material has proved successful when an adequate number of boats can be built to amortize the cost of toolings. Also, aluminum, which is often a most expensive building material, has been very successfully used in some small seiners and larger shrimpers of North America. In all of these cases, the investment required in design and construction limits use to the building of large numbers of boats. It is beyond the means of the individual workboat builder, who continues to build with his unique, instinctive skill borne of an experienced eye. Such a builder is free to exercise his individual creativity, but is usually restricted by his inherited conservatism and traditionalism. A decreasing number of these traditional builders remains. They are the source of true maritime heritage.

ANCIENT BOATS
IN A MODERN WORLD

As mentioned previously, some of the methods used in prehistory still survive, very often side by side with the most advanced techniques. This is true of the Welsh coracle and the Irish curragh, the contemporary portable frame-skin boats with ancient origins in the British Islands. The coracle shown in Figure 1-35 is obviously improved very little from the original. However, the "skin" is no longer an animal's hide. It is now an impregnated canvas fabric. The frame is woven of supple green limbs that have been

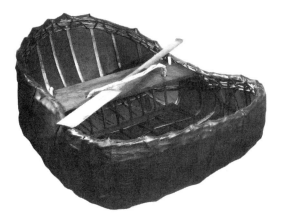

Figure 1-35. One of the oldest and most primitive boats. This frame-skin craft is a coracle from the River Teifi, Wales. (The Science Museum, London)

Figure 1-36. The Irish curragh (pronounced "corack") is the Hibernian version of the ancient Neolithic skin-frame boat. The frame of the curragh is more sophisticated than the Welsh coracle, as this plan shows. (The Science Museum, London)

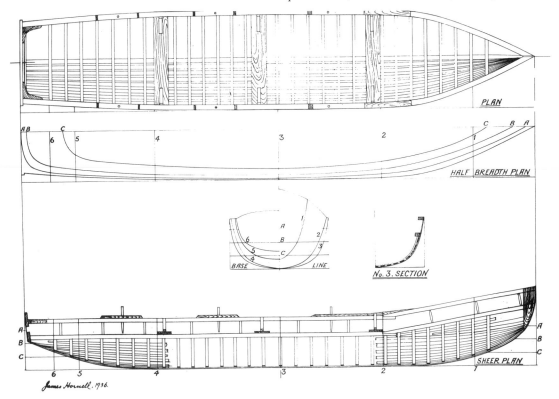

Figure 1-37. A Chesapeake log canoe. The boats were originally developed for crabbing and oystering by individual watermen, and this racing rig is not typical of the original working sails. Working log canoes often had only one mast.

barked and split. The rim (it can hardly be called a gunwale or sheer clamp) is woven of small, whole willow branches, which hold the peripheral shape and provide a reinforced edge to which the fabric is lashed. This craft is an elemental vessel that provides the itinerant fisherman a basic method of buoyant support. It satisfies needs that, in some regions, have become no more demanding than they ever were. Subsequent needs, elemental as they were, produced the curragh, shown in the drawings of an Aran Island craft in Figure 1-36. The form of this skin-frame craft is here elongated to a basic boat form with a rounded stern and pointed bow for directional control. The frame consists of light, flat wood strips running both longitudinally and transversely with a heavier sheer strip containing the oar tholes. These boats are 15 to 25 feet long, but light enough to be carried overhead by two men. They are still used in Ireland, launched from the beach to pursue lazy but powerful basking sharks. Both types of frame-skin craft are attractive to fishermen needing portable transportation.

The dugout canoe has been referred to previously as a ubiquitous and prehistoric type, fundamental in construction. Before the dugout canoe, there were only floating logs. Yet in this age of voyages to the moon, there are still more utilitarian log-hull boats in use throughout the world than any other single type of boat. There are some of fine and sophisticated line, such as the Chesapeake sailing log canoes. These graceful overrigged sailing craft, which originated first as simple crabbing boats, are now used only for the exhilarating sport of exhibition sailing and racing for pleasure. Built generally of several logs fastened transversely, they are literally carved and sculpted into double-ended sailing hulls with fine lines, 25 to 35 feet long. They carry a large crew for live and transferable ballast on hiking boards to counter the lofty spread of sails set on their raked and unstayed masts. They are no longer working boats.

The more humble working log canoes are used by primitive communities such as those in the Pacific islands, Caribbean islands, Indonesia, or the West African coast. They are generally hollowed and shaped from a single large tree. They are restricted in size by the workable size of tropical trees. Inasmuch as the observations of this book are concerned with the Western cultures, it is the log dugouts of the West African coast that are described below.

On the coast of the African bulge, which is the area from Nigeria to Senegal, there are more than fifty thousand working dugout log boats. These boats are not river canoes, although there are many more similar dugout boats on the rivers and lakes of this area of Africa. The dugouts of the coastal communities are ocean-working, surf-launched boats. The fishing industry is so rewarding here that a single well-manned boat of 30 to 35 feet might be responsible for as much as 50 tons of fish per year. Approximately 90 percent of the total protein diet of the people of these coastal countries is obtained from the seafood caught from these very primitive boats.

Figures 1-38 and 1-40 illustrate the typical form of two different styles of boat, which are the basic models for many thousands. Figure 1-41 shows a fishing boat on a beach in Senegal, and Figure 1-38 shows the type of boat

Figure 1-38. The efficient form of a Ghana canoe makes it superior to the Senegal canoe. It is round-bottomed with less rocker than the Senegal canoe.

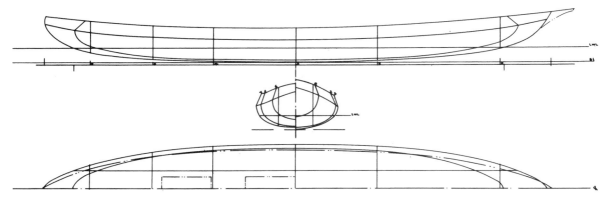

used along the coast of Ghana and Dahomey. The Senegalese boat has much the same form, in the rockerlike profile and the sections, as some of the boats of ancient Egypt.

The most common length of the West African log dugout is between 25 and 30 feet, with a beam of about 4½ feet. The logs are from selected large trees, often found deep in the interior as much as 150 miles from the nearest navigable water. The wood that native builders find most choice for dugouts is the best red African mahogany—prized also for decorative wood by the builders of the most modern yachts. The African boat "maker" uses only two tools to sculpt his boat, and these tools have been used the longest in man's boatbuilding experience. The adze and a broad chisel are the cutters, shapers, and carvers of a dugout log boat, as well as of the most modern wood keel or stempost of the finest modern wooden yacht or workboat. It

is remarkable to observe the trueness of form that these African craftsmen achieve with these tools in the finished canoe. Some evidence of this can be seen in Figure 1-39.

The canoes of Ghana, which are more abundant than those of Senegal, have nicely rounded hulls with a rocker sheer, as can be seen in Figure 1-38. The bow and the stern are almost identical in shape, though the afterbody is slightly fuller in the larger models. These canoes often have drawn-out stern and stem pieces that can best be described as a bill. The hulls, which are often carved by one man, require about three months' work, and are about six inches thick at the bottom and taper off to about three inches at the sheer rail. The sides show a flat in the section, which results in a tumblehome of the entire form, as well as what appears to be a continuous broad sheerstrake. The seats or thwarts are often loose or sometimes fastened across the upper edges from side to side.

The boats were originally built for about six to eight paddle-wielding fishermen, who were the prime propulsion system. In a few regions, however, a very simple and unstayed mast with a low-cut lugsail is used.

In recent years, the most progressive West African fishermen, utilizing the United Nations's Food and Agriculture Organization aid as well as U.S. foreign aid, have been motorizing their canoes. They generally use an outboard engine of 20–25 horsepower mounted in a centerline well in the afterbody as shown. This simple application was first studied by testing models in towing tanks to find the most advantageous location and shape of the aperture. Such modern research technology has probably never before been used for the improvement of such an ancient and primitive watercraft.

A variation in dugout form is found on the coast of Senegal, where beach boats have essentially the old dory section with a flat bottom and flared-out sides. These also have an added sheer plank, which increases the freeboard and pro-

Figure 1-39. Even though they are worn and weathered, these canoes show the true shape given by the skilled use of an adze and a broad chisel.

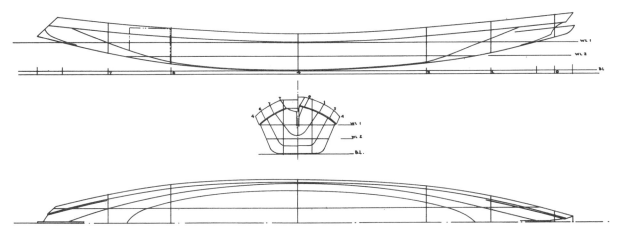

Figure 1-40. The shape of a primitive but finely made canoe is shown in these hull lines of a Senegalese canoe. There are thousands of this type of canoe along the West African shores.

vides a drier hull and greater capacity—a living example of the first step in the evolution of boat construction.

Launching and beaching these boats have always been haphazard procedures, which on a day of reasonably high ocean surf often appear foolhardy or even impossible. Launching a dugout manned only by paddlers can be a most discouraging way to begin a day. The boat can easily capsize, pitchpole, or broach. The crew will consequently be cast out of the boat, and the confrontation ends with all hands going home to await a better day. Mechanization of the canoes has improved this launching operation. A motor-powered dugout's success in moving through a surf is about 60 percent better than the paddle-propelled boat, and fewer crew are needed. Landing with a full load of fish in a significant surf is generally quite simple. The boat, as it approaches the line of breakers, is simply abandoned and often deliberately overturned. The crew swims ashore and picks the fish up from the beach as they roll in. Much fine fresh fish is harvested by these common boats, perhaps more than is con-

Figure 1-41. A Senegalese log canoe returning with a small catch of fish. Note the planked-up sides of this dugout hull, living evidence of the first step in the evolution of the planked boat.

sumed in the United States. The Senegalese dugout, shown in Figure 1-41, is a capacious craft that, in the course of history, has advanced to the point of metamorphosis from a dugout log to a plank-sided boat. It is about 35 feet long and has a beam of about 6 feet.

The discussion of log canoes, particularly single-log canoes, cannot be put aside without mentioning one other lesser-known and infrequently encountered type. It is not found in a Third World country nor a land of lesser industrial culture. It is a boat of modern Scandinavia, namely Finland. It is remarkable primarily in that it is fashioned from a single log native to a land whose climate is not conducive to growing large trees, unlike tropical or subtropical lands. It reflects immediately the resourcefulness and ingenious craftsmanship of its builders.

The age of this Norse method of converting a log into a thin-walled shell of a boat is not known, nor is the extent of the present use of the graceful wooden shell. The two illustrations shown here (Figures 1-42 A and B) reveal the simple but skilled, labor-intensive method of building. The resulting boat with one plank per side, to enhance the freeboard, is approximately 3.7 meters or 12½ feet in length. The beam of the boat may be as much as 3½ feet. It is light and transportable and ideal for use on the many inland waterways and protected bodies of water in Finland. It is likely the only log canoe type that makes this maximum use of the tree's circumference. (This statement totally ignores the watercraft of the Native Americans, which were fabricated so well and carefully out of the bark of a mature birch tree. This type of watercraft is omitted from our discussion of origins of boats only because we see it as a vessel that was not one of an evolving maritime methodology, as is also true of the reed boats of Egypt and the inflatable skin boats of ancient Mesopotamia.)

Figures 1-42 A and B. A Scandinavian log canoe. This is an old process of producing a canoe of adequate breadth from a single tree. The trunk of a birch tree is hollowed from the log (above) using nearly the whole log's circumference. It is then steamed and/or heated and slowly expanded. It is further widened (left) by attaching side planks to build up the freeboard. This is a boat from Finland. (National Maritime Museum, Finland)

Another type of primitive boat still survives, not along the edge of the sea but in rivers and marshlands. This boat is made of woven and bound reeds and can be found in Lake Chad in the upper reaches of the Nile valley, in Central and South America, in the Caspian Sea marshes, and undoubtedly in other remote regions where primitive people live marginally. This form of watercraft was used in the predynastic eras of ancient Egypt. It has been used continually since, especially where men are considerably restricted by the adversaries of poverty, poor agriculture, and shallow wetlands.

In the emerging society of ancient Egypt, the reed boat or papyrus raft was fashioned carefully into a boat shape. Papyrus reeds were abundant, and consequently the craft were cheap, popular means of flotation for fishing and hunting in the marshes. These boats were and are extremely perishable, lasting about a month to six weeks when used regularly. They were consequently made to be disposable and economically replaceable. The early Egyptians apparently made craft of papyrus reeds in much the same way as they are made today in the Lake Chad region. They also apparently made them quite large, perhaps as much as 50 to 60 feet. It is a considerable extension of logic, however, to reason that such craft were used beyond the rivers. The gradual absorption of water combined with chafe from the motion of the sea would result in an unwieldy hulk that would soon lose its shape— convincing evidence that reed boats were unsuitable for use on saltwater seas such as the Mediterranean.

Primitive man built watercraft of whatever materials were close at hand, wherever he lived. As these first craft provided mobility, he utilized better materials and improved his structural techniques to build craft of ever greater mobility. Such progress in boat design and construction made civilization possible.

CHAPTER TWO

NORTHERN
EUROPEAN WATERCRAFT

NORTHERN EUROPE HAS PRODUCED some of the most capable small, indigenous working boats in the maritime world. Some of these boats have been models of excellence and were copied in other lands; others have remained unique because craftsmen from other lands did not understand them and were not adapted temperamentally to duplicate them. A combination of factors, such as a heavy weather environment, sturdy native woods, and disciplined craftsmen, have contributed to all of the native boats of northern Europe. These boats sail in the semiprotected but rugged waters of the Baltic, in the arctic waters off the Norwegian coast, and in the Skagerrak and the Kattegat. They are found in remote harbors in the fjords of Norway, the Danish islands, the lowlands of Holland, the Hebrides, the Orkneys, the Channel coast, and other ports or coves between. This is a most extensive environment, yet there is a common bond of purpose and cultural influence that produces a similarity of structure in all northern European boats. Since this is not a complete encyclopedia of boats nor a catalog of geographical types, I will not follow the system that *all* examples both good and mediocre, however remote, must be located and described. Instead, the best, and sometimes the most interesting, will be discussed.

NETHERLANDS—BOATS OF THE LOWLANDS

It is best to look at the Netherlands first, because of its central geographical location and because its extensive maritime tradition and centuries-old determination to wrest the land and a living from the sea have produced a rich variety of unique boats.

Along the coast of Holland there is much land lying below the level of the sea. This land is constantly being reclaimed from the sea and maintained by the Dutch, who must rely on watercraft adapted to shallow water and restricted channels. So these craft are not only indigenous, but they are also ingeniously unique.

Because of the lowland nature of Holland, with its network of canals and open, shallow waters, the most characteristic feature of Dutch watercraft is their shoal draft. Upon first view, these boats all seem to be molded on bluff, full lines. In a sense they are, but after fuller examination and study, one realizes their configurations, all basically similar, are of a more subtle and complex character. The orientation of their entrances as well as their runs is rotated ninety degrees from customary form. The bows are excessively full above the waterline, with a maximum beam noticeably forward of amidships. The form leads into a shallow bottom with a flat run, a shape essentially designed to allow a maximum of flow under the hull. These hulls, with a spoonlike forward end, do not cause a very deep bow wave when under way, under either power or sail at maximum speed. Disturbance of the water is relatively slight, amounting primarily to splashing, broken water at the stem and other forward surfaces. There is no cleavage of the water; it is not forced away from the stem or forefoot as by most hulls with vertical, sharp stems and fine waterline entrances. Hence the wave pattern is largely muted and progress through the water is most economical. These are general features, typical of the various shallow-draft inshore craft, which are essentially the indigenous ones. The varied construction features of these boats produce types that differ from region to region and with the nature of their employment.

There are three or four predominant types of smaller Dutch workboats, up to approximately 50 feet in length. These are: the botter, the hoogaars, the boeier, and the schokker. These craft are shown in Figures 2-1 through 2-4. A larger but more bargelike craft is called the tjalk.

At times, these characteristic Dutch craft seem contrived when viewed against a backdrop of windmills and wooden shoes. There is no doubt that the people of Holland know how unique these boats are and, perhaps with official approval and assistance, maintain them as an attractive link with a nineteenth century Holland—the same Holland tourists want to see.

Figure 2-1. The form of the botter is uniquely Dutch. This half-model shows the flat bottom of a botter in contrast to its complex, curved hull. (Nederlandsch Historisch Scheepvaart Museum, Amsterdam)

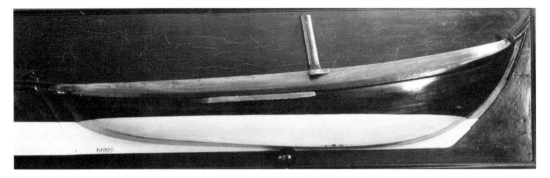

Figure 2-2. The hoogaars has a simple, rugged hull with flat sections and a flat bottom. It was originally the poor man's workboat and was indigenous to the region of Flushing and the island of Walcheren, Holland. (Nederlandsch Historisch Scheepvaart Museum, Amsterdam)

Figure 2-3. The boeier has a full, round bottom. Undoubtedly it is the oldest Dutch boat form, and quite likely it is the most basic of all Dutch boats. (Nederlandsch Historisch Scheepvaart Museum, Amsterdam)

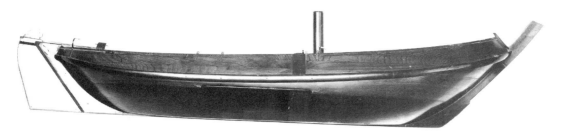

Figure 2-4. The schokker is similar in basic form to the hoogaars but is generally larger and smooth-planked. This type is frequently found in western Holland in the Scheldt estuary region. (Nederlandsch Historisch Scheepvaart Museum, Amsterdam)

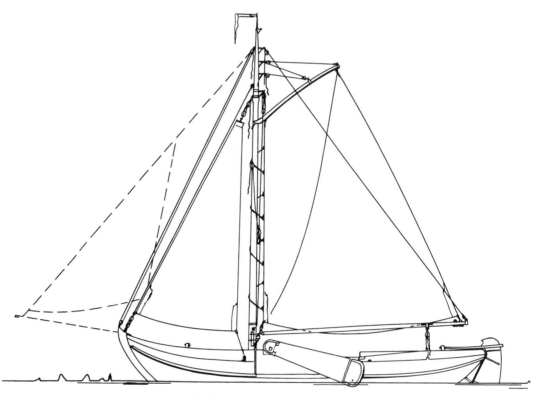

Figure 2-5. The sail plan of a boeier is similar to that of the botter. This example shows the lower rig of a working boat. This unique bezan-type sail plan has a characteristic pleasing proportion and, when seen on the waters of the Ijsselmeer, has a grace and simplicity typical only of Holland. These boats are being restored as pleasure boats and participating in local regattas.

These traditional boats deserve description, however, because they contain the origins of whatever indigenous qualities still lurk in modern Dutch boats. The motor barges, produce boats, and small freight boats largely evolved from the characteristic shapes of the traditional craft. The indigenous freight carriers, where they exist, are most frequently tjalks of 50 to 70 feet, most commonly built of steel. They are still working under power carrying produce and commercial goods. Some sailing workboats have become yachts and so they still have their rigs preserved.

The boeier is the most shapely and graceful of the traditional craft. It is also perhaps the generic one, in that it is the model that the seventeenth and eighteenth century Dutch yachts were built on. It is characterized by its lapstrake planking, rounded sections with noticeable deadrise, distinctive tumblehome in the sheer plank, and

Figure 2-6. A botter that has been converted to a pleasure craft. These boats are comfortable and cruise capably in semisheltered waters. Their popularity is evident in their frequent appearance in Mediterranean and British ports, and sometimes on the Chesapeake Bay.

Figure 2-7. The lines of a botter show her characteristic fullness over the flat bottom. This boat, with her full bow, tends to ride high and create less of a bow wave system than would be expected.

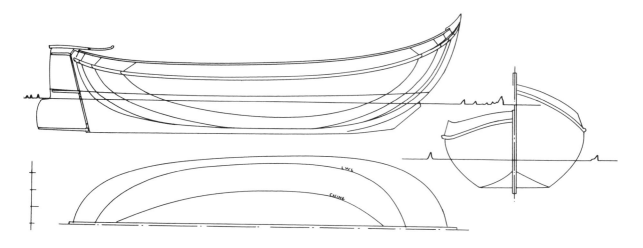

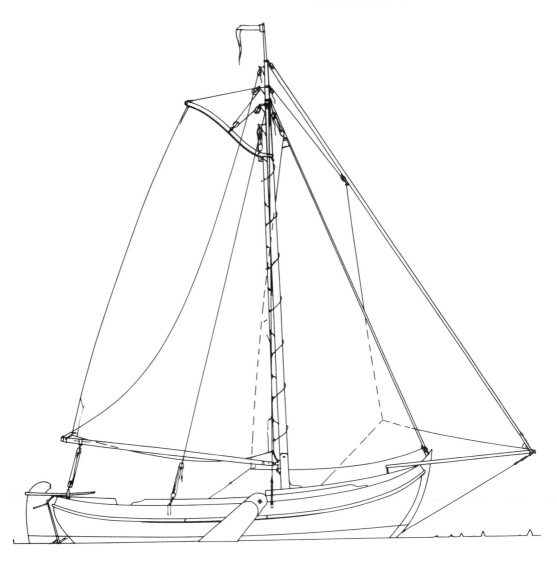

Figure 2-8. The sail plan of the botter in this example is somewhat loftier than generally seen on working boats. The stays are rigged on running tackles for lowering the rig frequently.

upswept ends. Often the bottom planks are carvel and laid parallel to the keel for most of the length. The fullest beam is forward of amidships.

The botter is similar to the boeier. The most distinctive difference between the two is the flat bottom of the botter and its carvel planking throughout. The stem on both the boeier and the botter is gracefully rounded in profile, generally terminating with a sharply defined crescent-shaped end. The characteristic modern rig of these boats is called a bezan. It essentially consists of a loose-footed gaff-rigged mainsail with a short, hooked gaff; an overlapping staysail; and in light weather a jib from a bowsprit rigged on the starboard side of the stem.

The boeiers and the botters today have mostly been converted to yachts and private craft, sailing for pleasure on the Ijsselmeer (formerly the Zuider Zee) or providing pleasant houseboat accommodations in a quiet canal. They vary from 30 to 50 feet in length. The original construction was of the heaviest sort of sawn frame with thick planking (either lap or carvel as indicated).

When the boeiers and botters were working boats for either freight transport or fishing, they had a large hold in the full hull that could be almost completely uncovered by a system of removable hatch covers. A graceful house with a pronounced crown as well as sheer was located well aft. The leeboards were fairly deep and tapered, and the rudder was broad and high with a curved tiller sweeping down from a rudderhead that was most frequently decorated with a head, a fish, or another carving that pleased the builder or owner. In the last thirty to thirty-five years, because of the scarcity of wood, steel has been resorted to as the basic hull material, although the original form of the types was retained.

Figure 2-9. The hengst is a smaller and older hoogaars still found in the Scheldt and the waters of western Holland.

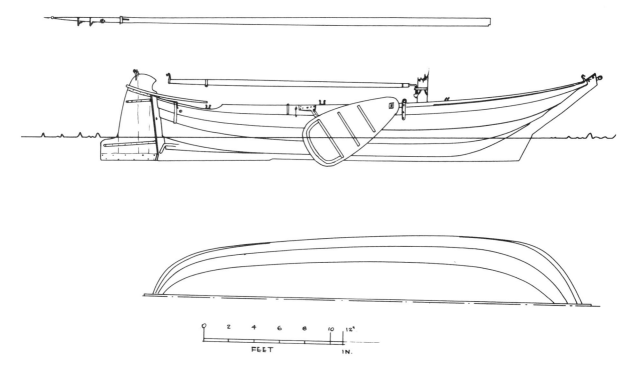

The schokker and the hoogaars are identified by their forward-raking, straight (rather than curved) stems. The schokker has a similar body form to that of the botter but with a straight sternpost as well, to match its stem. The hoogaars has straight sides flaring out from a flat bottom and is generally lapstraked with three or four broad planks per side. (See Figures 2-9, 2-10, and 2-11.) Both of these craft have the characteristic tumblehome washboard plank above the sheer gunwale, a line which adds necessary freeboard and provides for a base on which to hinge the leeboards.

A fleet of seiners that do not have the characteristic shape of the traditional "Dutch shoe" boat sails out of Volendam on the Ijsselmeer. Whether these boats can be classified as indigenous is debatable. While their general form is suggestive of most North Sea boats, their rig and appurtenances are typically Dutch, down to the traditional rigid wind vane at the masthead. These craft, with their only partially closed cabin shelter and large after wells, all painted a solid and somber black, have a round stern, straight stem, broad beam, and length of 45 to 50 feet. They have nondistinctive and graceless hulls.

Holland is like other countries of western Europe, and more aggressively progressive than most, in her industrial leadership. Her watercraft have become large, efficient, mechanized, instrumented, professionally designed, and thoroughly modern. They are thus vessels of the modern world and no longer indigenous to the Netherlands.

Figure 2-10. The lines plan of a hoogaars. Note the flat bottom and flaring sides. This is a simple and unpretentious form.

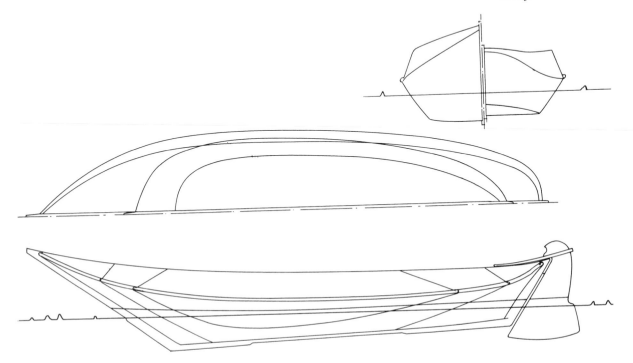

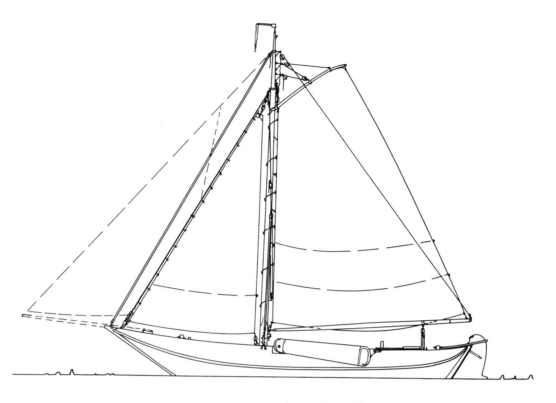

Figure 2-11. The sail plan of a hoogaars. This is the low rig of the original working boat. The common rig now is loftier, since most of the boats have been converted to pleasure craft.

Before leaving the discussion of Dutch boats and their heritage, we must hesitate for an overview of what is taking place now in this last decade of the twentieth century. It has been briefly observed in the foregoing paragraphs that boats of Holland ply protected waters. The canals and the harbors are protected from the sea by a system of dikes. The most outstanding is the great barrier holding back the North Sea. And essentially behind this long and massive elevated dam was shut in a smaller, inland sea, once called the Zuider Zee, now the Ijsselmeer.

For many years this inland sea was home for fishing craft—the various types of sailing craft discussed above. It is now and has been for some thirty years undergoing a massive land reclamation project. Ultimately, these large reclaimed islands lying northeast of Amsterdam, which is on the southwest corner of Ijsselmeer, will reduce the

Figure 2-12 and *Figure 2-13*. *In Ketelhaven, Netherlands, a small community of nautical archaeologists is working on recovered wrecks from the polders, where much of the old Zuider Zee, now Ijsselmeer, has been replaced by landfill. Some of the old wrecks are impressive size vessels when reassembled and/or restored, as is this example showing its dried-out hull on port and starboard at the stern. Note the massive sternpost. It is better to name it a vertical skegpost. The square tuck stern is typical on seventeenth-century ships. (Ketelhaven Marine Museum)*

original area of the sea behind the North Sea dike by more than half. The reclaimed islands, which are called polders, are already becoming occupied with modern housing projects and roads. However, there are low land and seemingly endless prairie-like scapes between habitations.

Yet our interest here lies in the Dutch awareness of their nautical heritage. Over the hundreds of years of the Netherlands' past, countless watercraft of all types had entered and sailed on this semi-landlocked and undeveloped great bay. The dikes were localized, and while efforts were forever slowly pushing back the sea, the technology was not developed to today's extent.

So in the years that passed, ships that became

Figure 2-14. This boat, built for four oarsmen, was recovered intact from the polders in the Ijsselmeer archaeological project in the Netherlands. Its age is roughly two hundred years. (Ketelhaven Marine Museum)

old, leaky, and weathered, were sunk or lost and disappeared in the Zuider Zee. During the recent great land reclamations, the dredges have located many, many sunken and partially sunken shipwrecks and boat wrecks, World War II airplanes, etc.—more than can presently be raised and recorded or, preferably, restored. Some have been raised, however, and partially restored or reassembled.

The results of these first restoration efforts are located at a small marine archaeological community at the north end of the polder island Flevoland. This place is called Ketelhaven. More wrecks are found than can be studied and brought to Ketelhaven, but when found, they are located and marked. While we were driving in Flevoland we saw many markers in the fields, each indicating the location of a sunken wreck.

The wrecks that have been brought in to the shops and reconstruction buildings at Ketelhaven vary in size and style—large, small, deep, and shallow

Figure 2-15. This is a reconstruction model for the ultimate assembly of recovered pieces of a wreck. It is made up of the scaled-down duplicates of the recovered pieces. It is a procedure originally used by Profesor Richard Steffy of the Institute of Nautical Archaeology, at Texas A & M University. (Ketelhaven Marine Archeological Laboratory)

Figure 2-16 and *Figure 2-17*. *Professor Richard Steffy, in dark suit, examines a partially reassembled wreck at the Ketelhaven Museum. The construction shows her single sawn frames and futtocks on the keel with a single mast step in place. The vessel was probably an early fore-and-aft rigged gaff sluep or sloop of the seventeenth century, about 60 feet in length.*

Figure 2-18. A rather precisely reassembled model at Ketelhaven. From its proportions and keelless bottom, it is probably a canal or market barge. (Ketelhaven Marine Museum)

hulls, most old beyond a century or more—for diversity is the goal of the current salvage procedure. The wood is in remarkably good shape. Some needs treatment, of course, before assembly. Other wrecks are fairly intact and remain so while treated. The illustrations in Figures 2-12, 2-13, and 2-14 show two interesting salvaged wrecks. The larger vessel is perhaps 18 to 20 meters in length and has a depth of 3 to 3.5 meters. Her transom stern exhibits the old square tuck and diagonal planking of the sixteenth to early seventeenth century. She was once a coastal or North Sea trading vessel.

Figures 2-16 and 2-17 show the well-known American restorer of ancient Aegean wrecks, Professor Richard Steffey, at the Ketelhaven establishment examining the reassembly of another vessel type. These bare bones of the frame immediately stamp the original vessel as having a broad and shallow hull. This is also very old but indicates the typical Netherlands type for shallow water, perhaps the Frisian Islands or canals, beamy and bluff in the ends.

When wrecks similar to the ones described above are discovered, their parts are usually collapsed, decayed, and scattered by tidal currents. Fortunately, here in the Ijsselmeer there was little tidal current and water disturbance, and the hulls are found in situ with remaining parts. This is not to say that the wrecks are intact. Depending on their ages, they are proportionately ravaged by natural decomposition. However, during salvage, the surviving timbers and other parts are properly marked, and because the metal fastenings have long since vanished through natural corrosion, the remains are individually and carefully transported to the reassembly area. Individual parts are reproduced to model scale and reassembled in miniature as study-guidance models. (See Figures 2-15 and 2-18.) This process was first successfully developed in the reassembly of wrecks in the Aegean by Professor Steffey. Those wrecks dated as far back as 450 BC and will be discussed in Chapter Four.

Here on the polders of the Ijsselmeer the study and archaeological restoration of the Netherlands' maritime antiquity continues.

DENMARK

Scandinavia begins just to the east of the Dutch lowlands, beyond the Frisian Islands where Jutland lies. Some of the most capable and thoroughly

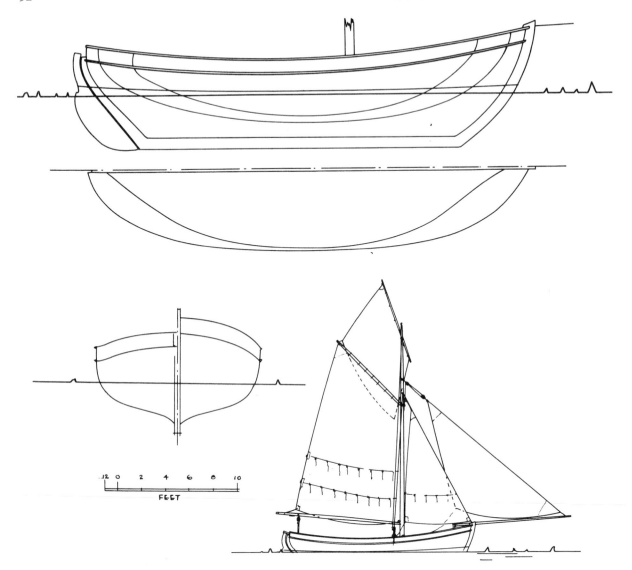

FEET

Figure 2-19. A Hornbaek sildebåd (herring boat) of Denmark. This boat exists today only in motorized, mastless fishing craft. This drawing shows the old sailing rig on the heavy old double-ender. They were once ubiquitous in the Danish islands. The long bowsprit and jack-yard topsail carry the light-weather sails that could be quickly taken in for the treacherous North Sea weather. (Handels-Og Elsingor, Kroneborg Maritime Museum)

Figure 2-20. A model of the graceful Danish sildebåd exists in the Maritime Museum in Kroneborg Castle at Helsingor, Denmark. Variations of this boat in different sizes are found throughout the Danish archipelago.

Figure 2-21. A small Danish coasting vessel of a type developed nearly two centuries ago to trade among the Danish islands and in the Baltic Sea. This boat still retains her low ketch rig and has found a sympathetic owner who makes his home aboard. Sometimes called a "Baltic trader."

indigenous small seacraft sail amongst the islands of Denmark's protective peninsula, as well as in the Skaggerak and the Baltic.

Here, as elsewhere in the modern world, sail has largely given way to power. Most of today's boats, while they are borne on hulls whose lines are old and traditional, have diesel engines in place of masts and sails.

The most typical hull form used in the small, heavy workboats and fishing craft in both Danish and Swedish waters is descended from the herring and plaice fishing craft of a century or more ago. The boats employed in the vicinity of the island of Sjaelland to the north of Copenhagen, where the old fishing ports of Hornbaek and Skovshoved lie, originated the form and style found in the contemporary small, powered fishing boats. Figure 2-19 shows the lines and rig profile of a nineteenth-century fishing boat of Hornbaek; she is typically double-ended, with a full heavy form, straight keel, and curving stem that is typical of the old Scandinavian style. While the hull above the water is full, her sections, both fore and aft, show a shallow wineglass form that provides a fine entrance and run below the water. The sternpost is typically curved inward, also, in the Scandinavian manner. The original rig on these boats is fairly lofty, with a club topsail and two headsails and an extremely long housing bowsprit. (This was a summer rig, no doubt.) The mainsail is typically loose-footed. She is 36 feet long, 13 feet in beam, and 5 feet in draft. This typically Danish style is repeated in many sizes. The model of Figure 2-20 shows a smaller one revealing her open interior.

A larger and even older Danish boat of much this same form is shown in Admiral Paris's well-known survey. This boat is a coaster 50 feet long with

Figure 2-22. The lines of this old Danish coaster can still be seen in Denmark's present-day coasters. These lines were drawn from those by Admiral Paris in his Souvenirs de Marine *in 1882.*

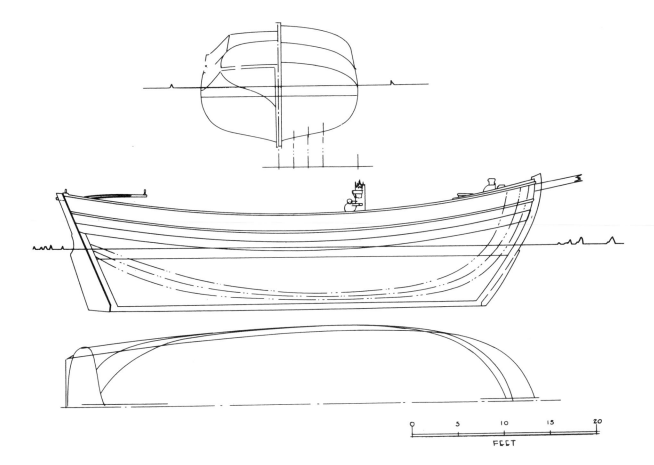

FEET

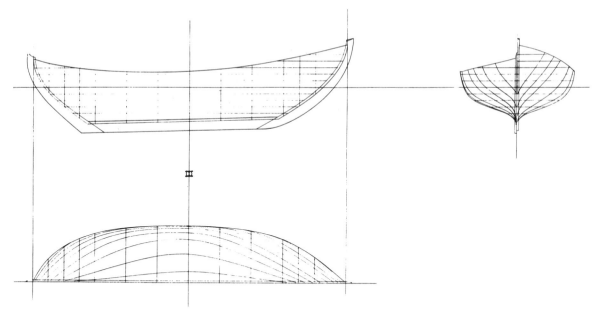

Figure 2-23. The lines of this Skovshoved sildebåd reflect at even a
casual glance her Norse working
boat influence. The boats still work
the inshore fisheries but are today
refitted for power. (Christian
Nielsen)

a transom stern, which is quite typical of the Danish coastwise boats. Her
lines and rig are otherwise quite similar, indicating a well-established local
form. (See Figures 2-21 and 2-22.)

The herring boats of Skovshoved, not far from Hornbaek, were a variation of the Hornbaek type. They had more grace and lightness, with a suggestion of Viking form. The lines (Figure 2-23) show a boat of smaller
dimensions than the Hornbaek type, with greater curvature in the ends and
with a typical old sprit rig. These boats were extremely numerous under sail
in the Danish Oresund east of Copenhagen only fifteen years ago. Figures
2-24 and 2-25 show the structure and sail plan of a Skovshoved boat. The
construction is predominantly lapstrake, particularly in the boats of less than
40 feet.

The Danish islands as well as Jutland are rich in small rowing craft, all of
them of typical Scandinavian mold. These craft are used today more for
pleasure and recreational fishing than for commercial work. They are, however, indigenous. They vary from approximately 12 feet to 16 feet in length
and are typically of lapstrake construction. They are finely modeled double-
enders. Figures 2-26, 2-27 and 2-28 indicate the size, shape, and construction of one of these rugged little beach craft.

The most unusual beach boats of Scandinavia, and perhaps the most functional contemporary beach craft anywhere, are the boats of the northeast coast
of Jutland. Essentially, these hard-working boats are all of similar construction
and style. They are built in three sizes: small rowing boats approximately 16
feet long, open motorcraft about 20 feet long, and larger decked motorboats

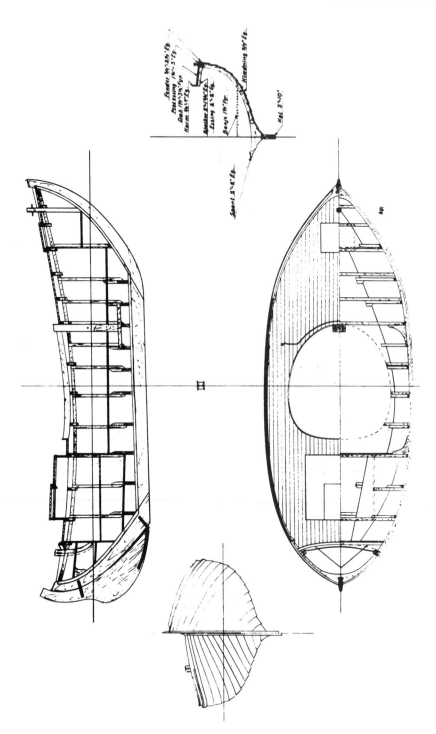

Figure 2-24. The structure of this Danish herring boat is rugged and reflects ancient Norse building methods and character. She has sawn frames with an integral floor timber. (Christian Nielsen)

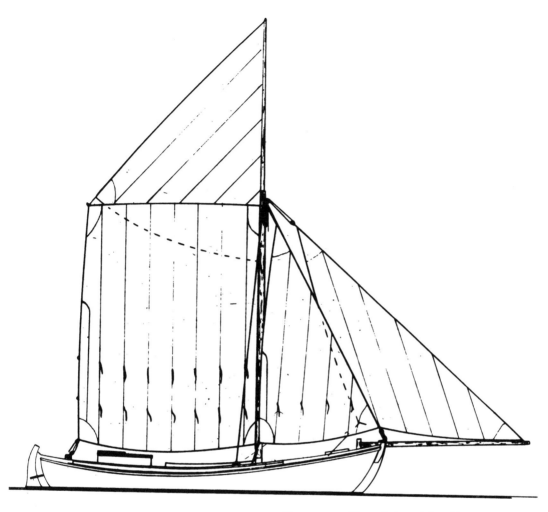

Figure 2-25. *The sail plan of the sildebåd is typical of all of the small Scandinavian fishing boats sailing in the Orsund for the past one hundred years. Unfortunately, these rigs have given way to diesel power. (Christian Nielsen)*

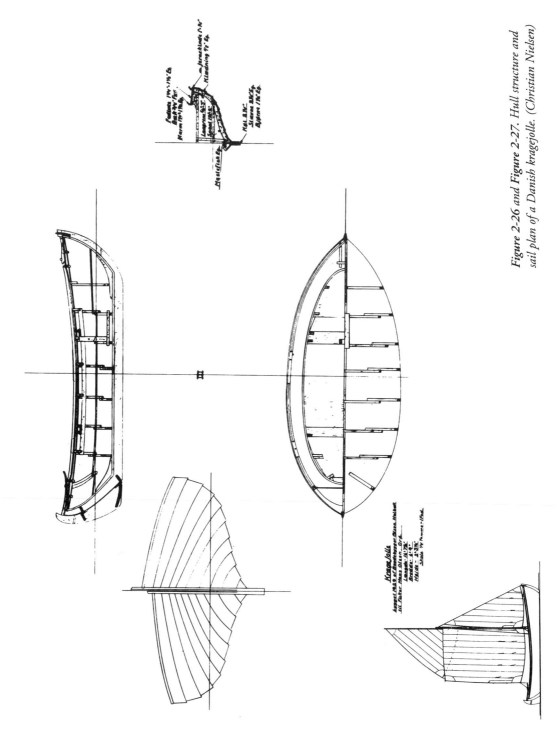

Figure 2-26 and Figure 2-27. Hull structure and sail plan of a Danish kragejolle. (Christian Nielsen)

from 30 to 40 feet long. All of the boats are heavily constructed to withstand daily launching and beaching on coarse, steep, open strands. The beaching process is unique and complex. It is carried out cooperatively by the crews of several boats with the aid of powered winches, a cluster of anchors holding a heavy outhaul pulley block, and, on the beach, a system of fixed pulleys and a sliding pulley. The boats, after being attached to the cable, ride up on the beach over metal rollers (in the past, wood sleepers were used).

Figure 2-28. This beach skiff, drawn up on the pebbled shore of the Kattegat, is typical of Danish skiffs with her fine double ends and curved-back sternpost.

Figure 2-29. The klitmoller boat is distinguished by its full hull and deep sheer. It is the largest beach-launched boat of Europe with the exception of some Portuguese seiners.

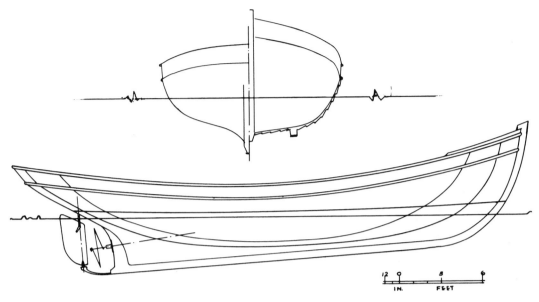

Figure 2-30. The hull lines of a klitmoller boat show her full and rockerlike hull. She is comparatively flat-bottomed for a lapstraked hull.

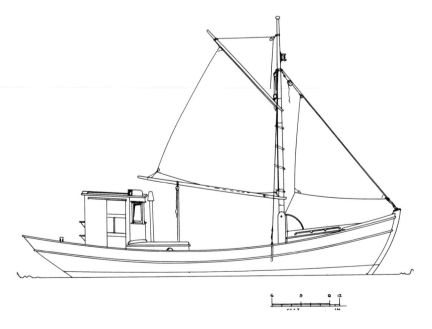

Figure 2-31. The klitmoller boat's short sail rig is used primarily today for steadying. The sail plan indicated here is representative of the present-day gaff-headed sail. The older rig still occasionally seen is the sprit.

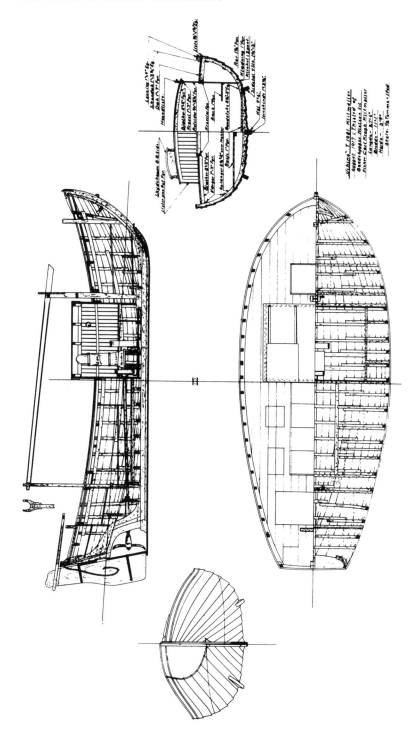

Figure 2-32. The structure of this old-style klitmoller boat shows the full hull and heavy sawn frames of Norse construction. Note the heavy beaching keels. (Christian Nielsen)

The boats are full bodied with lapstrake hulls. They are planked in oak with about seven planks per side for the rowing craft and thirteen planks per side for the larger decked craft. The smaller craft are similar in form to the beach craft described earlier, but the larger of the powered Jutland boats are fuller amidships with a broad transom, or with a high, full, elliptical stern as shown in Figures 2-29 and 2-30. These larger boats have a deep gunwale that provides more security to the fishermen working their hand gear on deck. There is a wheelhouse aft with access to the engine casing and engine just ahead of it. The engines of these boats, as in most Scandinavian fishing boats of this size and character, are hot-bulb semidiesels of one, two, or three cylinders. The propellers are controllable pitch because these engines have no reverse gear.

The larger, decked boats carry a standard mast and auxiliary sail rig consisting of a small gaff main and a short storm jib. The rig is most useful as a steadying sail in choppy seas. Figure 2-31 shows a typical profile of one of these boats whose dimensions are 37 feet overall, 14 feet beam, and 4 feet draft when loaded. Her displacement at the load waterline is about 15 tons.

These beach boats are built by local builders entirely by experience and eye. They don't work from drawings or models, and their boats are consequently excellent examples of indigenous art.

The scantlings of the beach boat in Figures 2-32 and 2-33 are typical. The keel is 10" by 9" of Danish oak with a steel bar shoe 3½" by 1". The frames are 3" by 5" fastened to the keel and floor timbers by natural grown knees. The planking is American oak 1" thick.

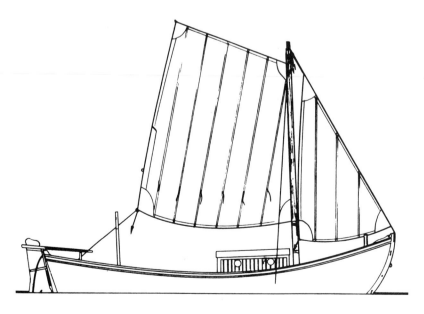

Figure 2-33. The outboard profile and sail plan of an old-style klitmoller boat. She measures 27'6" length, 11'1" beam, and 3'9" draft. There are still a few of these older models in service. (Christian Nielsen)

It is rather unusual to encounter beach craft in the Scandinavian countries. Where there are no convenient natural harbors and artificial harbor breakwaters are prohibitive, the use of beach craft becomes the only solution to working the sea for fish, providing of course that there are beaches in the area. The weather and the sea are so harsh on the Jutland coast that the days of the year fit for launching fishing boats never number much more than one hundred. The larger motorcraft can stay at sea for several days run-

ning, but both the smaller and the larger boats normally fish from sunrise to dark.

SWEDEN

The Scandinavian style of larger fishing craft is used extensively in the Baltic, among the Danish islands, on the coast of Sweden, and in the more protected waters of Norway. (The boats sailing from the western coast of Norway to fish the North Sea will be discussed in Chapter Three

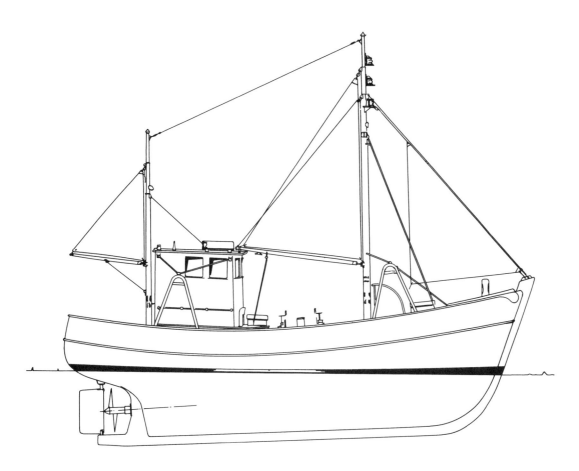

Figure 2-34. Outboard profile of a twentieth-century Danish trawler.

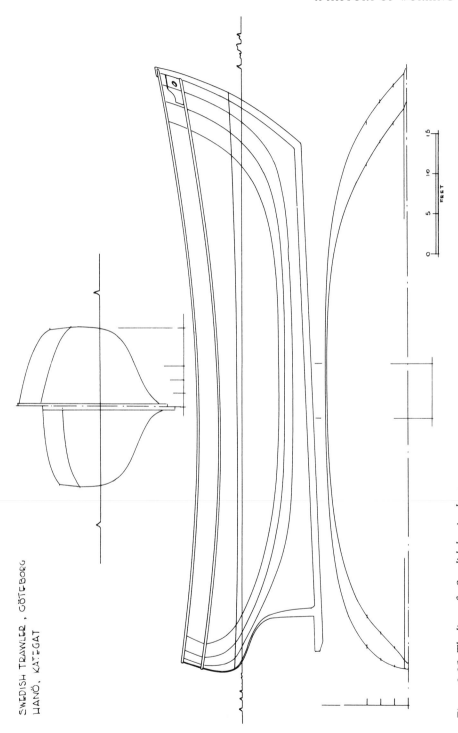

SWEDISH TRAWLER, GÖTEBORG
HANÖ, KATEGAT

Figure 2-35. The lines of a Swedish herring boat. This hull is rugged but graceful, with an inward-raking sternpost and gently curving stem.

Figure 2-36. The bottom of a Swedish herring boat. Her large controllable-pitch propeller indicates she has a heavy, low-speed diesel engine with one forward speed.

Figure 2-37. A modern Danish trawler at rest alongside a fish pier in Copenhagen. This style Danish boat roams the North Sea and the North Atlantic as far west as Greenland.

with the North Sea boats of other lands.) There are local variations, of course, that to an expert eye identify not only the national identity of the fishing craft but also their locale. Before the variations are discussed, however, let us look at a typical contemporary working boat of the Scandinavian character.

This boat is first of all indigenous on a broader scale than perhaps any other type discussed in this book. It is indigenous to the Scandinavian protected and semiprotected waters and has its roots in nineteenth-century boats, such as those of Hornbaek and Skovshoved. The traditions behind this boat's construction, however, began one thousand years or more ago with the Vikings. The most critical non-Scandinavian must admit that the Vikings were the most original and gifted boatbuilders in northern Europe. A composite profile of this typically Scandinavian contemporary working boat of the fisheries is shown in Figure 2-34. She is approximately 45 to 50 feet in length, 16 feet beam, and 6½ feet in loaded draft. Her loaded displacement is perhaps 75 tons.

In the fishing ports of Sweden from Goteborg to the north, many similar boats can be found. The bows of the Swedish boats are fuller with a bit more of the "apple-cheeked" feeling and have stems with a continuous gentle arc. This feature is evident in the herring boats in the harbor of Hono, Sweden.

The Swedish boats in the Baltic as well as those of Denmark and Finland have similar form but crisper lines with a straighter stem. Sometimes they have two masts for steadying sails, as shown in Figure 2-37.

In the protected waters of the Baltic there is a need for small freight carriers to trade among the islands and small ports. These boats are generally nondescript in character but have the recognizable features of nineteenth-century hulls that have been converted to power. Some still have reduced masts and short bowsprits for auxiliary sail. While these boats cannot be classified according to form, they are recognizable as a type, even though they are generally loaded almost to their gunwales and their deck loads of miscellaneous crates obscure their shape (Figure 2-38).

The hulls of the Baltic coasters may be of iron or wood, and often their form is that of the Danish or Swedish schooners that were built nearly a century ago for Baltic and North Sea trade.

A profile of one of these schooners is shown in Figure 2-39. The original schooner, as the illustration shows, was three-masted with topmasts, topsails, and three headsails. The mizzen, unlike that of the American three-masted coasting schooners, was slightly shorter than the fore and main. Sometimes these schooners carried two or three square yards on the fore, making them a sort of topsail schooner. Their hulls, however, were typically Scandinavian, generally with broad transom sterns and sometimes outboard rudders. There were occasional variations with double-ended hulls. The present-day power conversions of these boats will preserve their hulls for

Figure 2-38. This diesel-powered coaster does not disguise the fact that she was once a graceful boat powered by sail alone. She now carries cargo into the out-of-the-way ports of the Danish islands and Swedish coast.

Figure 2-39. Solid lines show the profile of a twentieth-century Baltic coaster. Dotted lines show her nineteeenth-century schooner rig.

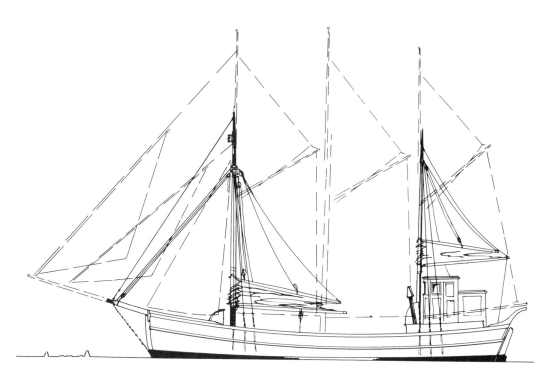

perhaps another quarter century. Whatever their replacements will be, it is certain they will not be of such interesting, graceful, or indigenous design.

There are few evident small beach craft in Sweden, but there are many small, graceful, varnished lapstrake boats. These are used as utility craft and inshore fishing boats. Typical of these are the pram-bow craft, 12 to 15 feet long, found along the west coast of Sweden and the east coast of Denmark. These prams are found elsewhere in northern Europe as well. For instance, in England they are popular for both pleasure craft and utility boats. In Holland the blunt-bow form was first used as a variation of larger working craft and soon became popular for small rowing craft.

The Swedish-Danish version of the pram, as seen in Figures 2-40, 2-41, and 2-42, is long (about 18 feet), light, and narrow, with a bow drawn out nearly to an apex. It is a graceful lapstrake-planked craft, handy under oars or sail, with pronounced rocker in the bottom and a lifting but broad transom stern. These prams are generally varnished bright, as are most of the very small craft in these waters.

As recently as fifty years ago in the Swedish, Estonian, and Finnish waters of the Baltic, there was a type of sailing workboat with pronounced individual character. The most obvious feature of these boats was their great beam, which was sometimes almost half of the length. Their graceful hull form, however, did not give any impression of the bulkiness often associated with such excess width. The ends were deep and fine with a body flaring upward. The boats were lapstrake-planked in oak, had flush decks with an open

Figure 2-40. The Scandinavian pram can be found in most ports along the Skagerrak and Kattegat coasts. Her lines indicate an able and uniquely graceful boat. (Christian Nielsen)

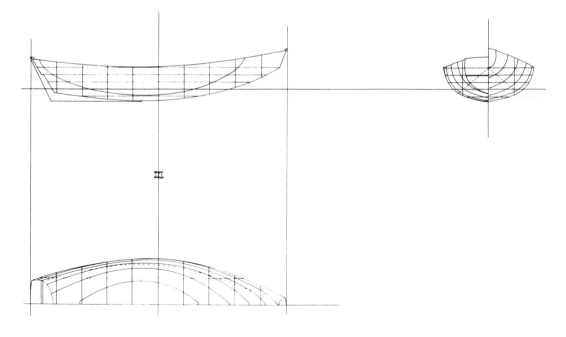

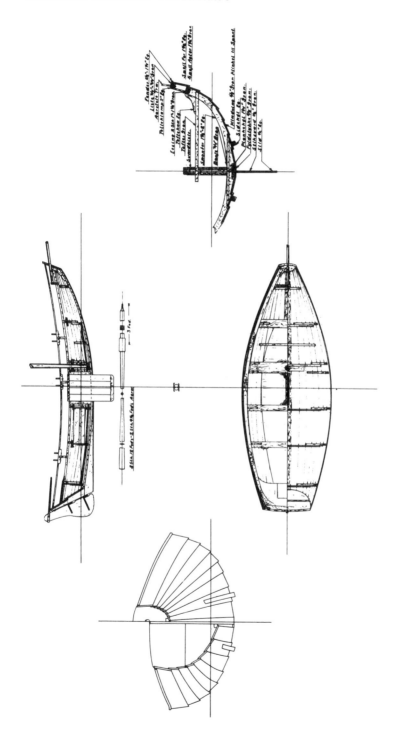

Figure 2-41. The structure of this 18-foot pram is light and strong in the best Norse tradition. As a centerboarder she will perform well and efficiently to windward. (Christian Nielsen)

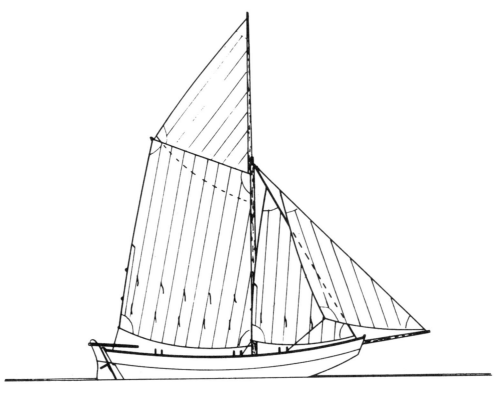

Figure 2-42. The sail plan of the pram in Figures 2-40 and 2-41 indicates a sprit rig with a topsail and two headsails—an exceptionaly well-proportioned rig. This boat measures 18' long, 6'4" beam, and 2'4" depth below her rail amidships. (Christian Nielsen)

heavy rail, and sailed under a lofty sprit rig. They were powerful sailing boats, perhaps as capable as any sailing workboat anywhere at anytime. While they are for all practical purposes now extinct, a remaining example may be encountered here or there under reduced rig and power. They are basically similar to, but larger than the Danish boats of Figures 2-26 and 2-27.

The North Sea is a body of water shared by Norway, Scotland, England, and the Lowlands. It is a large gulf, really, slightly larger than the Aegean Sea but brutally exposed to the Norwe-gian Sea and the Arctic Ocean to the north. Its outlets to the south and east are the Dover Strait to the English Channel, and the Skagerrak to the Danish islands and the Baltic. This North Sea region, more than any other, proves the theory that boats assume like character from the waters they sail in and their employment. The North Sea has for centuries been one of the world's richest fisheries, and the boats that have sailed it regularly have acquired similar character, as have, to an extent, the boats fishing the Grand Banks or those working in many regions of the Mediterranean. For this reason, North Sea–type boats are discussed in further detail in the following chapter, where the Norwegian, Scottish, and British varieties of this boat are covered.

NORWAY

On the Norwegian coast, which borders both the North Sea and the Norwegian Sea, ancient boatbuilding lore persists to a surprising extent in the small inshore working craft. This ancient character is strikingly evident in the inshore boats of the island-fjord region north of Bergen. The craft there are basically all that remain of the once numerous types of powerful offshore fishing and working boats of the last century and early twentieth century.

It is not surprising that Norway has contributed significantly to the finest of seagoing

Figure 2-43. The Nordland boat of the northwestern coast of Norway is classic. The characteristics of this boat, which descends directly from the Norse longships of one thousand years ago, are reflected in many lapstrake boats of Norway today. While this particular boat passed from the active scene in the early 1900s there are smaller rowing models still in use, and a few larger craft similar to this are owned by fishermen in the north islands.

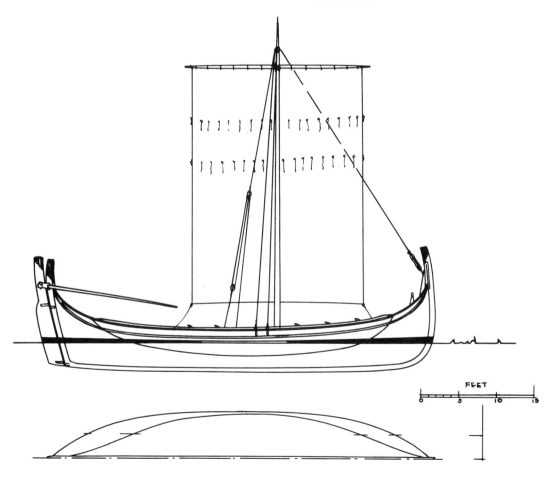

designs. This region of mountains and fjords was the birthplace one thousand years ago of the finely modeled watercraft of the Vikings. These Viking boats were those that carried the fearsome plunderers, the invaders and ultimately the colonizers of Iceland and Greenland. Their boats had to be good for these tough sailors. The skills of the Old Norse shipwrights directly influenced the boats of England, France, and Germany for more than five hundred years. The heritage of Norway has always been the sea. Two-thirds of Norway's population lives on the coastline; 90 percent of its commerce is carried out on the water. The influence of Norwegian maritime knowledge and skill is most currently evident in modern ship design. The great tankers, cargo carriers, naval vessels, yachts, and even tugboats of the world bear the marks of Norwegian designers and the results of the research in their Trondheim Station for Ship Model Testing.

Only the small inshore boats of Norway, especially the rowing craft, retain characteristics of ancient design. Some of these little boats are almost miniature Viking craft. After seeing their natural-grown V-frames and their swept-up stems and sterns, one's first reaction is that they forgot the carved dragon's head. The construction is basically shell-first, edge-fastened lapped strakes, typically only three planks per side in the rowing craft.

The Nordland boat, shown in Figure 2-43, is the true but practically extinct ancestor of the small, so-called bindel boats. This Nordland boat of the nineteenth and early twentieth century is very close to the original model developed a millennium ago. It is a coastal boat used in fishing and transport. It has a single midship mast, a squaresail, six or seven oars per side, and is open from end to end with high stem and stern posts. There are some that have a small covered cuddy cabin aft. About the only concession to modern design is a long rudder mounted on the sternpost by conventional pintles

Figure 2-44. The bindel boat is a small model of the Nordland boat. These can still be seen in use in the western fjords of Norway.

Figure 2-45. Replica boat much the same as a bindel boat rigged for sail with old sprit rig. These boats are very popular in Oslo, where a number of them sail in their class competitively.

Figure 2-46. Two recreational craft similar to Figure 2-45. The dark-hull boat carries a squaresail with the same proportionate profile as the Nordland boat in Figure 2-43. These boats are purely recreational today and are skillfully made and finely finished. They are beautiful re-creations of the Norwegian maritime past.

and gudgeons. (The side steering oar was abandoned sometime during the thirteenth century.)

Figure 2-44 is a photograph of a bindel boat. This particular one is 16 feet long and 5 feet wide and is built in the same ancient manner as the Nordland boat, with grown frames and knees and three planks per side below the painted sheerstrake. She has the ancient Norse curved rowing tholes or *kabes* instead of thole pins (a later invention).

The old Norse type of rowing-sailing boat 15 to 20 feet in length is very popular today about the coast. Similar to the bindel boat described, these

Figure 2-47. This natural-crook cant frame from the bow of a Norse boat of the eleventh century is identical in shape to those used in today's Norwegian skiffs and bindel boats.

Figure 2-48. This graceful Norwegian skiff reflects ancient Viking construction.

Figure 2-49. The Norway skiff, or faering as it is called in Norway (basically indicating four oars), is planked and framed much the same as those of the Vikings one thousand years ago. They are made with only three planks per side. (Owen Wicksteed)

Figure 2-50. The faering seen bottom up shows the true sheer attained by the three-plank sided hull. This is a Hardanger faering; they are the ubiquitous inshore boat among the fjords. (Owen Wicksteed)

Figure 2-51. The Hardanger faering bow showing clearly her simple planking. (Owen Wicksteed)

Figure 2-52. The Gokstad two-oared skiff and faering found in the Gokstad wreck of 900 AD. (Oslo Museum)

boats are used for pleasure now. Their owners take great pride in their style and maintain them in the most painstaking way. Much like antique autos in America, the boats (Figure 2-46) are kept brightly visible and shown in regular meetings or rendezvous. They are handsome boats with a direct and proud link to the past.

Figure 2-47 shows a natural-grown V-frame from a Norwegian boat recently uncovered by archaeologists in Bergen, Norway. The boat from which this frame came was built during the mid to late Viking era, about AD 1100. As a structural member it was significantly a part of all Viking craft (see Figure 1-9). It is still to be found forward or aft in today's Norwegian boats, and in most small lapstrake Scandinavian boats. While these natural-grown crotch frames may not be startlingly unique, they are excellent examples of the persistence of ancient practice. Another and even more localized example of Viking-type framing is a built-up inverted A-frame. This type of frame is found in the earliest of Viking craft and is particularly evident in the Gokstad and Oseberg ships, preserved in the Oslo Museum, of AD 900, as well as the Danish Roskilde ships of AD 1000. (See Chapter One.) It is most evident in the interior structure of the ubiquitous present-day Norwegian small craft known as *faerings*, meaning four-oared (Figures 2-49, 2-50, 2-51, 2-52).

If there is any watercraft anywhere that is reduced to the simplest *essence of a boat* it is the Norwegian faering. John Ruskin wrote a century or more ago about such a boat:

*. . . the bow of a boat—a common undecked sea boat, lying aside in its furrow of
beach sand; the sum of navigation is in that. You may magnify it or decorate it as
you will: you do not add to the wonder of it. Lengthen it into a hatchetlike edge of
iron, strengthen it with a complex tracery of ribs of oak, carve it and gild it till a
column of light moves beneath it on the sea, you have made no more of it than it
was at first. That rude simplicity of bent plank, that can breast its way through the
death that is in the deep sea, has in it the soul of shipping.*

To extend this thought beyond Ruskin's bow of the boat, the Norwegian
faering has in its whole length the essence and "soul of shipping." Though
this skiff has only three planks per side—often unfinished with the mill saw
marks still showing—these planks are spiled and bent to form the most
graceful of boat shapes. The form of the Norwegian skiff is quite consistent
among the many examples that can be found along the west coast of

*Figure 2-53. The lines, structure,
and rig of an authentic Hardanger
faering built in 1896. (Owen Wicksteed)*

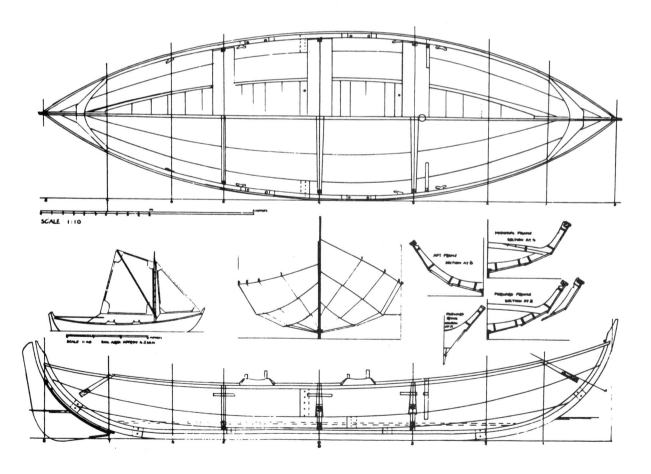

Norway. It is most easily described by reference to Figures 2-51, 2-52, and 2-53. It is a rakish little double-ended hull that reflects at a glance its lightness and rowability, as well as its stability and capability in rough water. There are few frames in the average skiff of this type, perhaps four at the most. The forward and aftermost V-frames are canted as shown in the illustration. Sometimes these boats carry a short mast with a lugsail or a loose-footed gaff sail and jib. Whether the propulsion is by oar and ancient hooked thole or by sail, the boat is always most simple and functional. If there is such a thing as the "basic boat," it must be here. Figure 2-53 shows the hull lines and detail of a classic faering.

These handsome little boats of the Norwegian coasts are all-purpose workboats. For a locale such as the west coast of Norway with its rugged mountainous shoreline, cut into by deep fjords for hundreds of miles, such boats are adaptable. The seacoast extends above the Arctic Circle and as far south as the Skagerrak, the stormy water separating Norway from Denmark. There are rocky islands all along the coast with thousands of inlets for protected landings and isolated domiciles, villages, and towns. At any of these places scores of small craft are tied up or dragged ashore. As well as being the vehicles for fishing and hauling, boats are the only transportation and connecting link to the world. And the smallest of these is the faering. It is light enough to be launched or hauled ashore by one man or two. It is buoyant enough to carry six to eight times its weight. Its stability is similar to a New England dory—the more it is loaded, the greater its waterline widens. It rows easily and sails well.

In fact, it is a boat so impressive that it has been the subject of scholarly research by the British National Maritime Museum and the University Museum of National Antiquities in Oslo. Its modern version became ubiquitous in Norway's fjords. A replica of the original Gokstad faering, found in the gravesite with the great Viking Gokstad ship, was built and thoroughly tested. This boat, Figure 2-52, was in remarkably good condition.

Figure 2-54. (Right) The great fjord region of Norway when studied in this map quickly convinces one that it is a place requiring water transportation. The broken lines mark the ferry routes for regular travel. The residents of the fjord villages must themselves rely on their small sailing and rowing craft such as the faerings for local transport. The land about them is rugged mountain terrain, mostly snow-covered year round. (Owen Wicksteed)

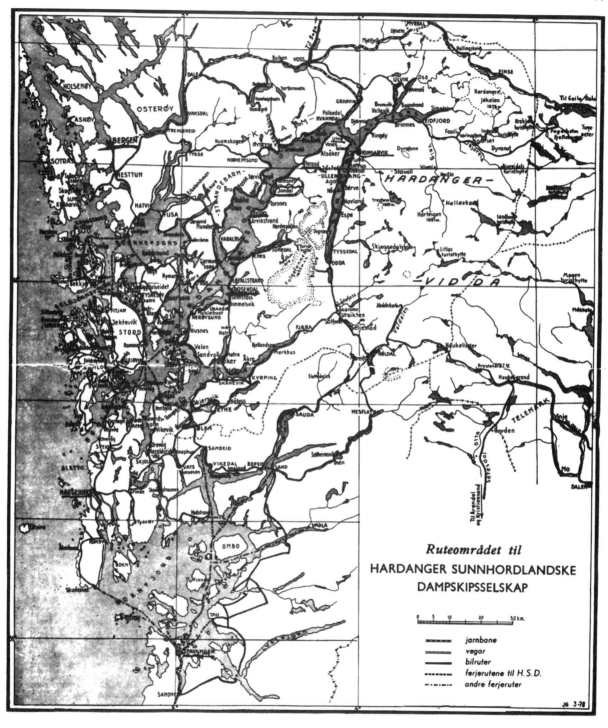

Ruteområdet til

HARDANGER SUNNHORDLANDSKE
DAMPSKIPSSELSKAP

Figure 2-55. A detailed view of a model of the Gokstad faering rigged for rowing. Note the side rudder on the starboard quarter.

This original, dating more than one thousand years past, actually to AD 870, is a longer boat than presently used and of less beam. The contemporary (AD 1900) Hardanger Fjord model is 5.46 meters (17.9 feet) length overall and 2.60 meters (8.5 feet) maximum beam. The Gokstad faering is 6.56 meters 21.5 feet) overall and maximum beam of 1.438 meters (4.72 feet). Thus the length/beam ratio is 4.56 for this ancient boat and 2.124 for the Hardanger boat. The contrasting ratios show only a difference in application of the two faerings separated by 1,030 years. They are both designed and structured nearly identically. They have three planks per side, the same number of identically structured transverse frames, and the same V-cant frames forward and aft. The proportions vary primarily because the Gokstad boat was carried aboard the larger Gokstad ship where her beam would be critical.

The dimensions of the replica of the Gokstad boat built and tested by the British National Maritime Museum are interesting:

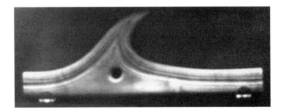

Figure 2-56. A typical oar thole carved for the Gokstad faering; a Viking style seldom used today.

Figure 2-57. Preserved and restored section of a wrecked Norse ship of the medieval period in Sweden. The ship dates from approximately AD 1250. The construction shows basically the earlier Viking construction with elaboration of deck beams, solid floor futtock, vertical post-stanchion support under deck windlass. This windlass is mounted aft for the main halyard, which hauls up the heavy main yard. The Viking-type boat has progressed. (State Museum, Stockholm)

Figure 2-58. This is a one-of-a-kind boat that cannot disguise its native Scandinavian character, although it may be trying. It is a privately owned boat with cabin accommodations and a comfortable cockpit built on a lapstrake, seakindly Scandinavian hull. It may be a miniature pilot boat, with its rubber tire fenders along the side. It was photographed in Bergen, Norway, in 1966.

Length overall	21.53 feet (6.56m)
Maximum beam	4.72 feet (1.43m)
Vertical height of hull at B max	1.63 feet (0.496m)
Stripped (empty) hull weight	237 lbs (107.96 kg)
Prismatic coefficient	.514
Maximum loaded displacement	2,000 lbs

A further but more significant difference between the ancient Gokstad faering and the contemporary faering is the oar length. The standard formula today for oar length on most Norwegian boats is the max beam of the boat plus ½ of the max beam: (Bmx + Bmx/2) = Oar Length.

The oars found with the Gokstad ship for the small boats were approximately 15 percent longer than today's. This simple difference between the basic propulsive instruments, otherwise the same—carved in the same manner, with the same looms and blades and thole diameters—prompts questions. Were the Viking men stronger with more endurance? Could they row the boats faster, or had they not yet figured out the easier way?

The construction of both the larger and smaller Norse hulls is remarkably well thought out. Because the foregoing description has been piecemeal, the Norse construction system should be further considered. The Viking style and method for wood vessel construction, especially in Norway, was used in boats of all sizes and employment, and it still exists in some vessels. It was applied in wood construction until wood ceased to be the basic boatbuilding material.

It began in the Dark Ages, sometime before the eighth century AD, when the only building tools in this early Iron Age were sharpened blades and hammers. The early Norse did not use saws—they did not want them.[1] The lapstrake planks were split to proper thickness and adzed or planed to smooth the surfaces. The floor frames were formed from natural crooks, with beams connecting the sides shaped by adze from natural-growth knees. Figure 2-57 shows a section of a larger Norse-built vessel taken from a wreck of approximately AD 1250–1300.

The reader should not conclude from the discussion here that Norway's native watercraft are confined to bindel boats, Nordland boats, or faerings. There are perhaps more individual types of local watercraft along the almost limitless shoreline of Norway's rugged coast than in any other country. The very interesting book *Inshore Craft of Norway*, edited by Arne Emil Christensen of Oslo, describes nearly fifty locations along the Norwegian coast with their native boats and variations. The word *variations* is key in studying these watercraft. They all exhibit the character and basic structure of the Scandinavian heritage first developed by the Norse people more than a thousand years ago. It is regrettable that it is not possible to reproduce their images in photographs and lines drawings on these pages, but for that we heartily recommend Arne Christensen's book. You will understand what I mean about variations.

[1] Saws were used in the Bronze Age in the Near East and the ancient Aegean countries.

THE FRENCH CHANNEL
AND NORTH ATLANTIC COAST

Aside from the erosive effects of time and the gradual changes of economy and technology, the factor most destructive to small indigenous workboats has been the great wars that have swept northern Europe in this century. Both World War I and II combined to eliminate effectively the most picturesque as well as capable sailing workboats of the continental English–French Channel coast. The small luggers that sailed out of the fishing ports of Brittany, Normandy, and Flanders are now gone. They were doubtless doomed anyway, but would have lingered perhaps a while longer had not they and their industry been overwhelmed by the violence of war. These craft were sunk by passing gunboats and U-boats for target practice and were commandeered by invading troops. It was not profitable to replace them with boats of the same form and rig. The fisheries of Belgium are now served by modern boats of larger and more efficient design. The inshore fisheries of the French coast are no longer productive for smaller craft. There

Figure 2-59. The older fishing craft under sail along the Normandy and Brittany coast are distinctive in their lug rigs. Many are being restored and rebuilt today as a pleasure type for racing. They are all particularly in evidence during the Maritime Festival in Brest, which has the promise of being a regularly recurring event. In July 1992, the three-day festival attracted 955,000 visitors. These boats are reminders of the great fleets of luggers of the last century where the chasse-marée originated (Figures 2-60 and 2-61). The vessel in the foreground is the well-known type called Bisquinne. The boat in the center mid-distance is called a Plougastel. (Tom Price)

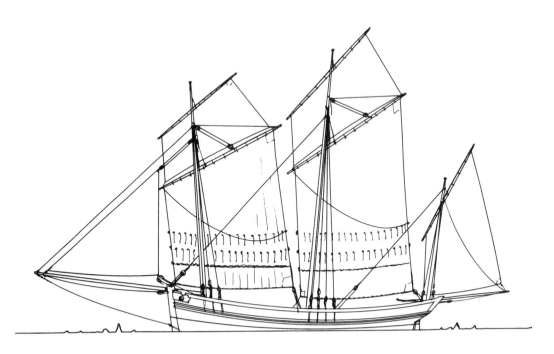

Figure 2-60. The classic profile of a chasse-marée of Brittany on the French coast of the English Channel. This boat is the origin of much of the rugged construction and hull form of today's modern French and Flemish trawlers. These boats originated in the early nineteenth century and continued to be used until World War II.

are thus precious few boats on this coast that can be described as indigenous originals.

It is interesting to reflect on an example of the life of an old European boat. Probably many more boats than are readily evident have a number of lives and experiences as they grow old and pass through good times and bad times. Some old hulks are never restored, like a number of the great clipper ships of the 1850s and 60s that ended their days as coal barges. On the other hand, some that began their lives in very humble circumstances lived on through much brighter days after restoration. I am thinking of old fishing vessels such as the Gloucester schooner *Ernestina*, which was rescued in the Cape Verde Islands as a rotting hulk, returned to the United States for salvation, and is now a celebrated sail training vessel. And others—in addition to *Gazela Primeiro*, beginning as a Portuguese fishing barkentine, now a tall ship of Philadelphia. Some privileged people now have the delightful experience of

Figure 2-61. A double topsail Bisquinne of Brittany, popularly called a chasse-marée. (National Maritime Museum, Paris)

traveling in the Burgundy Canals of France for a week or two, dining on the most delicious French food freshly gathered and prepared each day, aboard a very happy boat moving slowly through the wondrous Burgundy countryside. This one particular boat, restored with some seven state-rooms, a dining lounge, and other luxury appointments, began its life sometime before World War I as a small steam collier in a firth of northern Scotland. It was sold into the British coastal trade, and was commandeered during World War II to help evacuate the British army from Dunkirk. It eventually found its way to France as a river barge, and was ultimately purchased, restored, and rebuilt in 1975 to become a canal cruising barge that I experienced. That old boat has had a full life.

Figure 2-62. The profile of a powered fishing craft of the French coast of the English Channel. Many of the older boats are converted luggers, though the more recently constructed boats follow the same basic form and profile. The similarity of this hull with that of the chasse-marée is evident.

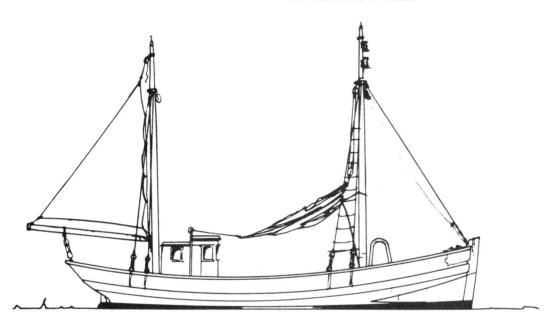

Figure 2-63. *This post-World War II fishing boat of Normandy is rigged in the tradition of the old plumb-stemmed luggers.*

Before passing over the English–French Channel to the working boats of the British Islands in the following chapter, it might be appropriate to discuss briefly a former boat of the Brittany coast and its descendants as a respectful tribute to a shining seagoing tradition. Figures 2-60 and 2-61 illustrate a French *chasse-marée* or "sea hunter." The profile of this boat shows the basic character of these powerful luggers.

They came in different sizes and detail, these luggers of Brittany. Chasse-mareé is the traditional name for the old luggers, which vied with one another in annual races and competed among themselves in their regular races from the fishing grounds to market. The old ones carried towering layers of lug sails. The survivors today are mostly from seaports in West Normandy and North Brittany, such as Granville and Cancale. Along this latter coast were localized three-masted luggers of similar form called Bisquinnes—now called "queens" of the old French fishing boats. (See Figure 2-59.) A two-master from Cancale is smaller and has only single lugsails, but its masts are tall enough to set lug topsails on occasion. The masts on these boats are rugged and lightly stayed, the main raking aft and supported longitudinally by a heavy mainstay; the foremast is supported laterally by shrouds run to chainplates well forward, as the mast is stepped well into the bow. A long, near horizontal jibboom is run out to port of the stemhead—a housing spar—and carries a broad lowcut jib set flying. Altogether, these boats of the French coast carry on today a most respectable seagoing tradition of restoration and preservation. Annual festivals are held at which as many as one hundred boats gather to show themselves and compete. They are all of a single character, but of individual stripe. They are lovely, beautiful, and impressive deepwater boats.

This type of boat most represents the feeling and character of all the sailing workboats of the northern French and Flemish coasts that last operated commercially in the first part of the twentieth century. It cannot be possible that the traditions and skills of indigenous boatbuilders were lost when these boats ceased to exist. Their sailing rigs and some of their form and line are still part of an occasional contemporary boat found sailing from Britain, such as their modern trawlers. Indigenous tradition, for the most part, is immortal.

CHAPTER THREE

TRADITIONAL WORKING BOATS OF THE BRITISH ISLANDS

On THE NORTHEAST COAST OF Saxon England in the latter part of the eleventh century, one fine day in mid-September, a troop of Viking warriors had assembled. It was east of the city of York along the Derwent River. They had departed the Orkney Islands several weeks past with some 250 Norse longships fitted out and supplied for an expedition of invasion as well as plunder. They were commanded by a Viking lord named Harald Hardrada (Harald the hard leader), a scarred veteran of many plunderings and a lifetime of armed aggression. No question, he was a leader of men, and his intentions this time were to take over the kingdom of England from King Harold Godwinson. His strategy was to begin his invasion here in the North Sea coast near York, to subdue and consolidate the people, with his partner Tostig, the brother of the English king. They had already plundered and burned a small town south of York and defeated a troop of defenders outside the city.

Harald Hardrada waited with nearly half his army of berserkers for a negotiating group of leading British citizens from the city of York just over the hill to the west. He would talk about hostages to be given to him to prevent that city from plunder and worse. As the Vikings waited, they saw the British truce party appear over the rim of the hill, or so they perceived. The hilltop was less than a mile away, beyond which was the outline of the York Cathedral. As they watched the group approach along this road from York, it grew, and there were the misty silhouettes of men on horseback. The bright sun at the Vikings' back to the east was being reflected in flickering flashes off polished steel—armored negotiators? It was soon evident that Harald from Norway was being approached by King Harold of England and his army, an army that had been waiting all summer on England's southern coast to repel the rumored invasion by Duke William of Normandy.

This day along the River Derwent by Stamford Bridge was the beginning of the beginning of the permanent establishment of the sovereign kingdom

of England. It began here with the face-to-face encounter between Harold of England and his Viking enemy, Harald of Norway.

King Harold's forced march from the south of England to York is one of the most significant feats in military history. The ensuing battle there at Stamford Bridge near York and the total defeat of Harald's Vikings set in motion a series of events that determined the destiny of the English-speaking world. The Vikings who survived were expelled from English soil, and never did any return. During the nearly two hundred years preceding, they had left their mark: part of their language, their system of money, and much of their tradition. They had done their thing, and in departing, had left an everlasting maritime heritage.

Following the Battle of Stamford Bridge, while King Harold was at a banquet in York

Figure 3-1. The segment of William the Conqueror's story in the Bayeux Tapestry at the bottom of this illustration is reflected above by two of his ships as they more likely appeared. His flagship or command vessel is to the right with the cross and lantern at the masthead, as seen in the tapestry. His amphibious operation was one of history's most significant invasions. He landed some seven thousand armed soldiers together with three thousand horses for the cavalry troops. Not until World War II was this sort of amphibious maneuver successfully repeated—in the reverse direction—nearly nine hundred years later.

celebrating his victory, a messenger who had been riding three days from the south entered the hall and proceeded to the king's table. He told King Harold that William of Normandy had landed on the English shores at Pevensey on the Channel. The year was 1066.

In a single, amphibious maneuver, William of Normandy landed nearly seven thousand men at Pevensey. Accompanying this horde of knights and soldiers were three thousand horses, together with an arsenal of weapons, armor, and supplies to sustain a protracted invasion. The boats, about 450, that carried this formidable amphibious conquest were Viking-type longships, authentic down to their decorative dragon heads and tails at stems and sterns, striped and otherwise decorated single squaresails, shields along the gunwales, and long curved steering oars. The boats crossed the Channel at night under sail, for William wisely waited for a favorable wind rather than prematurely exhaust his men at the oars. Most of the boats were fitted with thirty-two oars. They were built of lapstrake oak planks by skilled Norman shipwrights at the mouth of the River Dives on the Norman coast. There is no reason to believe that these ships were different in size, shape, and construction from those that had been used by Viking raiders and Norman settlers for the several hundred years prior to William's invasion. They were longships like those found intact or nearly so in modern Norway and exhibited today (see Gokstad ship, Chapter One).

William's ships are illustrated in a remarkable work commemorating his conquest. The invasion story is told on a 321-foot tapestry 20 inches wide that was hand-woven at the bidding of William's wife, Matilda. This tapestry illustrates the actions of Duke William from the time he was promised the English throne by King Edward the Confessor to his bloody victory over King Harold at Hastings. This original picture-history can be seen today in the city of Bayeux in the French province of Normandy. On it can be seen the boats being built for the conquest, their

provisioning, their Channel crossing, and their landing (Figure 3-1).

Before William's conquest, England was ruled piecemeal by jealous Saxon lords who were unable to prevent frequent landings and pillagings by aggressive Danish raiders. Many of these raiders chose to settle, and a succession of Danish and Saxon kings before King Harold sat on uneasy thrones. William consolidated these factions in the eleventh century, and England became a unified nation of sea-conscious people.

The digression into early Anglo-Saxon, Viking, and Norman history is justified to establish the evident links of the ancient boats of more than a millennium past to the existing maritime structures and maritime arts in the British Isles.

The lapped plank boats are strongly evident where wooden boats exist. The building techniques are common to all down to the square-cut copper rivets with the same shaped heads and ferrules on the inside plank surface. In the northern waters of the British Isles, in the Orkneys and the Shetlands, the shapes of hulls are recognizable extensions of old Norse craft—or were until local people stopped building wooden boats. Somewhere in remote waterways and near small fishing villages there may still be survivors.

The Norse-type boats and later ships that developed were to follow the solid, no-nonsense structure of the boats of the Norsemen. These boats had a fine entrance at the waterline with hollow abaft the forefoot, flaring bows, and a lifting sheerline. In the centuries that followed, their kind led to a number of cumbersome larger craft, ordered, no doubt, by seapower-conscious monarchs.

We must look at the environment surrounding the British Isles, including the North Sea, as we note specific British small craft. The British Isles, in the context of this chapter, refers to the waters surrounding England, Scotland, and Ireland, as well as the small island groups such as the Shetlands, Hebrides, and Faeroes. The political boundaries within this region are of minor importance to this study.

SCOTTISH-NORSE HERITAGE

At the northern limits of this region, the coast of Scotland on the North Sea is closer to the fjords of Norway than to London or the southern shores of England. It is natural that common working of the rich North Sea fisheries should bring about close similarities between Norwegian and Scottish craft, as does the ancient inheritance from Viking occupation.

The small working boats of Scotland and the east coast of England have been influenced through history almost totally by the fortunes of the herring industry. Salt-cured herring has been a staple of diet for the people of northern Europe for at least a millennium, and for several centuries this industry was dominated by the thrifty Dutch. Until King Charles I in the seventeenth century demanded the large fee of 30,000 pounds from Holland for the privilege of catching the fish near the English and Scottish coasts, neither the English nor the Scots had engaged seriously in this industry. Until then, the fishermen of Britain had only fished inshore from small open boats to provide for their own families or, at most, local communities. Their boats were similar to the Norwegian skiffs and boats described in Chapter Two. They were open boats of lapstrake construction, propelled by oars or a very simple sailing rig. Such boats have prevailed in isolated regions in small numbers until now (early to mid twentieth century), especially in the islands

Figure 3-2. This old Norwegian herring boat's ancient line is closely related to the old Scottish boats and to the earlier Viking type. (The Science Museum, London)

Figure 3-3. The Shetland ness yole was simply an enlarged version of the Norway skiff. The component parts were often imported from Norway, prefabricated. (The Science Museum, London)

Figure 3-4. The North Isle yole, a harbor and coastal boat, is almost a direct descendant of the Norse craft. (The Science Museum, London)

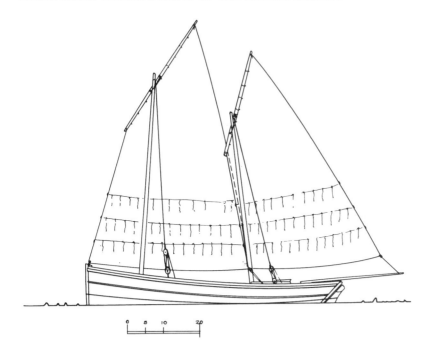

Figure 3-5. The Scottish zulu was essentially a fifie with an extreme rake to the sternpost. This same type of hull with the raked sternpost is still evident in some trawlers of Scotland and Ireland today.

north of Scotland. However, the demand for herring brought on the Anglo-Dutch wars of the seventeenth century and ultimately resulted in the development of larger fishing craft supporting a thriving industry from the bays and firths of Scotland.

By the nineteenth century these Scottish-built fishing craft dominated the coastal and offshore fisheries in the British North Sea waters and were sheltered from any serious foreign threat by the great navy of the British Empire. The boats were of many categories but were generally two-masted, lug-rigged sailing craft varying in length from 35 to 70 feet. Many of them were unattractive, marginal-design products of builders with limited skills. On the other hand, there were a few types "designed" and built by craftsmen of considerable capability. These boats were to be the ones that prevailed and survived the transition from sail to power.

Before considering these present-day power craft, the smaller open fishing boats that preceded the upturn in the herring fishery industry should be described. In the Shetland Islands and the Orkneys and south as far as Moray Firth, a type of open fishing boat called a sixern established a notable reputation. The name refers to the boat's complement of six oars. Its style and configuration was definitely Norse, being clinker-built double-ended with upswept stem and stern sheerlines similar to Nordland boats. These boats evolved into larger craft and ultimately, in the nineteenth century, became known as scaffies. At the same time, the enlargement of many

Figure 3-6. The sixern was a heavier boat than the ness yole and operated farther offshore. Sixerns were about 32 feet in length and 10 feet in beam, and were lapstrake-planked of fir in the Norwegian manner and iron fastened. They were used extensively until the beginning of this century for deep-sea line and net fishing and carried a single, dipping lugsail. They contributed, together with the other Scottish boats of this and related character, to the well-known fifie type and, later, to the contemporary trawler. (The Science Museum, London)

Scottish harbors and the population growth resulting from the Industrial Revolution brought greater demands on the fisheries, and larger, decked boats were built. These larger fishing craft lacked most of the Norse or Viking flavor of the earlier small craft but still retained the double-ended form and the lugsail rig. The most predominant type was called a fifie. The predominant features of a fifie were its "melon-seed" double-ended hull, nearly vertical stem and stern, and rather flat sheer profile. (See Figure 3-7.) Individually they were not distinguished by their beauty; however, a fleet of them running for harbor with a fresh catch in a North Sea gale should have been a most impressive sight.

These boats and similar craft performed most ably for nearly three-quarters of a century in the North Sea herring industry. As a matter of fact, this entire North Sea enterprise continued to

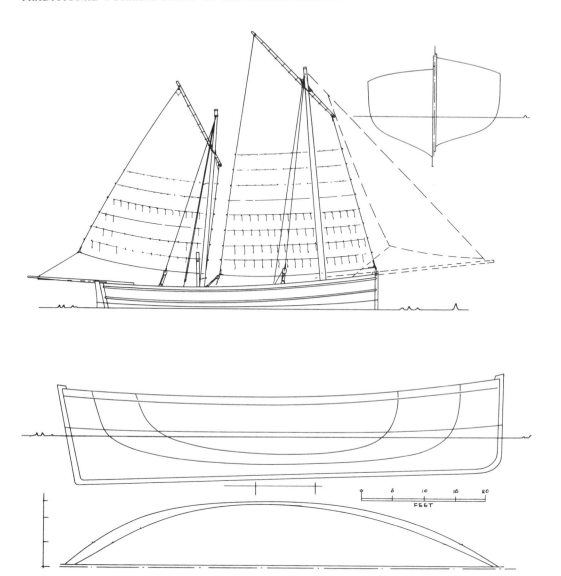

Figure 3-7. *The outboard profile and lines of a Scottish fifie. This boat, when mechanically powered, became the prototype for the later modern wooden trawlers and ring netters.*

enjoy increasing prosperity. At the turn of the century there were no fewer than eight distinct types of sailing herring drifters operating from Scottish and English harbors, with the Scottish boats predominating in size and number. The largest were the Scotch fifie and a similar craft called the zulu, which was basically a large fifie with the raked sternpost of the scaffie. Such boats were up to nearly 80 feet in length. With the introduction of power to the drifters and trawlers, steam power predominated, but finally succumbed to diesel engines.

The first motor fishing vessels were actually fifie-type hulls with a short steadying sail rig on two masts. The subsequent development of fishing gear and improved methods brought a new type of net called the ring net, which made catching herring simpler and more dependable. This development in turn brought a fundamental change in hull design, primarily because handling the ring net required a more maneuverable, quick-turning boat. The outboard rudder and extreme aft location of the propeller used on boats of the fifie-type hull were awkward and unresponsive,

Figure 3-9. The contemporary Scottish ring netter is a most powerful and impressive boat. In this fine example built by Miller and Sons of St. Monance, Fife, Scotland, in 1966, the strong Norse heritage is still evident in her sweeping sheer, the rise of her stem, and her fine entrance. She is 58 feet long overall and 18½ feet in beam. (James N. Miller and Sons, Ltd.)

Figure 3-10. This Norwegian seiner is very similar in style to the Scottish model. This similarity is the result of the need to perform the same function in the same environment and is not necesssarily the result of imitation. (Jenssens Foto, Hougesund, Norway)

and the propeller frequently broke water in a seaway. Consequently, the canoe stern or modified cruiser stern was adopted. Boats of this configuration, as illustrated in Figures 3-8 and 3-9, are the basic, indigenous North Sea herring fish boats of today. Similar fishing craft sail from Scottish, English, and Norwegian harbors as well as from many Dutch and Belgian ports.

In this industry, boats are generally becoming larger. Their more sophisticated designs and steel hulls (especially if they are Dutch) consequently destroy their indigenous character. However, the Scottish and Norwegian boats hold closely to the old traditions. They are built of wood, largely pitch pine on oak frames. The Norwegian boats invariably have bright-varnished

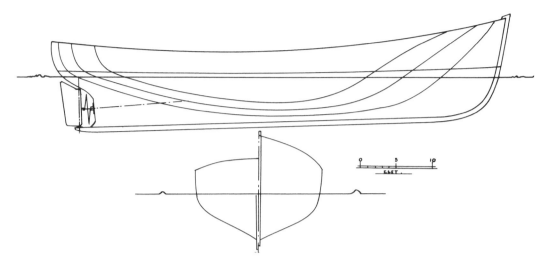

Figure 3-11. The hull form of a typical Scottish ring netter is shown in this drawing of the lines profile. This hull is taken from the compilation of towing tank tests by the Food and Agriculture Organization, Fishing Boat Section. The boat was built in Dunbarton, Scotland, in 1945.

hulls showing the yellowish wood-grained planks. They also carry a white stripe at the sheer below the rail from stem to stern. The only characteristic difference between these Scottish North Sea boats and those from Bergen and Stavanger and other Norwegian ports is the straighter stempost of the North Sea boats. Norwegian herring drifters have decks that are quite wide forward, which produces a flaring bow, and sometimes they have a counter stern and a large deckhouse aft. Essentially they are indigenous to the North Sea and have established a reputation over the world for their seaworthiness and handiness in foul weather.

To better illustrate the hull configuration and proportions of these splendid North Sea boats, the hull lines of a typical Scottish ring netter are reproduced in Figure 3-11. These modified lines

have been redrawn from a tank test report provided through the Food and Agriculture fishing boat section of the United Nations. This North Sea boat was built in 1945 in Dumbarton, Scotland. Her dimensions are 62 feet overall, 17.4 feet beam, and 7.21 feet draft aft. She is powered by a four-cylinder diesel engine developing about 140 horsepower, which produces a top speed of about 10 knots. Note that there is a definite flattening in the run from amidships to the quarter. The bow sections show a nice flare, and a full deck line carried out to the stem indicates a dry hull.

I had occasion several years ago to tank-test a hull very much like this one in a series of rough-water tests comparing her with a more sophisticated and more contemporary trawler hull. The newer hull had a more rakish stem with a fuller stern and finer waterlines. There were other subtle differences in coefficients. Needless to say, but surprising to the students conducting the tests, the older boat proved markedly superior in waves that were progressively increased in height. With both boats loaded similarly, she was able to hold a modest cruising speed in waves that would have required the more modern boat to heave to. Throughout the entire sets of wave spectrums in which the tests were conducted, the power required for equivalent speeds was less for the Scottish herring drifter. A modern designer would be well advised to look closely at this boat's form if it is an able seaboat hull he or she is to create. It is not difficult, for one accustomed to studying hull lines, to see the obscured reflection of an old Norse hull in this Scottish boat. This basic hull form persists with slight variations throughout the British Isles, and may be seen in some boats of North America.

To uncover the purest indigenous boats, those that reflect the ancient forms with the least obscurity, it is necessary to look to the most isolated communities—communities where the people live in environments remote from contemporary society. The most fruitful locales are usually islands, displaced from the trails of commerce and the technological paraphernalia so common to twentieth-century civilization. Such communities are becoming increasingly rare, but one such still thrives in the seas north of Scotland, equidistant from Norway, Iceland, and Scotland. This is the small archipelago of the Faeroes.

The Faeroes were occupied more than a thousand years ago by Norsemen following the earlier Viking raiding parties. It is said that the Vikings drove out or killed the Celtic monks who first settled in the seventh century as a recluse order. There are still ruins of an ancient and forgotten abbey there. The Faeroese of today are unmistakably the descendants of the early Norse settlers, and their lives, their habits, and their traditions of dress bear striking similarity to the old Danish and Norwegian styles. While their culture is not primitive, they have adapted to a lifestyle caused by centuries of self-sufficiency. Also, while they have been a part of the Kingdom of Denmark for many hundreds of years, they speak a language of their own more similar to that of the ninth- and tenth-century Norse than to any modern Scandinavian tongue. Although their diet is varied and somewhat similar to other Scandinavian diets, their most basic staples are air-cured mutton, seabirds and their eggs, and processed whale blubber, which is a delicacy. Until only recently in this century, their homes were of rugged old stone with sod roofs. It is natural to expect that the boats used by these people would have much in common with the boats that the Norsemen first brought to these shores one thousand years ago, and this is the case; today's Faeroese boats are practically the same in structure and form as the ancient Viking craft, but heavier. They are in configuration roughly similar to the shapely Norwegian faerings but have a greater variation in size, from 12 feet to nearly 40. They carry two to eight oars, and have eight to thirteen lapped strakes per side. These Faeroese boats have retained a remnant of ancient style that is unique.

A typical eight-oared boat used in the inshore fisheries is nearly 35 feet overall on a beam of 8 feet. (See Figure 3-12.) She is lapstrake-planked over sawn double frames widely spaced, and is undecked even to the ends,

Figure 3-12. Boats of the Faeroe Islands show the character and detail of ancient Norse construction, but at the same time retain their own individuality. The Faeroe Islanders are direct descendants of Viking colonists who settled in the Faeroes during the ninth and tenth centuries. Until recent years, they had little trade with the outside world. (The Science Museum, London)

with stem and stern post elevated about 12 inches above the sheerline. Both the sternpost and the stempost are curved in profile from keel to head.

Some Faeroese boats carry an outboard rudder but a steering oar is common. They do not have the extreme upswept sheer in their ends reminiscent of the Viking longboats, but instead have the more natural, lively sheer of the Norse working boats, and perhaps of the ancient knorrs, which were tenth- and eleventh-century Norse trading boats. These boats, needless to say, are superb boats in rough water. Their origins are basically the same as the small beach craft and inshore boats of Denmark, the skiffs of Norway, the transplanted lapstrake boats of Nova Scotia,

and the New England whaleboats of the past century.

In a number of the Faeroese boats, an outboard motor is often observed sputtering in a central well cut into the hull alongside the keel. The lines and structure of the boat are intact, but I wonder how long these sailors, accustomed to oars, will live with this smelly, noisy mechanism before becoming aware that it is more efficient at the stern of a flatter bottomed hull.

On the North Sea coast of England there are few indigenous craft, and those that remain are slowly becoming extinct. This coast, as well as the rest of the British coast, was not too long ago the home of a multitude of sailing workboat

Figure 3-13 and *Figure 3-14.* This small, rugged Scottish boat is locally known as a pot hauler. Anywhere else she would be called a lobster-boat. Her heavy construction is similar to her larger sister, the Scottish ring netter, as they are both descended from the same sailing drifters. She was built in St. Monance in 1965 with larch planking on an oak frame. She is 28 feet long, 10 feet in beam, and 3 feet in draft. She is powered by a 28-h.p. diesel. (James N. Miller and Sons, Ltd.)

types. Now it is a region of small working power-boats that are beyond categorization. Most of these boats are modern examples of independent or experimental design that have lost all traces of heritage. There are some, however, that show the influence of Scottish builders and are variations of the powerful North Sea drifter type described previously. The skills of Scotland's building yards have been used extensively by the English for centuries. Scottish yards have built craft ranging from the largest Cunard ships to the smallest fishing boats.

The smaller fishing boats used for prawning, lobstering, and scallop dredging are essentially smaller versions of the same hulls as those of the herring drifter and even larger trawlers. They average about 30 feet in length and are double-ended beamy hulls with diesel engines of about 30 h.p. A typical Scottish type used for lobstering is illustrated in Figures 3-13 and 3-14. She was built in St. Monans, Fife, Scotland, for a fisherman of Bournemouth, England. She is 28 feet long, 10 feet in beam, and 3 feet in draft, and is powered by a 28-h.p. diesel. Built in 1965 of larch planking on oak frames, she has a large, roomy well deck with a combined wheelhouse and engine aft. She has a single mast with steadying sail which, unlike the triangular sail on Danish craft of similar style, is a regular gaff sail. This type of boat reflects the best and most traditional in Scottish building. Her appearance alone, with well-formed hull and natural sheerline, heavy rails, and a straight-reaching stemhead, projects an air of seagoing confidence to any observer. These boats are affectionately referred to as "pot haulers."

We cannot leave the northeast coast of England without another look for a ubiquitous, indigenous boat. This coast of Northumberland and Yorkshire, where long ago Harald Hardrada landed and prepared to inhabit the area with his people from Norway, has not generally developed into a land with distinct Norse maritime heritage. Other than boats with lapstrake con-struction, there are few other distinguishing marks that would suggest any such heritage. The watercraft, due perhaps to the movement in the eighteenth century toward offshore fishing, are mostly undistinguished in their form and style. That is, except perhaps for one—pictured in Chapter One was a lapstrake type of craft worked from the beach that had a unique form. The coble comes in various sizes and guises now, but originally it began as a sailing craft launched from the beach, and this fact explains its unique form of hull. The profile and lug rig are shown in Figure 3-15. The sheerline curves up sharply aft and tends to hook downward forward, a feature that helps it through the surf on launch. The heavy bottom plank with bilge keels are essentially for beaching. These are the original features, but over the years of development other characteristics appeared. The stem curves under into a short keel ending about a third of the distance aft. Abruptly it scarfs into a heavy center plank called a ram. From that point on aft the center plank is paralleled by heavy bilge keels called sand strokes. Outboard of these on each side is a ridge set into the plank lap on each side that becomes thicker toward the transom; it is called the rising stroke. The whole after bottom is reinforced by filler pieces in the grooves of the plank lap. These boats are built essentially as beaching craft and thus the bottom is strengthened and thickened for this wearing process.

The flat transom sterns are of considerable rake, and for the boats with sail a deep outboard rudder is hung that rakes down forward. These rudders are rigged after reaching deep enough water. The other unique feature is the boat's tumblehome. This tumblehome is of a purpose perhaps more unusual than elsewhere it might occur in other boats. It is apparently a feature that allows the boat to be turned over, bottom up, with less effort than a boat with more conventional flaring sides. Cobles are built nowadays with a tunnel stern to provide for propeller drive in a protected space.

Figure 3-15. A Yorkshire coble. This is a unique boat of Great Britain—one of several. It seems to have no ancestors between the Vikings and the present, although its relation to Viking or Norse vessels seems to be only its lapstrake planking. This model clearly shows the unique bottom form of the coble. Today's cobles still operate occasionally from the beach, but they are heavy boats and are now fitted with diesel engines. The owners of modern cobles are more inclined to moor them in the harbor than to haul them out on the beach. (The Science Museum, London)

Figure 3-15A. A coble sitting in the water is a graceful looking boat. This one is aptly named Willy Nilly. (D.R. Goddard, Exeter Museum)

Cobles vary in size. The smaller ones are about 22 feet or less and are and were used in salmon fishing—traditionally were four-oared or rigged with one lugsail. The winter fishing cobles were upward of 25 feet and carried a jib and a storm jib in addition to the lugsail. These old operating cobles were transom stern beaching craft, heavy enough to require a tractor for beaching and launching.

Similar but larger craft, double-ended and about 40 to 42 feet, are called mules, and they operate out of ports such as Scarborough and Whitby. At the present time cobles of any type are becoming very rare.

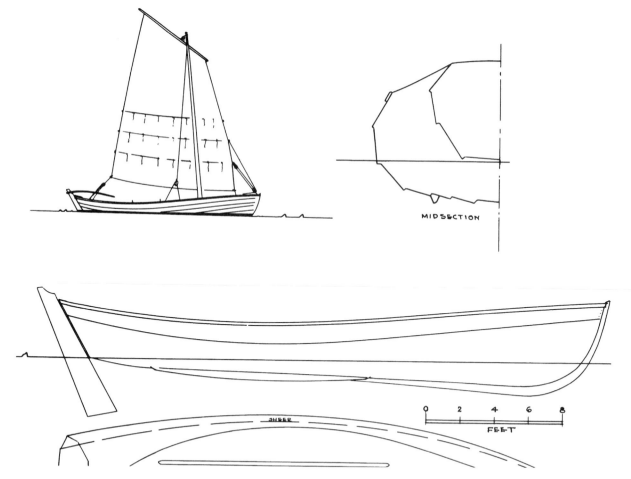

Figure 3-16. The lines and sail plan of a Yorkshire coble, a lug-rigged workboat that still survives.

Figure 3-17. This is an exceptional view of a Thames spritsail barge hard on the wind as seen from the deck of another sailing barge. These hardworking barges have been common to the Thames and the Thames estuary region in England for two hundred years or more. They have now expired, and since the late 1950s have been replaced by power barges. Some, however, have been restored and sail, as here, as pleasure vessels racing regularly in regattas with others of their kind. (Den Phillips)

Farther along down the eastern English coast there is such a typical craft that it is difficult to categorize among the indigenous craft of the fishermen, lobstermen, and rural watermen of the coastline. It is not one of them at all. It is an urban craft and it was extremely common for several centuries—and now it has vanished except for the nostalgic remnants in watercraft museums in London and sailing cults along the Thames. I am talking about the old sailing barges of the Thames and Medway. These vessels—it is difficult to call them *boats*, or *cutters* or *yawls*—are sailing barges. They are barges and were used as such. They hauled almost anything up and down the Thames. A great city needs such craft to transport heavy bulk cargo that cannot be carried conveniently in trucks (lorries) or by rail to any specific waterfront destination. The sailing barges have now left the scene. A pity. They were picturesque—James McNeil Whistler, the great American-expatriate-English artist, took great pains to place them in the foreground of his somber scenes of the Thames. They were photogenic—every postcard scene of the Thames and Houses of Parliament in past years included a sailing barge or so. They rafted together along the quays of the Thames standing by for cargo loading—or unloading—or just standing by. Their great masts and confusing rigs, with some pointed upstream and some downstream, tied together alongside, added to the confusion. To add to this rig mix, their masts were also mounted in gallows frames for lowering to pass under bridges. So some of these photos and paintings of a nest of Thames sailing barges could require some time to sort out. This is particularly true when some had their masts partly lowered and the mainsails partly drying out, some with single-mast rigs, some with spritsail rigs, and some with a yawl jigger rigged on top of the rudderhead. The history of Thames sailing barges can consume volumes. But even so, when it is all recounted, a barge is a barge—especially when it is carrying a load of hay 12 to 15 feet above the deck.

I have, of course, grossly slighted the character of them here, particularly for barge lovers. There were so many of them. I can only say again that they were picturesque and they were certainly working craft on the water. There were the great coasting barges that left the rivers and sailed the coasts. They ranged between 80 and nearly 100 feet in length. These usually carried the yawl rig with a great gaff mainsail and large club topsail, a fore staysail of proportionate dimensions with a jib and flying jib on a heavy bowsprit, and a small yawl jigger aft by the rudder.

Their flat-bottomed and flat-sided hulls were maximized for sailing by rounding with a short chine forward to a stem and a chine up to a transom aft. The later barges were fabricated of steel. To further enhance their sailing requirements they carried large leeboards on each side together with heavy hoisting tackle. The larger of these coasting barges could carry up to 300 tons of cargo.

While these sailing barges were of a common style barge hull—flat bottom, keel-less, and flat, near-vertical sides—the ends were varied and individual. As mentioned above, the bows and sterns turned into shapes for sailing. The middle body was of constant dimensions, that is, had parallel sides for approximately two-thirds of the length. The stems were straight and nearly vertical, some raking slightly aft. The transoms were often of wineglass profile, but also in vertical transverse plane.

Their rigs were essentially and characteristically based on the sprit mainsails, a style of sail rarely found elsewhere—hence their native name the "spritsail barge." There were some boat owners that preferred a traditional gaff and boom, although the mainsail was often loose-footed on the boom.

The gaff-rigged barges were locally called "boomies" to separate them from the older spritsail rig. The head rig varied. Some carried bowsprits, some not. Their head rig could be, according to weather and employment, as many as three sails—staysail jib and flying jib, and commonly a small jigger-mizzen, most useful as a balancing vane.

The descriptions above are for the general run of sailing barges. Their history and heritage show some classic variations that were still among the typical basic barges some sixty to seventy years ago. Some of the older wooden barges had "scow"-type bows instead of stemhead bows. Some would fly a squaresail downwind. And for many barges the bowsprit was a movable feature of mobility. It generally was a running bowsprit—to be run in and run out. It also was held against the stem when rigged by a hinged iron gammon ring, and was found useful in acting as a leveraged boom for hoisting. Barges often sailed with the bowsprit run in or sometimes rigged up at a high steeve

Figure 3-17A. The outboard profile of a typical spritsail barge on the Thames. Note the long sprit with its heel in a sling at the starboard side of the mast. The sprit is a useful boom for lifting cargo. The mizzen-jigger, sheeted to the rudder, is useful as a steering sail in the heavy Thames traffic.

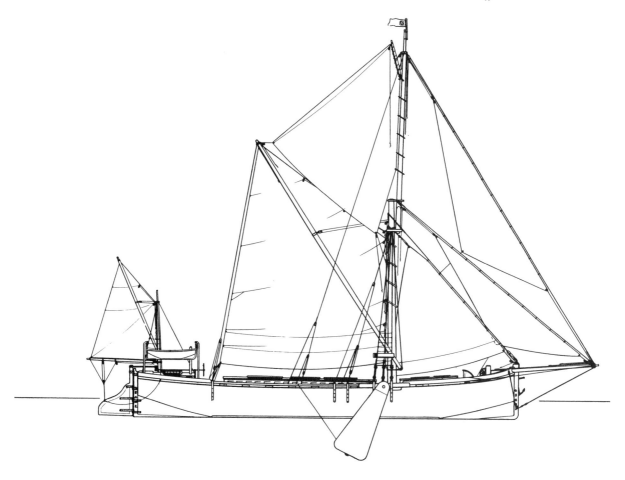

Figure 3-17B. A bawley, restored for pleasure use and competition sailing. Bawleys were formerly fishing boats common on the southeast British coast. They are square-stern, outboard-rudder, lapstrake hulls of handsome shape. They carry a large-area sailing rig for light weather, the large gaff topsail and jib set flying on a long, heavy bowsprit. This rig can be run in quickly. (Den Phillips)

or angle under staysail and main. Again, a spritsail barge was a many-splendored thing! There were hundreds of them before World War II. In 1952 some fifty still sailed, and twenty years later two survivors were working. Today there may be a few for collections, barge yachts, and restorations. Their useful days are long past. Figure 3-17A is an approximate profile of a latter-day Thames spritsail barge.

An inshore English craft typical of the Cornish coast, long renowned for its sailors, is shown in Figure 3-18. This boat is slightly smaller than the fishing craft of the North Sea and Scotland; she is 36 feet long, 11 feet 8 inches in beam, and 4 feet 6 inches in draft. She is similar to a majority of English-built motor workboats of the south of England, showing some of her own, rather than Scottish, regional influence. The most dominating feature of British building, evident immediately in this boat, is the overall restraint. To the eye of a naval architect, the boat seems to lack the natural flow and shape of the sea that was so easy for the Norsemen to introduce so long ago and pass on to a considerable degree to the Scots. Simply put, this boat lacks any sense of heritage. To use an apt description

Figure 3-17C. A Colchester smack, named Charlotte Ellen, *running hard on a reach. A smack, like a bawley, was a substantial fishing boat type in the southeast where the Channel meets the North Sea. Most of these single-masted vessels of about 30 feet are restored today, if they still exist, for local type competition. The smack is a traditional cutter-type rig with a long boom and a long housing bowsprit. Unlike the bawley, the smack is a smooth-planked hull with an overhanging counter. This allows a longer foot on the mainsail. (Den Phillips)*

common among American yacht designers when confronted with a boat impressing them as this type does me: "She looks as though she hasn't been taken out of the box she came in." A description as disparaging as this deserves qualification.

These boats of Cornwall and elsewhere along the south coast of Britain are sturdy craft. They differ from Scottish boats primarily in their flat sheerline and square transom stern. Their stems are quite plumb and their entrances and runs are fuller than those of Scottish-built boats. Boats such as these are of traditional Cornish design and are suitable for most types of inshore fishing. The hull of our example in Figure 3-18 is of round-bilge form, carvel planked, and properly built to the most exacting and conservative specifications. Her keel and backbone structure are of oak, and her planking is of larch. Her fastenings are either copper or galvanized steel, and her floor frames and futtocks are natural grown-to-shape oak. Her decks and cabin structure are clear pine. She is fitted with a heavy, wood outboard rudder, protective rubrails, and a steel stem and keel shoe. Her engine is an 85-h.p. Rolls-Royce diesel, which produces a speed of 8 to 9 knots. She is a proper little fishing boat typical of the best British seagoing tradition. As such, she has become an indigenous type. There is little evidence of heritage from her forbears, the Cornish luggers of the nineteenth century. They too were ruggedly built boats that had flat sheers, plumb stems, flat bows, and boxy sterns. They did not sail as well as their French competition. The old Cornish luggers competed with the great French luggers out of the ports from St. Malo to Brest across the Channel in Normandy and Brittany, which was written about in the previous chapter. The Cornish luggers out of Penzance and Mouse Hole and other ports of Cornwall and Devon have disappeared completely, and left but

Figure 3-18. The coast of Cornwall in England is renowned for its sailors and tough, seagoing boats. This boat from Penzance is quite typical of the Cornish fishing craft that replaced the plumb-stemmed luggers. Note the straight sheer and vertical, square transom stern with outboard rudder. (John Burgess)

little behind in present-day watercraft to remember them, except as noted below in Falmouth estuary.

There are still some interesting workboats under sail that survive. On the Cornish coast in the Carrick Roadstead, a stretch of water reaching inland from Falmouth, there is a type of small gaff cutter surviving as an oyster dredger. It "survives" much in the same manner that the Chesapeake skipjack survives—under protective conservation laws prohibiting the dredging of oysters by powered fishing boats. The oyster industry is so favorable at present that many new boats are even being built for the business. There are about twenty to thirty boats at work during the season. There is no "fixed" boat type here except in rig. Most boats are between 25 and 30 feet in length with transom sterns and plumb stems. They have, most of them, the characteristic shape described above for other Cornish boats. In fact there is good reason to believe, from the

Figure 3-19. A Cornish lugger that has been converted to power. She originally had two masts. (Steven Lang)

age of many of the boats and their hull styles, that they were related to the fishing luggers sailing out of the Cornish coves at the turn of the century. The original rig of these luggers was most often two-masted, with short lugsails and no jib. Whether this was the origin of the oyster boats or not is open to question. A Cornish lugger that has been converted to power is seen in Figure 3-19.

At present the oyster boat rig is essentially that of the celebrated English gaff cutter. The long horizontal bowsprit, with two headsails, and the well-peaked gaff set on a mast stepped nearly amidships produces this handsome and well-proportioned nineteenth–century–type cutter. The jib is set flying and, while the boat is working the beds, is frequently slacked down onto the bowsprit, while the main is reefed. Dredging with

Figure 3-20. A Cornish oyster dredger under sail. This boat carries her summer canvas with a square-headed jack-yard topsail. She was built as an open lugger about seventy years ago. Like the Chesapeake skipjacks, these oyster boats participate in an annual race to open the season. In England, however, the prize is a keg of ale. (Basil Greenhill)

Figure 3-21. A Falmouth quay punt under summer rig. A number of these punts have been converted to pleasure craft and still sail. They are the prototypes of many of the present Falmouth oyster-dredging sloops that are still being built in the old manner. (The Science Museum, London)

reduced sail is not, as often assumed, a shortening of sail because of foul weather; rather it is to hold down the dredging speed and prevent the dredge from jumping along over the oyster bed.

The small sailing oyster smacks, while not uniform in size or hull characteristics, are sufficiently similar to be categorized. They are most similar in appearance to a former type of this same region that was a most noteworthy boat. The Falmouth quay punt, of which there are none still at work and perhaps less than a half dozen still extant as pleasure craft conversions, was a fine workboat. (It may be worth noting that I designed and owned a modified quay punt a number of years ago which I sailed about the Chesapeake for several years with a great deal of pleasure. This boat is shown in frame under construction in Figure 1-34.)

The Falmouth quay punt was generally an open craft with a gaff yawl rig and two headsails. Her hull was about 25 feet in length and 8 feet in beam with a plumb stem and a transom stern. She was employed originally carrying stores and ferrying passengers to and from the large square-rigged ships lying-to off Falmouth or anchored in the roadstead. However, these fast little boats differed from the fishing luggers of this locality in an important respect other than their rig. Their hull sections had a nice wineglass shape, which, with their relatively light, buoyant body, gave them a good bearing on the water. Figure 3-21 shows a quay punt in her summer rig in the early part of this century. Figure 3-22 shows a model of an old quay punt in her winter rig. The summer rig

Figure 3-22. A model of a Fal-mouth quay punt in her winter rig. (The Science Museum, London)

was the same rig with the addition of a long bowsprit and large jib.

Hastings, on England's southeast coast, has a steep, pebble beach where another unique working boat survives in an environment uninviting to more normal craft. The Hastings lugger is a deep and full lapstrake boat. It has two masts with a reduced lugsail rig, considerable beam, and most unusual mechanical power arrangements. This boat, while substantially handsome, can best be described as eccentric. The means of propulsion provide for almost any contingency. The boats are fitted with two to three propellers driven by diesel or gas engines, or both, with widely differing horsepower.

The Hastings lugger of the eighteenth and early nineteenth centuries was very similar in hull but with a two-masted lug rig (Figure 3-23A), and was used primarily in service and rescue work for larger vessels in trouble off the beaches of Hastings and Deal. The boats were maintained in readiness for

Figure 3-23. The Hastings lugger of today is still the same basic boat as that of the eighteenth century. Note her easily stepped rig, protected propeller, and high freeboard. This boat still operates from the beaches of Hastings and Deal and is even seen occasionally on the beaches of the French side of the Channel.

launching into the surf, and their state of reliability was the chief concern of their owners. It is reasonable to assume that this penchant for dependable functioning has carried over to the present-day types and owners.

A typical Hastings lugger today, shown in Figure 3-23, displaces 7½ tons, and is 28 feet long, 11 feet wide, and 3½ feet in draft. The sails consist of mizzen, main, and jib, and fishing was and may still be done by nets, lines, and small trawls. The most distinctive feature of Hastings luggers aside from their many means of propulsion is their stern form. Originally, they had a large, conventional transom stern with an outboard rudder. Such a stern was eventually recognized to cause difficult handling at sea and in surf during beach landings, so a modified form was developed. The result is a sort of tucked-up rounded stern that is unique and apparently an

Figure 3-23A. The modern Hastings luggers are showing their wear and age. This boat, photographed on the beach at Hastings in the spring of 1993, no more carries a sailing rig. They are rigged for power trawling, and the old hulls look tired. There are some twenty of them left. (Alec Tilley)

Figure 3-23B. There are three types of sterns on the old hulls. This one is an "elliptical" stern. She is the smaller type of lugger without pilot-house and is referred to by the locals as a "punt." (Alec Tilley)

Figure 3-23C. This is an example of a "round" stern lugger at Hastings. (Alec Tilley)

operational improvement. Altogether, the Hastings lugger is a most unusual, genuinely indigenous fishing boat.

Another sailing working boat of England survives on the west coast, north of Blackpool on Morecambe Bay, facing the Irish Sea. The prawns taken here are well known, perhaps as tasty as those from Dublin Bay on the opposite shores. Prawning is inshore work that does not involve heavy nets or power blocks on heavy booms. It is done in these protected waters by a fine-looking sailing cutter with a rig similar to that of the oyster boats of Carrick Roadstead, discussed earlier, but a different hull form.

The Morecambe Bay prawner actually has a hull form similar to some of the turn-of-the-century knockabout sloops of the Cape Cod region. The stem has a nicely curved profile, and the stern has a rather long, overhanging counter with the raked rudder hung well below and forward of it. There are some variations in form and dimension, but typical dimensions are 30 feet overall length on a 25-foot waterline, a beam of 9 feet, and a draft of nearly 4 feet at the sternpost. These boats are, because of their fine appearance and sailing qualities, often converted to pleasure use. The basic working prawner is decked, with no cabin, but has a large open cockpit abaft the mast. Prawning, like fishing, under sail is becoming rare, but there are still a few of these boats working (now with auxiliary motors) from North Wales as far north as Solway Firth.

BOATS OF IRELAND—LARGE AND SMALL

England and Ireland are separated by more than the Irish Sea. It has been difficult, because of England's historic greater power and discernible patronizing attitude, not to lean in the Irish direction, and the feeling is recipro-

Figure 3-24. A modern boat of the Royal National Life-Boat Institution. A boat such as this must be capable of operating in any weather or any season. This lifeboat was designed in Ireland and built in Scotland. She is 70 feet long, 17 feet in beam, and 7½ feet in draft. (John Tyrell and Sons, Ltd.)

cated. Early in this century a well-known English authority on ships and boats wrote that the Irish were not a seafaring people and that the only boats they had of value were those built in England and acquired from Cornish, Manx, and Scots fishermen who fished in Irish waters. If this was the situation when that opinion was written, I do not find it so today—even the reverse may be true. There are excellent products of native Irish boatbuilding and boat designing skills that are commissioned by no less than the Royal National Lifeboat Institution. As an example, Figure 3-24 shows the 70-foot *Grace Patterson Richie* flying the British flag, designed and built by John Tyrrell and Son, yacht and boatbuilders

Figure 3-25. The coracle originated long before recorded history. Today's version has a frame of woven barked tree boughs and a covering of tarred canvas. Originally, the covering was the hide of an animal.

of Arklow, Ireland. While this example may not qualify as an indigenous boat, she is a magnificent vessel and is cited here to dispel any prejudice concerning Irish abilities to build the best seagoing craft.

The Irish tradition of dealing with the cruel seas surrounding her insular realm reaches back to the first days of Christianity in Ireland. There is evidence that Irish Christian monks sailed north to the Faeroe Islands and eventually to Iceland as early as the sixth century AD. Like the Scottish and English coasts, the Irish shores also were raided, exploited, and inhabited by the Vikings. There were Norse settlements and strongholds at Dublin, Sligo, and other localities in Ireland, and it is illogical not to conclude that the boatbuilding skills of these settlers found some root.

On the other hand, the more primitive watercraft of the Celts also influenced Irish boatbuilding. Both the Irish and the Welsh can lay claim to surviving remnants of a Neolithic culture—the coracle and the curragh.

No one knows, of course, where or how these watercraft were first introduced. It is clear, however, that the primitive ancestors of the early inhabitants of the British Isles first transported themselves to those shores in similar frame-skin boats. The isolated Celtic races, whose energies and motivations were more agricultural than nautical, found these craft always adequate for their simple requirements on streams, rivers, and even the rocky bays of Galway. They have thus survived for countless centuries with few changes in their original form.

A coracle is a skin- or fabric-covered woven wood frame shaped much the same as half a melon. It seldom has a capacity of more than one man and his small burden and is rowed or paddled with a scooplike paddle. After a log raft and an inflated animal hide, this sort of craft was, no doubt, prehistoric man's first waterborne transport. These craft may still be seen occasionally in the vicinity of the River Teifi in Wales. Figure 3-25 shows an example of a Teifi coracle. A very similar type of coracle is indigenous to the River Boyne on Ireland's eastern coast. The Irish generally refer to the fabric-covered frame craft as curraghs.

A slightly more sophisticated curragh is found in Galway, the Aran Islands, and Achill Island on the west coast. This curragh is a step closer to a boat in form as well as construction. The frame is "built" rather than woven (Figure 3-26 shows the construction of an Achill Island curragh). The island curraghs are larger craft holding three or four men and four to six oars. Their primary advantage is their lightness and transportability. They are truly indigenous craft, and it is a curiosity to find them in such a small land side by side with the finest examples of the modern boatbuilder's art and science.

One of the best of today's Irish boatbuilders is John Tyrrell and Sons in Arklow. This yard produces boats that are as notable in their fine line and form as those of Scotland. These boats follow the traditional form of the North Sea in their pilot-boat models (see Figure 3-27), but in the fishing

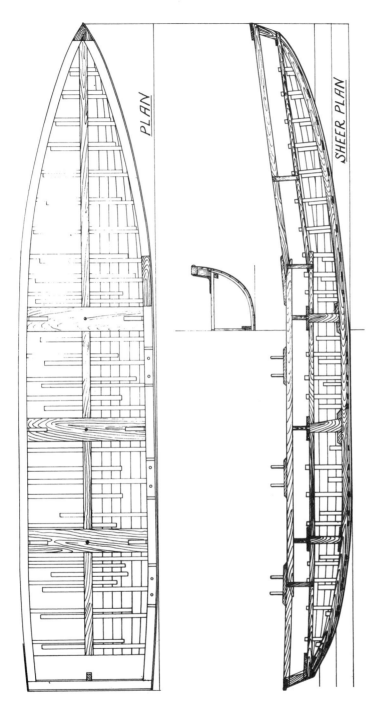

Figure 3-26. In Ireland a coracle is called a curragh and is more often elongated into a boat form with a more sophisticated frame than the Welsh version. It is still a primitive type of frame-skin boat. (The Science Museum, London)

Figure 3-27. This modern pilot boat sets the style and standard for many Irish work-boats. She was built in Arklow, Ireland. (John Tyrell and Sons, Ltd.)

craft the basic hull form often favors a transom stern.

It is interesting to compare the small lobster-fishing boat of Ireland to the similar fine boats on the opposite side of the Atlantic. Figure 3-28 depicts an Irish lobstering boat that shows considerable similarity to a Maine coast lobsterboat. She is, of course, a heavier boat with a full displacement form and carries less power. On the other hand, she is perhaps more comfortable in a heavy chop offshore. Her dimensions are 34 feet by 10 feet 6 inches, by 4 feet, and she is powered by a 36-h.p. Lister diesel that drives her at 7½ knots. Unlike her Scottish relative, she has her wheelhouse forward and is transom-sterned. Generally, most of the older boats engaged in the Irish fisheries are double-ended with the traditional aft wheelhouse.

A recently built, most sophisticated Irish trawler comparable in size to the Scottish boats is shown in Figure 3-29. The pleasing sweep of sheer and reaching bow of this hull reflects the best of North Sea and old Norse influence, yet her practical lifting transom stern provides a broad platform aft. Her wheelhouse and rig are most modern. She is 65 feet long, 19 feet 3 inches in beam, and 8 feet 6 inches in draft, and is powered by a 240-h.p. Boudouin-type diesel. She is equipped with the latest navigational and electronic aids to fishing as well as auxiliary generating gear and powered deck equipment. Her crew's quarters are centrally heated.

Figure 3-30 shows a typical Irish drift net fisherman tied astern a pilot boat in the harbor of Tramore. The fishing boat here has a raking stern, the old-style stern similar to the Scottish luggers of the past century, and an outboard rudder. The pilot boat is a more modern cruiser-stern double-ender. Both of these are hull forms, however, that are typical of Scotch, Irish, and the North Sea traditions.

As pointed out in the preface, it would be impossible to describe every boat in all the corners of any geographical region. It is particu-

Figure 3-28. An Irish lobsterboat. She is similar in style, though heavier and slower, to the Maine lobsterboat. (John Tyrell and Sons, Ltd.)

Figure 3-29. This modern Irish trawler is a large, comfortable boat. She is built of African iroko and Irish-grown oak. (John Tyrell and Sons, Ltd.)

Figure 3-30. These two boats in the harbor of Tramore on Ireland's south coast are two different working types. The boat on the left is a modern pilot boat with a trawler stern. The one on the right is a fisherman with a double-ended hull.

larly difficult in regions of generally similar cultures, such as the British Isles, where the people have been separated politically yet have been united by their industry on the seas. In many respects the trawlers and drifters of Ireland, especially those of Northern Ireland, are quite like the boats of Scotland. Their indigenous quality is created by individual Irish builders and is reflected in the outboard-rudder double-enders and transom sterns.

The Irish did not have a great assortment of workboats under sail in the recent past, and few have survived until today. A few sloops, known as Galway hookers, were still at work in 1970, however, satisfying the need for basic transportation among the islands of Galway Bay. Used essentially to transport peat fuel to the Aran Islands, the very few barely surviving hookers are

over a century old. These boats are poor indeed. They were originally built heavily but economically. They have been patched and marginally maintained through the many years. The character of these boats, however, is still clearly unique. They are between 30 and 35 feet in length, carry a gaff main, a staysail, and a jib on a long bowsprit. The mast and rigging is heavy to the point of being overscale. The sails are black. The hull form is most unusual in its high freeboard, very full shoulders, tumblehome, and hollow forebody. The hull has a rather straight, flat run in the afterbody with a full transom stern and outboard rudder. The keel is long and straight, not unlike that of the Danish Skovshoved silde-båd (see Chapter Two).

The smallest craft of any locality often retain the most ancient characteristics of the boats that preceded them. This is true of the craft in Scandinavia, the Scottish and North Sea islands, Portugal, and the Mediterranean, to say nothing of the coracles and curraghs of Wales and Ireland. There is a small skiff of Ireland that is more refined than the curraghs but less sophisticated than the ubiquitous lapstrake rowing boats and

Figure 3-31. The oldest and one of the few surviving sailing workboats in the British Islands is the Galway hooker of Ireland's west coast. Note the unusual setback of the laced mainsail from the mast. (Kevin MacLaverty)

dinghies so common in all British and Irish harbors. This fine rowing skiff is found along the Shannon estuary and is about 16 feet in length. It is essentially a flat-bottom boat with the flaring sides of a banks dory, but with four heavy lap planks per side. The stem is gently curved and the narrow transom is roughly wineglass in form. This causes a slight hollow in the counter that is unaccountable in purpose. Because of the resulting curvature in the sections, the sawn frames must be curved. It is on the whole a very handsome skiff and is generally rowed by four oars or nowadays more often pushed by a small outboard. Figure 3-32 shows the form and structure of a typical Shannon skiff. It provides native rural water transport and is a fine vehicle for tending nets or handline fishing in western Ireland.

Most of the rowing skiffs and dinghies of Ireland are similar to those of Scotland and England. They are round-bottom boats of conventional lapstrake construction. They have either transom sterns or double ends. Their form is severely conservative and has not changed noticeably for nearly a century and a half. They have become the model for the tenders and lifeboats of larger vessels and are a standard around the world.

Figure 3-32. A Shannon River fishing skiff. This is not a boat built to an individual's whim; there are many like it in the area and it is quite different from a common "flattie."

It might appear that I have skipped over many important English boat types in my discussion of the British Isles. This is not true. There are simply no great numbers of surviving indigenous English boats. The multiplicity of distinctive types of working sail that operated in English waters three-quarters of a century ago are now extinct. There were Yarmouth luggers, Lowestoft drifters, Mounts Bay drivers, nickies, nobbies, Humber keels, Thames spritsail barges, East Cornish luggers, West Cornish luggers, and many, many others. These boats are all well documented in massive detail in English sources. It is too bad they can be seen today only in books.

CHAPTER FOUR

MEDITERRANEAN BOATS—THEIR LINEAGE AND STYLES

IN RECENT YEARS SOME ANCIENT wrecks from the Mediterranean Sea's prehistory and early history have been brought up to the light of day. At present, work is progressing on one from the Bronze Age off the southern coast of Turkey. We do not yet know all there will be to know about this vessel. Nothing has been revealed about its shape or structure except that there is a keel and that its planks were attached to it by mortice and tenons similar to those of nearly one thousand years later. This knowledge alone is startling—to know that the shell-first system existed at least one thousand years earlier than previously established. This vessel of Ulu Burun, which it is known as, was a coastwise trading ship. She was carrying a cargo of bronze ingots and valuables that included a gold chalice, gems and jewelry, and other articles of trade. All of this stimulates the archaeologists to put together a story of her voyage to add an early fragment to the knowledge of Western culture. But at this point in our narrative of maritime structures we are pleased to know the facts about her keel and planking.

There was a more complete wreck of a trading vessel discovered in 1967 and gradually and carefully reassembled. This boat of about 50 feet in length was wonderfully complete in its wreckage.

Now, at the twentieth century's tail end, it is becoming increasingly difficult to convince a new breed of historians that there once was something known as Western culture—even a Western civilization. Whether or not they believe in it, it existed—it has lasted waning and waxing, rising and falling in darkness and brightness, and it began somewhere in the eastern end of the Mediterranean. It no doubt was nurtured in the tenuous beginning, about four thousand years ago, by the Egyptian Empire.

GREEK CRAFT

In Chapter One we noted that in the Aegean Islands there were those great maritime people who identified themselves on and about the island of Crete.

It is in this vicinity that it is best to locate the maritime roots of the Western world. It is the land and the territory lying about the shores of the Mediterranean that is rich in our history of Western culture and maritime lore. The Mediterranean Sea holds the wrecks of ships and boats beneath its surface that could trace the development of the world's seacraft from its beginning. It is in this eastern basin of the great middle sea that the wrecks of the *oldest* boats have been found.

We have mentioned two wrecks, and our interest is the second of these two found along the north coast of Cyprus, near Kyrenia, by a diver named Andrea Cariolou. In 1967 he led Michael Katzev and his team of archaeologists from the University of Pennsylvania to a pile of amphorae in 30 meters of water. The subsequent excavation here revealed a most remarkably intact ancient wreck.

The ship's timbers were raised, preserved, and ultimately reassembled. It had survived from the classic age of Greece, dating from about the fourth century BC. The ship was a merchantman that had a cargo of some four hundred

Figure 4-1. Kyrenia II, *at sea in the Aegean under shortened sail. She is an exact replica of the original Kyrenia ship of the fourth century* BC, *the wreck that was raised with hull and cargo nearly intact. The original is now on display in the museum of Bodrum Castle, Turkey.*

Figure 4-2. The lines from the reassembled Kyrenia ship drawn by Richard Steffy, the archaeologist reconstructor, in 1983. Her dimensions are: length between perpendiculars (inner faces of stem and stern) 13.88 meters; beam, 4.2 meters; tons burden, 25.

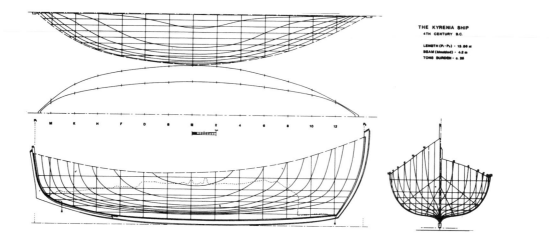

amphorae, some of wine and some of oil. Her sailing load also included stone ballast that weighed more than 1,650 kilograms (3,638 pounds). The archaeologists believe the ship was manned by a crew of four based on the assortment of eating and drinking utensils found in her galley. They locate her home port at Rhodes. She was found on the bottom in open water near the southwest coast of Turkey and her sinking was, as reconstructed by the archaeological team, the work of pirates. The coins found on board indicate her loss some time between 300 and 310 BC.

The hull was remarkably well preserved with about 75 percent of her timbers and 65 percent of her planking in place. The ship, now called the Kyrenia ship after her location and reassembly, has now, with the support of a Greek preservation society, been replicated with the name *Kyrenia II*. See Figure 4-2, the lines drawing, as restored to full size by Professor Richard Steffy.[1] Her principal dimensions are: length, 13.86 meters (45.5 feet); beam 4.2 meters (13.7 feet); draft of water about 1.5 meters when loaded (4.9 feet). She is now afloat and her performance under sail is most revealing. (See Figure 4-3.)

Probably no other true replica ship has been so objectively finished and so conscientiously sailed and tested as *Kyrenia II*. (See Figure 4-4A and B.)

[1] *Professor Steffy directed the reassembly of the original wreck.*

Figure 4-3. Kyrenia II *sailing on a beam reach with her squaresail yard braced up hard, and the sail tacked down hard to the forward deck cleat. She was having some temporary problems with her port-side rudder when this photo was taken, but she is holding her course well with the starboard rudder. She sails well, and her cruising between Cyprus and Greece has dispelled the historians' unfounded statements that squaresails in the classic period could only carry the vessels with the wind.*

Her construction was carried out under the direction of the archaeologist discoverer of the original vessel, Michael Katzev. He writes:

The project of building a replica of the ancient Kyrenia ship has taught us much. We have learned that modern shipwrights can readapt to the method of shell-first construction and relearn the mortise-and-tenon joinery method last used by their ancestors almost a thousand years ago. We have shown that the shell of a hull can be built up to its load waterline by mortise and tenon alone, virtually no internal bracing. We have proven that Steffy's lines drawings of the Kyrenia ship can be precisely duplicated. He calculated the distance between the rabbets in the stem and stern posts of the Kyrenia ship to be 13.86 meters (45.6 feet). In Kyrenia II it is 13.76 meters—a difference of only 10 centimeters (4 inches). He calculated the molded beam to be 4.2 meters. In Kyrenia II it is 4.20 meters!

Of course there was no mast or rig that sur-

vived the millennia since this early classic ship sank. However, the mast step in the wreck indicated it was a single-masted rig, and of course it carried a squaresail. There is enough iconography surviving of the period to fairly closely duplicate her sail plan. It is obvious in being reasonably accurate.

Kyrenia II has been tested in good weather and bad—particularly in the seasonal heavy winds of the Aegean (the meltemi).(See Figure 4-5.)

Kyrenia II was built in Pergamum, Greece, and launched in 1985. In September 1986, she sailed from Piraeus, Greece (a seaport near Athens) to Paphos in Cyprus. This first voyage in part nearly duplicated the route of her ancient predecessor. The distance is 600 miles. The weather varied between flat calm to heavy. She averaged about 3 knots for the entire voyage which, considering alternating winds and flat calms and unfamiliarity with a single-squaresail rig, is not too bad. On the return voyage she encountered whole gale conditions (Force 10) but again also encountered total calm. She aver-

Figure 4-4A. Kyrenia II *in the Piraeus port of Athens, shortly after her construction and launching. Her planks are held by mortise-and-tenon fastenings and connected to internal frames after the planking has been built up to the waterline. These plank-to-frame fastenings are copper nails like the originals and clenched over on the inside.*

Figure 4-4B. Side view of Kyrenia II *in port at Piraeus showing her port-side rudder. The helmsman stands between the two tillers and works them together, one forward, one aft, according to the direction of course change.*

Figure 4-5. Kyrenia II *sailing downwind in a good breeze— probably between 20 and 25 knots. Her sailing rig was reconstructed according to ancient iconography. Her yardarm is doubled in the ancient Mediterranean fashion. The sail is made of linen with furling lines led over its surface to the foot. The yard is lowered and the lines hauled in, bringing the sail up to the yard much like a curtain. Thus the sail area is reduced to any desired amount.*

aged about the same time, logging 660 nautical miles. She recorded under sail conditions alone an average speed of 4.4 knots for 22.5 miles. When sailing under good conditions, her best speed is close to 5 knots steady. These figures have been taken from the record kept by the archaeological experiment team while they closely observed the ship's performance. These people were not aboard when, on a more recent voyage, it is reported by Mr. Katzev as follows:

> As dull as the third day was the fourth was exciting, encountering a storm—with easterly gale winds with gusts over 50 knots. Kyrenia II *sailed through high seas spread with spindrift on a quarter to broad reach. For the first time she sailed through rain. Although heeling considerably, no water came over her sides and the hull remained relatively dry. Furthermore, some 35 amphorae, alas empty of wine, mold-made by Sophocles Mourides of Nicosia (Cyprus) and representing about a tenth of the ancient ship's cargo of Rhodian amphorae, laden atop sacks of gravel, did not move at all. Around noon with winds now about 25 knots* Kyrenia II *reached speeds of 12 knots sailing downwind.*

The boat sails well on reaches (wind on the quarter or the beam). She seems to have been tested mostly that way. She will also sail close-hauled, as reported. Regrettably, Katzev's report does not record how close. At one point the log states that while sailing along the south coast of Turkey near Kos in relatively heavy wind one night, she "averaged over 7 knots on a close-hauled tack, frequently with speeds of 10 to 12 knots." This was at night in a storm with gusts reported to over 40 knots.[2]

We should remind ourselves that we are talking here about the sailing performance of an ancient boat from the period of classic Greece—the fourth century BC. She is observed and sailed by late-twentieth-century men who are learned and honest sailors. I think that we can revise our beliefs about ancient boats of the pre-Christian era, which have been said to have been indifferent under sail, sailing by day and staying close inshore, from port to port along the coasts. And a general statement by one classic maritime historian that boats of antiquity could sail only in the direction the wind was blowing—what rot!

But also let us return to Figure 4-2, the lines drawing of the Kyrenia ship. The drawing shows the hull configuration as taken off the reassembled wreck by Richard Steffy, the archaeological reconstructor. Below the dotted line, on the profile view, is the original hull that survived to be carefully put in place after the wood was restored in a bath of polyethylene glycol. This is essentially the sailing hull below the waterline and in the middle body extending significantly above the waterline. This is the form as created by the ancients. In the body plan, observe the keel and garboard area and how the whole end view of the sections is like a stemmed goblet—a wineglass section, well known today.[3] Again, observe the longitudinal profile form, with

[2] *It must be noted that Kyrenia II's theoretical hull speed is 9.00 knots.*

[3] *This sectional hollow shape along the garboard and keel produces a low-pressure region while sailing on a reach or a close-hauled tack that keeps the boat from making excessive leeway.*

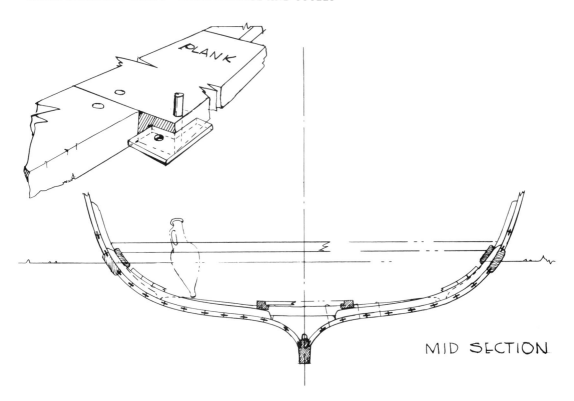

Figure 4-6. The structural section of the Kyrenia ship. It shows a shape that in a modern sailing craft would produce an excellent cruising boat with windward ability.

the keel from stem to stern not a straight line, but arched down in a rocker shape. This is also well known today for sailing hulls and to add strength for beaching or grounding on hard spots. The lines of the bow and buttock traces, particularly aft of amidships, show a flat run back to the quarters, where they quickly turn up—an excellent sailing characteristic. In fact, I believe we are looking at a sailing hull here that, for her requirements as a coastwise sailing merchant vessel, could not have been much improved upon today, except for her sailing rig.

Finally, let's look at her construction. In Figure 4-6 is the midsection showing the basic structure. This drawing shows her timbers and planking, etc., as reassembled from the wreck, to just above the waterline. The planking shell is, of course, held in place first by the mortise-and-tenon system as shown in the enlarged sketch above the section. The hull has a wale strake at about the waterline that is backed up by a stringer on the ceiling inside. When the planking is built up to about the waterline, it is reinforced by placing the transverse timbers inside—these are the frames. They are alternated with transverse center frames or floors that extend to the turn of the bilge on both sides adjacent to the half frames, which extend to the height of the wale strake from above the garboard strake. The frames are fastened to the planking by copper nails clenched over on the inside and through trunnels on the stem and the stern.

There are quarter decks aft and forward for

the helmsman and for working the ground tackle and sails. The cargo hold is not decked—the cargo in the ancient shipping world was protected by matting and other fabrics. As noted in Michael Katzev's report above, she took on remarkably little water while sailing in rain and heavy weather.

Altogether, we must conclude from studying this operating replica that she is most convincing as an offshore sailing vessel. Conscientiously copied from the original hull, she was completed with knowledgeable skill. She must be taken very seriously as a historic fourth-century-BC seagoing merchant vessel. Her sailing performance was remarkable, although some of her speed notations were made under poor conditions. Without reliable instrumentation, they are probably extended beyond the actual. Although she may have been surfing down a wave slope at the reported 12 knots, the duration of the gravity-induced speed would have been very brief. While her hull speed is calculated based on Froude's well-known equation, $V \times V/ \sqrt{L} = C$, or $1.34 \times \sqrt{L}$ = speed in knots (in *Kyrenia II*, close to 9 knots), we must reserve our analysis of the speed under sail to similar limitations. She carries enough sail, she has a fine sailing hull, she was not heavily loaded, and the crew had obviously learned to handle her sail on various sailing points. Her double rudders are of narrow high-aspect ratio and create only a minimal drag. When sailing close-hauled, hard on the wind, braced hard up, the crew learned to harden the yard down, and also to brail in the leading "foot" of the sail. This sort of sail handling led ultimately to a fore-and-aft sail—it is mystifying why it took so long.

Our modern terms such as *reefing, foot, quarter deck*, etc., do not strictly fit this ancient craft. They have been introduced into our language or languages only centuries after the ships of antiquity. The fourth-century sailing vessels had sails without reef points. Sail was shortened by a sort of brailing system with lines at regular intervals

dropping from the yard to the long lower edge of the squaresail, and held to the sail and guided through small lead rings. This arrangement does not create a very sharp leading edge to the sail when it is close-hauled, and in light winds is not very efficient. On the other hand, in the case of a single mast and sail as *Kyrenia II*, there is not much adverse windage in the rigging. Again, this archaeological experiment with a 2,500-year-old example is convincing.

At the same time or, to be precise, a century before the Kyrenia ship was sailing, there was a grander type of Greek vessel, used in an entirely different occupation. It was a larger vessel and significantly more important politically and strategically. We must describe it here first because of the sharp contrast with the Kyrenia ship and, second, because a replication of it was built in 1985–86 in close conjunction with *Kyrenia II*. We are talking now about the great oared vessel of classic Greece known as a trireme. This type of vessel was most important to the Athenian Navy in the early fifth century BC. In 480 BC the Athenians, in some three hundred triremes, met and defeated the Persians, with reputedly more than six hundred similar galleys, in the first great naval battle between warship fleets. Using strategy and tactics in the Bay of Salamis, 65 kilometers west of Piraeus, the Greeks sank and otherwise destroyed the Persian force. This remarkable victory, which probably ended the Moslem world's westward expansion for more than two millennia, was not due to any great superiority in Athenian warship design. It was rather due to the intelligent strategic planning by the Greeks. A trireme, because of its early importance as the mechanism that preserved early Western culture, should be discussed, particularly viewing its structure and impact, if any, on future development of ships.(See Figure 4-7.)

Trireme is a word that nautical historians have trouble with. The word is popularly translated into English as "three banks," referring to the oars' placement. The problem is with *banks*.

Figure 4-7. An Athenian trireme of the fifth century BC. This reconstruction is similar to the Olympias *built in 1985–87 in Greece to a design by John Coates of England. However, there are some small differences in size and afterdeck arrangement. The differences are not of great consequence. She carries 170 oarsmen as well as 12 to 15 marines for boarding in battle. But the primary attack weapon of a trireme is her forward waterline-mounted heavy bronze ram. The ram was used on warships until the late nineteenth century AD. The vessel under oars may reach 9 to 10 knots for short sprints. Her cruising speed is in the vicinity of 6 knots using two-thirds of the rowers. (William Gilkerson)*

Derived from *bench*, it does not necessarily mean vertical tiers—the rowing benches or banks can be arranged in different ways. Literally, a single-banked rowing boat in naval terminology means rowers with a pair of oars each, port and starboard. We need not go any further in the seating arrangement of a trireme for it is today, rightly or wrongly, interpreted as three tiers of oars per side. It is further unfortunate that in all of the ancient art and sculpture of classic Greece there is no existing clear graphic depiction of a trireme. There is but one great example of a purported trireme from a panel of a marble frieze that was found in the ruins of the Athenian Parthenon. It shows in sculptured relief a section along the side of a galley, presumed to be a trireme. Called the Lenormant Relief, this is as good as any ancient graphic evidence of a trireme gets. The rowers along the top of the panel are clearly profiled with their hands and arms pulling on oars. The oars show their long looms from the upper rowers down to the waterline along parallel angled

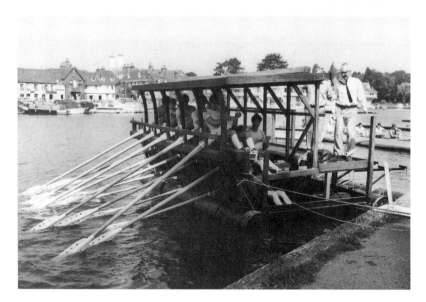

Figure 4-8. A mock-up of a trireme's seating and rowing arrangement, using a volunteer crew from Cambridge University at Henley-on-Thames. The ancient seating arrangement is not entirely as comfortable to the racing crew as that of an eight-oared racing shell. One of them said as much—"I would hate to do more than a half mile in this rowing rig." The seating arrangement of a trireme has been a lively controversy as long as can be remembered. It probably also was among the Athenians under Themistocles in the fifth century BC. (John Coates)

lines. There are many other presumptive oars coming out of the sides of this relief below the rowers, but from ill-defined sources. It is a frustrating study. As said above, we will not go any further in the discussion of oar placement.

The trouble is that classic historians seem to reconstruct their image of triremes around the seating arrangement of the rowers, assuming they are in three layers or assembly of tiers. It is the shipbuilders and ship designers who must suffer in trying to reconstruct, traditionally and logically, the vessel required for rowing on the sea before designing the seating arrangement.

At any rate, in approaching the problem of reconstructing a Greek trireme of 500 BC, or better, 480 BC, the project's leaders, Professor John Morrison of Cambridge University and John Coates, OBE, recently retired from the British Admiralty as senior naval architect, called together an advisory council. The council convened April 21, 1983, in a meeting room of the National Maritime Museum in Greenwich. There were representatives from maritime groups as well as independent nautical types, some thirty-five altogether. The Britishers were in the majority and included the National Maritime Museum director and his chief archaeologist down to the hands-on rowing expert and master of Ulysses' galley replica, Tim Severin. There was also one expert from Denmark and four from Greece, including the director of the Hellenic Maritime Museum and a shipowner from Athens. There were also two representatives from the United States, Professor Richard Steffy from the Institute of Nautical Archaeology and myself. This two-day meeting discussed the feasibility of the proposed design in drawings and model presented by Mr. John Coates, as well as the recommended construction techniques advanced by Richard Steffy. These discussions were informal, with questions and differing proposals and suggestions from the floor. The outcome was positive and the result was to recommend proceeding with plans for building a replica of an Athenian trireme of 480 BC with dimensions as follows: adequate for crew of 200 including 170 rowers, her length was to be about 42 meters (137.5 feet). The length as approximated and ultimately built was based not on the

Figure 4-9 A and B. The construction of the present-day trireme Olympias *was undertaken by the Greek navy at their navy yard near Piraeus, built to the design of John Coates, naval architect from England, along with John Morrison, well-known classicist and retired Cambridge professor. These views of her underbody and oar ports show her under construction. Her hull was built up shell-first with the ancient mortise-and-tenon plank fastenings. The locking wooden pegs can be seen protruding here from the bottom planking before the hull was finished. The quality of the wood structure of the hull is excellent. (John Coates)*

required distance between rowers for adequate rowing space but on the length of the shipsheds for storing in the small circular port at Piraeus, Microlemano. The beam of the ship was determined from the width between supporting columns of these ship sheds.

The triremes originally and also rationally were light-displacement vessels, carrying no ballast and built from lightweight wood (pine) and of minimum scantlings. The original engineering for such a structure must have been state-of-the-art. This is not a poor presumption when considering Greek structures during the age of art and building in the fifth century BC. The draft of the trireme design was thus small, about 1.5 meters. However, the total weight of the complete structure without crew as built now is surprisingly some 25 tons (metric).

The trireme ship type or "trires," as the vessel is called by more-learned scholars, survived through the Greek dominance of the seas and passed over into the Roman supremacy when it was used in an only slightly altered form. The Romans also used great numbers of two-tiered rowing vessels in their navies. The ship was, of course, a warship whose primary offensive weapon was a beakhead or ram at the waterline. The earlier galleys of Greece used rams in the form of a boar's head, a heavy bronze casting extending beyond the stempost at the waterline with its base rooted into the structure. These were in the sixth and late seventh centuries BC. But as the culture developed and science improved, the ram improved into a more effective shape with a heavy center vertical and three ribs on both sides extending back and widening into a solid base. They were, of course, cast in solid bronze, and one of them was recently found by underwater archaeologists working along the Israeli coast at the ancient harbor of Caesarea. It is no coincidence that no other remains of these ancient and strangely significant powerful warships have ever been found. By their own nature only the bronze casting was capable of surviving. Triremes were unable to sink as did the more ubiquitous trading vessels. They carried no ballast and, to the contrary, were made excessively light in weight of pine and other light soft woods, which had little resistance to deterioration. They existed only for their relatively itinerant employment—rather like emergency vehicles. None have ever been found, nor has much evidence of their existence survived for us to see today. It is perhaps questionable that we should take space here to mention them—when our inferred policy is to include and describe essentially the boats whose origins and survival are of indigenous nature. We try to emphasize only the wooden boats that have existed into the twentieth century or nearly so by their timeless qualities passed along from hundreds of generations of sailors and boatbuilders. War vessels seldom have such characteristics; certainly the great grandfather of all warships, the Greek trireme of the fifth century BC never did, or we would know more about what it really was. It was, and as its current replica, *Olympias*, is today, largely a complex extended arrangement of seating on benches mounted in a floating wooden shell, with a canopy-deck above the rowers and a heavy bronze casting at the forward end at the waterline. These features were never of much importance to maritime commerce—except as they have made warships the guardians and the security for our passing cultures. If it had not been for the exceptional skill of the Athenians under Themistocles at Salamis in 480 BC, we may today have been speaking Arabic instead of English.

There is no question that a trireme was a very formidable vessel, certainly a historic ship in the hands of the Greeks. There were literally hundreds upon hundreds of great oared ships that developed to the optimum of their militant purpose during the middle first millennium BC. Yet who can say that, from a maritime point of view, they were more important than other and smaller watercraft and contributed more to the development of the nautical arts?

While oared ships were extant for some three thousand years or more (the last naval battle in which galleys were used was at Matapan in AD 1717) their end was permanent. After multiple cannons mounted on large sailing vessels became the dominant seagoing weapon, an oared galley was literally dead in the water. Such war galleys are helpless when in range of such large sailing warships. Their cruising range held them close to base and the human propulsive power required an enormous logistic system. When weapons become outmoded, so do their carriers.

So it is with passing symbols of power. The ordinary, the unexceptional, the common, the sometimes coarse and vulgar—those things never die. And there is nothing left today to really identify the ancient trireme. But we have the Kyrenia ship, which has all the attributes of a good old ship. It was through that pipeline that traditions, the shape and eternal style of a sailing vessel, were carried down.

Now we can look toward development of maritime techniques in the waters where this little trading ship sailed. In her rig, like that of the

ship from the Thera fresco (Chapter One) in the Aegean Islands a squaresail, we see an early note of progress—the Kyrenia ship was in a newer millennium, about one thousand years younger at least. Her sail has no lower yard. It can also be reduced in area by the brailing lines, a first-millennium idea. This may have resulted from the motivation to cant down the leading edge of the sail to sail closer to the wind. While it can be done with a double-yard squaresail, brailing is not as awkward. This whole line of experimentation led ultimately to the triangular lateen sail and was followed by the familiar fore-and-aft sail.

This evolutionary development has many forms and was in process perhaps two thousand years. It is not known for sure whether it was first used in the Far East, the Near East, or the West. We can say, reasonably confidently, that it was finally developed to its present state of efficiency as a product of Western culture.

But we should admit the use of the three-cornered sail called the lateen. Its place of origin is truly speculative—there is little real evidence whether it was the eastern Mediterranean or the Indian Ocean. It had been in use earlier perhaps on the Nile River, and it is still used there. This is close to the center of the ancient Western world, and the roots of the earliest Mediterranean cultures cannot be disassociated from it.

On the shores of Lebanon there are still remnants of ancient half-sunken stone breakwaters of the harbors of Phoenician city-states near the sites of Sidon and Tyre. In a place once called Byblos, now Jubayl, there exists, as elsewhere on this coast, a type of remarkably refined inshore beach boat. This boat is natural and graceful with a gentle sheer, well-molded ends, and a proper beam-to-length ratio. Its coefficients of form are modern in the most approved sense, and yet its origin is unknown. It is possible to say that this beach boat could well be a model that is the basis for all Mediterranean beach boats. The beach and harbor boats so prevalent throughout this whole great sea have a common look, with, of course, many regional variants. This boat seems to be a recognizable root, as basic to boat design perhaps as Latin and Greek are to modern languages.

The Lebanese beach boat is a smoothly planked, typically Mediterranean double-ender with a rising stempost. Its distinguishing feature, and also the characteristic that reinforces my belief in its originality, is its restrained design. Its sheerline, for example, is more gently curved than that of most other Mediterranean beach boats; the stempost does not rise quite as high; and the hull is also of less depth. These are all features that were innovations when first devised. Essentially this boat has a clean canoe-shaped body with no abrupt changes in curvature, yet with sufficient curvature to have a natural hollow in the bow without a shoulder. The construction is on the heavy side, with sawn frames, carvel planking, and often a heavier rubrail plank below the sheer plank. The boat is from 16 to 20 feet in length, and is generally powered with a small one-cylinder engine. In the past, it was rowed, or sailed with a short lateen sail. It is a graceful boat whose ancestry is lost somewhere in the mists perhaps ten centuries past—or even more. It is regrettable that we have no photo here of this beach boat. I saw it only once, but we will see its sister and cousins later as we progress through the smaller boats and beach craft to follow in this chapter.

EGYPTIAN SURVIVORS

The oldest civilizations near the Mediterranean shores were those of the people of the Nile. While the Egyptians have never been a seapower, they have been water-oriented. Nearly the total population is confined to the fertile strip of land bordering the edge of the Nile and its estuary. The earliest inhabitants here were probably the first to exploit effectively boats of any sort. The primitive watercraft still used on the Nile are of interest primarily because of the origin of their

ancient sails. The sail form still used here, like the Lebanese boat described previously, is probably an original: The lateen sail was early in evidence on the Nile—sometime in the early Christian era. There is some evidence of lateen sails in Roman art as well. The lateen is now historically a popular and widely adapted rig. In Egypt, it retains its original form—a graceful, triangular fore-and-aft sail with a towering yard peaked high above the masthead.

In the dynastic periods of Egypt on the upper reaches of the Nile, sails had always been "square" or spread on yards. As shown in the earliest dynastic reliefs, the yards were often tilted

Figure 4-10. Before the Arab-Israeli wars, there were many varied types of boats working at the Mediterranean entrance to the Suez Canal. This stone lighter with a settee rig, a variation of the lateen rig, is representative of a mixture of Eastern and Mediterranean cultures. (The Science Museum, London)

Figure 4-11. Three two-masted gaiassas, heavily laden, sailing downwind on the Nile. Still taking advantage of the nearly constant upstream wind as all Egyptian boats have for over five thousand years, these boats could very well be the direct descendants of the very first boats to sail. (The Science Museum, London)

upward to reach for breezes above the trees or sandy cliffs. The part of the sail in the downward position was in the way and of little use, and so it was trimmed back. This sail can still be seen today above the second cataract of the Nile on a boat type called a nugger. This rig is also known as the "nugger lug."

On the lower Nile some sailing working boats today are notable for the great spread of their ancient triangular sails. In all of the regions where the lateen has recently been in any use—in Portugal, most Mediterranean regions, the Black Sea, the Red Sea, and the Persian Gulf, as far east as India and south to the African coast—no sailors can equal the Arabs of the Nile in maneuvering boats equipped with this rig. The boats using these great sails are not noted for their shape, structure, or anything else except their surprising performance beneath their bulging triangular canopy. This lower-Nile boat type is known generally as a gaiassa. It is sometimes two-masted, but more often nowadays it has a single, forward-raking mast carrying the long lateen yard. This yard, often 80 feet or more in length, is made up of sections, overlapped and lashed crudely together, a universal practice with large lateens. The yard is not generally lowered when the sail is shortened or furled, but the crew goes aloft, straddling the yard as if it were a sloping tree trunk.

The gaiassa's hull, Figure 4-12, is a flat, broad, barge form with a swept-up spoonlike bow for keeping the cargo dry, as the bow wave piles up when the boat is running against the river chop. This bow, with its exaggerated rise, is perhaps the last remnant of any likeness to the magnificent high-ended riverboats that sailed the Nile four thousand or more years ago.

To the Westerner, the method of sailing a gaiassa is unusual. When sailing on the wind, the yard carries the sail to windward of the weather rigging. As with the older lateens it is customary to wear around because the yard is above and outside the shrouds and riggings. When wearing, the gaiassa's yard is hauled around aft of the mast so that the yard is always on the windward side of the mast. When sailing free or off the wind, the tack ropes on the lower end of the yard are slacked off and the sail forms a lifting air foil overhead, carrying the craft gracefully along. The sailor of a gaiassa could probably not sail any other type of sailing craft, even if it were lateen-rigged, but then, no other sailor could possibly manage a gaiassa.

There were a number of small lateen-rigged harbor and delta craft on the coast from Port Said to Alexandria before the Arab-Israeli wars. These boats have suffered, as did the boats of the Brittany coast during World Wars I and II, from the ravages of war and the interruption of peaceful commerce. It is unlikely that these craft will be replaced.

The Bronze Age trade routes, carrying the first sea commerce, led first to the Levant coast (modern Lebanon, Israel, and Syria). The Egyptians, always in search of timber, found the cedars of the Levant most useful and valuable. But in the years of the second millennium BC, another people were trading and sailing, as seen in Chapter One. Egyptians called this new race of sailors simply the "People of the Sea." We know them as the Minoans.

AEGEAN CRAFT

It is likely that in the Aegean Sea, whether on the island of Crete (which was the power base for the Minoans under the mythical-real King Minos) or in the Cyclades Islands, the techniques of boat- and shipbuilding changed. It was gradual, of course. But there is now developing archaeological knowledge that a fundamental change in ship structure occurred here. Sometime in the early part of the second millennium, probably between the seventeenth and fifteenth centuries BC, the idea of a keel was born. There is no other conflicting or additional evidence of such a centerline ship's girder. The ship now being excavated at Ulu Burun, a coastwise merchant ship trading to and from the Aegean in the eastern Mediterranean, clearly has a keel timber with the garboard strakes attached. It is dated to the mid-fifteenth century BC, or late Bronze Age. The ships of Thera in the fresco (Chapter One) have recently been declared by the further archaeological finds at Akrotiri to be of the seventeenth century BC. These ships of Thera, with hulls and sailing profiles according to Egyptian styles, are most likely of the state of the art in Egypt at the time—heavy mortice-keyed planking on a flatter bottom with no vertical center timber.

Thus maritime knowlege develops and moves on. In this area we see the later Kyrenia ship and the succession of classic age ships becoming planked up with a more rational order of internal framing.

Boats are produced now, however, in a style indigenous to the eastern Mediterranean, and they are typically found in the Aegean and on the Turkish littoral. There is, first, a type of trading schooner frequently of Greek origin to be seen among the islands and in the small harbors of the eastern coast. Most of these schooners carry a conventional gaff rig nowadays, instead of the formerly popular sprit or lugsail rig. The masts are comparatively short with no topsails ("bald-headed" as the rig was referred to by American sailors). The hulls are deep and full, of heavy displacement, but with a nice sheerline culminating forward in a rising, flaring bow. The stem form is a fairly common Mediterranean profile, and Americans would describe it as a "clipper" bow. It is, however, a far older and more subtle form than the bow form of the American nineteenth-century clipper. It most surely evolved from the rakish stems of the old Turkish and Saracen galleys that were so impressively predominant as warcraft centuries ago. This stem profile can be seen on other Mediterranean craft, described later.

There seem to be no rigorous rules surrounding the proportions or form of the eastern Mediterranean trading schooners. The individuality of their builders is freely expressed. These vessels may have broad transoms carrying the heavy rudder stock outboard or they may have a more graceful rounded or elliptical stern on a short counter overhang. The gunwales are deep and heavily built, and they have wide decks broken by but one heavily framed hatch, a companionway, and a small deckhouse. The boats vary between 50 and 75 feet in length. The style and color are always unmistakably eastern Mediterranean.

The eastern Mediterranean hull, with its variable rig, overhanging stem, and either transom or short counter stern, is seemingly increasing in popularity in the smaller sizes, particularly the boats of approximately 30 feet in length. These smaller boats among the Aegean Islands generally have a short rig with a single mast. They depend on a one-cylinder diesel of large displacement. The sail may be a lateen, but usually it is a lugsail

Figure 4-13. The ubiquitous Aegean trading schooner is not always as graceful as this nearly completed hull. This boat, however, has the same basic style as most trading schooners found principally in Greek and eastern Mediterranean ports.

Figure 4-14. An Aegean trading schooner at work apparently at night with a fair and following breeze. She is sailing along with the lightest of a bow wave, recently out of the port on the island of Astypalaia in the Cyclades northeast of Crete. Her captain is standing beside the helmsman on the afterdeck while another crewman keeps a lookout amidships. This schooner, about 60 feet in length, is fairly heavily laden, and with the fullness of her hull will not make more than about 7½ knots even with the fair breeze. This is a model by William Bromell.

or conventional low-cut gaff sail. The most notable characteristic of these boats—they seem to have fallen into a recognizable style—is the attention that the builder pays to producing a nicely formed hull. These boats are purely Greek and can be seen in the crowded harbor of Piraeus or in any of the small island harbors between Hydra and Rhodes. They are used for inter-island transport, fishing, or more frequently these days, since the discovery of the Greek islands by tourists, as charter boats (together with an assortment of other nondescript types). They have been called caiques, and have been imported to or duplicated in Florida by Greek sponge fishermen. Although it is not the typical sponge boat now used in Tarpon Springs, Florida, the type is occasionally seen there. Figure 4-13 shows one of these boats in a builder's yard just after completion of the hull. The excellent workmanship is clearly evident in this well-modeled 30-footer. Note the typical Mediterranean bow bittheads extending from the bow rail. These bittheads are stan-

Figure 4-15. A contemporary version of an Aegean trading lugger. This type of trader is relatively common in the Greek islands and is closely related to the Turkish tchektirme. Many have two masts, but the sails are only auxiliary and are seldom unfurled. The unique bow form is a holdover from ancient times. Note the integrated construction of the traditional waist rails. (Greek National Tourist Office)

Figure 4-16. A double-ended Aegean fishing boat.
Note the built-up sheerstrake and the fabric spray
shield. (Ammanatides, Athens)

Figure 4-17. This sponger is typical of all of the
smaller boats of the Aegean. This type is identified
primarily by the shape of its raised stem. This broad
stem is always carved in profile with a semicircular
cutout in the after edge. (Half-model by William
Bromell)

dard in many types of Mediterranean boats, both eastern and western. Identical ones were used on the ships and boats of ancient Rome.

A common boat of the Aegean, yet one that evades categorization, is also an island trading boat. It is similar in size to the schooner type described previously. It is the nearest contemporary relative, sometimes an actual conversion, of the Greek and Turkish sailing coasters so common in the nineteenth century. These were great sprit- or lug-rigged craft of deep sheer with low waists protected by built-up strakes added as waist rails. (These are the modern version of the old woven fabric waist cloth that dates back to the second millennium BC and earlier.) The termination of this raised planking forward produces a unique bow and stem form that identifies the boat as Aegean.

Among the small ports of the Levant coast and in the Aegean Sea, there are still cargo-carrying boats with an unusual assortment of rigs. Some of these are related to the old polacres, or Mediterranean square-riggers with pole masts. These boats are sometimes conventionally square-rigged brigs or brigantines with single pole masts 60 to 80 feet in height, generally exhibiting the steep sheer of Mediterranean boats, or they can be stubby-masted schooners or large ketches with one lateen and one gaff-headed sail and perhaps a square yard on the main. Such odd craft are difficult to classify, because they combine experimentation with ancestral or ancient influences. They are interesting to study individually, but they are lost as indigenous types. They are mentioned here only to note their presence and to isolate them from more important craft.

Figure 4-18. A double-ended Aegean fishing boat. Note the tiller curving down from the high rudderhead. (Greek National Tourist Office)

Smaller but very common Greek fishing and sponger types are found in many individual variations throughout the Aegean area. They are typical of the Greek islands. (See Figures 4-16 and 4-18.) The boats have a deep sheer with rising ends, often have a spray curtain along the waist (an Aegean usage that can be observed on a Greek vase painting of a ship in the fourth century BC, as well as on one of the Thera fresco ships), and have a stempost that extends approximately nine to ten inches above the forward deck. This stempost frequently has a distinctive semicircular cutout carved in the after edge. The mast is comparatively short and the loose-footed sail is for steadying and can be used for auxiliary drive. These boats are generally double-enders but are now sometimes built with a broad wineglass transom by Aegean builders. It is interesting that the double-ended form used here is hollow with flaring after sections. Such a stern can be seen in the little Aegean sponge-fishing boat of Figure 4-17.

The sponge-diving industry in the Aegean has suffered in recent years because the local sponge beds have been depleted. The Greek boats now sail to the grounds off the African shore for sponges. Poor local fishing has had an adverse effect on the old boats previously used in sponging that were similar to but larger than those existing now. Some of these older types were prevalent in Tarpon Springs, Florida.

The Greeks have an instinctive feeling for line and form, which is their inheritance, and it is very apparent in all of their boats. The structure and form of the boats built, owned, and sailed by Greeks are the best and most seakindly in the whole Mediterranean. It has probably always been so.

Figure 4-19. A small Greek beach boat used for fishing. This type is indigenous to the Gulf of Corinth and sails with a light sprit rig. Because it does not have a high stem, this boat is unique. It is a fine-lined double-ender with a raking stem and stern. (Greek National Tourist Office)

TURKISH BOATS

Fishing craft and trading boats used beyond the Dardanelles in Turkish waters have successfully survived the transition from sail to power. In the process the Turks have retained and improved the strong regional character of their boats.

The boats of Turkey retain the quality of structure that began with the Ottoman Empire when expense was of very little consequence and the sultans imported the best craftsmen from wherever they were to be found. It was in the building of the Moslem galleys that the tradition of Turkish excellence in boat carpentry began. That the skills of the past have been passed on from generation to generation is obvious in the present-day boats active as fishing craft and coastal traders out of Istanbul and the Black Sea.

The most typical and well-defined Turkish boats are found in and around Istanbul and the Sea of Marmara. They are either coastal carrier boats or fishing craft, mostly engine-powered today but some with short auxiliary sailing rigs. Of the fishing types, the most notable is a seiner of the Istanbul locality known as a balikci. Although this boat type is a development of perhaps only the last fifty years, it has a regional character strong enough to be considered indigenous. This type is generally from 45 to 50 feet in length, and its form is characterized by a graceful sheer, fine entrance, powerful bows, and a trawler-type overhanging stern. The keel is straight with a slight drag, and its draft of about 5.5 feet allows fairly easy beaching when necessary. The general hull shape and structure is in the finest tradition of low-powered, seakindly

Figure 4-20. The hull lines profile of a balikci, a comparatively recent development in Black Sea and Bosphorus fishing craft. This boat, however, is an extension of older traditions that have for centuries characterized Saracen boats.

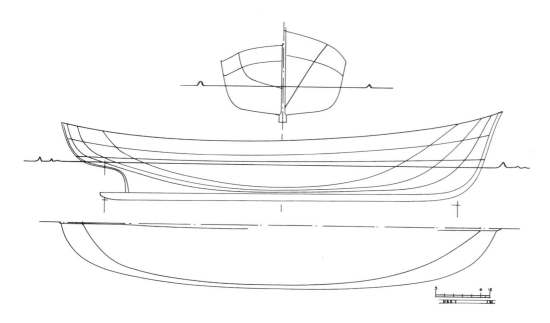

forms. (See Figure 4-20.) These boats have been studied extensively in towing tank programs sponsored by the Food and Agriculture Organization
under the direction of Professor Ata Nutku of the Technical University in
Istanbul. The builders have been most responsive subsequently to further
development and improvement of the type. These balikci are capable boats
in the most modern sense. Their structure is of the most conservative sort,
with closely spaced sawn frames together with heavy keels and keelsons. The
planking is carvel with deep gunwales and heavy railcaps.

An older type of craft on this northern Turkish shore is a freight carrier
called a tchektirme, shown in Figure 4-22. These boats, still abundant,
were developed from older sailing craft once fitted with a large triangular
sail. The identifying character of a tchektirme is its deep, exaggerated
sheerline. This sheerline sweeps down from a high scimitar stem to a waist
that, when loaded, may be at or below the waterline, and then sweeps aft
to a high sternpost. Above the guardrail of the apparent sheerline, however,
is a higher bulwark. This feature is reminiscent of the classic Aegean boats,
which required a wash– or sprayrail to protect the amidships area. This

*Figure 4-21. The hull
lines of a small tchek-
tirme. The tchektirme
is built in various sizes
from less than 30 feet
to more than 80 feet
in length.*

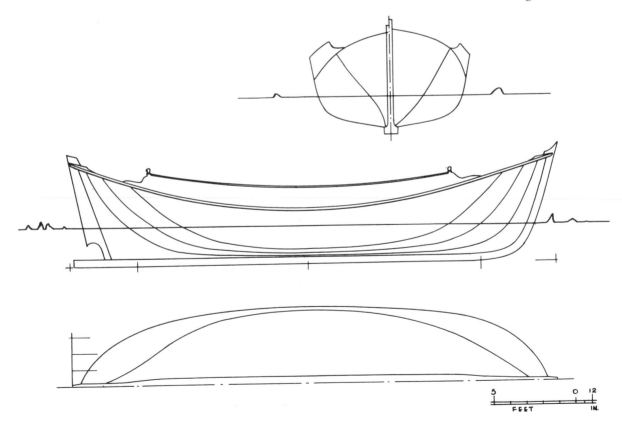

higher bulwark curves up from the upper guardrail abaft the bow chocks and again back down to the after rail line. The modified lines drawing of a small but typical tchektirme shown in Figure 4-21 indicates the classic profile of this type. It is notable that the deck line is always flatter than the apparent sheerline in these boats. Tchektirmes vary in size from small, almost miniature craft of less than 30 feet to quite large boats, sometimes as much as 80 feet in length.

Very seldom are contemporary tchektirmes seen under sail. However, when they do carry auxiliary sail, the rig consists of a short lug mainsail or triangular sail with a long foot and a conventional jib or forestay sail rigged to a housing bowsprit.

Figure 4-22. The Turkish tchektirme is certainly the most common trading boat in the Bosphorus and the Black Sea. It is also seen in the eastern Mediterranean, and its relation to the Greek island traders is apparent in the bows and the waist boards along the sides. Since World War II, the tchektirmes have all gradually been converted to power; formerly they carried a two-masted lug rig.

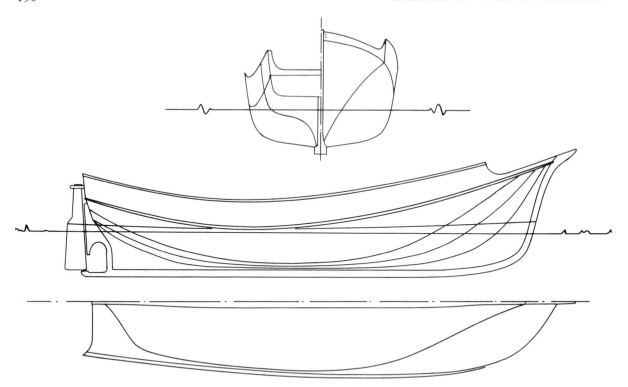

Figure 4-23. The lines of a taka in this modified profile show the curious features of this traditional Turkish boat. Note the high quarter rail and outboard rudderhead.

The taka is perhaps less numerous but no less distinctive in style than the tchektirme. Takas are distinguished first by the unusual profile of their upper stem. This distinctive shape has been unflatteringly, but very descriptively, called a "chicken-beak" stem. (See Figure 4-24). The sheerline of a taka is very extreme and similar to the tchektirme's. The upper bulwark is also characteristic of the tchektirme, but it extends all the way to the stern in a taka. The taka's stern form is also distinctive, being a square transom stern formed quite high on the sternpost. The sternpost is frequently set partially outside the transom, and the rudder is hung conventionally outboard with the curved tiller projecting across the transom. (See Figure 4-23).

Takas have generally well-proportioned hulls aside from their stubby-looking after end, which results in less than a clean, flat run. Their sections are nicely rounded similar to the tchektirme. The basic taka may range in size from a boat of about 18 feet up to a sizeable coaster of 60 feet carrying perhaps 250 tons deadweight.

It is most evident that in Turkey the type of boat developed is generally not dictated by a single employment. Very seldom is it possible to observe indigenous boats whose distinctive forms and character are the result of the specific requirements of their employment. The most usual circumstance is

Figure 4-24. The taka is a very short-ended boat distinguished by its unique false stem extension. The boat is stubby and flat-floored, and has a high, flaring bow—an inefficient but curiously attractive hull form.

that a boat type must be adaptable to several modes of employment to survive successfully. This general truth is well illustrated throughout the Mediterranean as well as in the craft at its eastern end. The takas and tchektirmes are built in all sizes and are employed as seiners, handliners, coastal carriers, traders, or in whatever water transport suits the owner or is most profitable.

In my discussion of Aegean boats, a caique was mentioned. While this term may often be used to describe Aegean craft, it is more properly applied to a specific small rowing craft in Istanbul and the Sea of Marmara. This boat is undoubtedly a descendant of a very elegant boat. The sultans of three to four centuries ago were transported with great pomp in a multi-oared, high-ended, decorated boat called a *caique* or *kayik* in Turkish.

Today the surviving kayik is a very graceful double-ender whose simplified profile lines are shown in Figure 4-25. The boat has a canoelike profile, but is quite broad of beam; the beam and fullness are carried well aft where the greater weight is carried. This boat type is still colorfully decorated and embellished with carving and has gracefully formed ends. Its name, however, like the names of many fine and functional artifacts and devices of men, has become popularized and extended to other like objects of lesser quality. So today we are not quite sure what a caique is when someone uses the name.

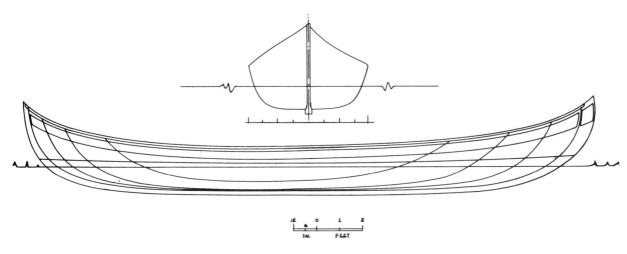

Figure 4-25. The long, graceful, canoelike hull lines of a caique. The Turkish caique is actually the one genuine caique of several misnamed types. It is used in contemporary Turkish fisheries as a net-handling boat and fishes in conjunction with the balikci.

VENETIAN BOATS

On the old trade route from the Aegean around Peloponnesus through the Ionian Sea and up the Adriatic there is a timeless quality to the sea. This is the ancient and classic sea of Homer. With only a little imagination one sees misty images of ancient ships against the blue haze of the mountainous shore. Long after the Minoan traders, Ulysses, Greek triremes, and the Roman merchant ships disappeared, this route led to and from the powerful Venetian state. The elaborate war galleys of Venice ventured forth from this seaway with flashing oars to diminish the power of the Ottoman navies. This heart of the Mediterranean today brings to mind many memories of world sea power, wealth, commerce, and a great progression of traditional shipbuilding. Today's boats in this area are but a poor and shabby reflection of such past glory.

There are several types whose operation and origin identify them with this region, but they are only the remnants of a recent coastwise commerce under sail. It is rare to encounter any of these craft under sail. Practically all are converted to mechanical power with auxiliary sail.

In the southern end of the Adriatic near the Ionian Sea, where Italy is nearest to Greece, the boats observed are much like those to be found in the Aegean and about the Greek harbors. But farther into the Adriatic there is a noticeable change in character. The most predominant boat, one that originated in the region of Ancona at least two centuries ago, is a very full and bluff coasting vessel called a trabaccolo. Trabaccolos were indigenous in the eighteenth century to both coasts of Italy. It is recorded that Commodore Edward Preble of the frigate *Constitution*'s squadron purchased or chartered several as gunboats for additional support in his campaign against Tripolitan pirates in 1804. This boat has two masts carrying two lugsails, and it has a large jib set flying on a steeply raked bowsprit. It has a colorful, striped, double-ended hull and a tall rudder. The boat's most distinctive feature now is the fullness of its ends, particularly its bows, which terminate in a backward-raking stem. It has an unusual round-bilge hull with shallow flat

Figure 4-26. The classic, centuries-old trabaccolo of the Adriatic is best illustrated by this native model. Note the full lug rig and housing bowsprit with headsail. These boats are still occasionally seen under this rig, but most often they have a cut-down mast and are diesel-powered. The boats are distinguished by their high, bluff, swept-up bows and heavy, carved oculus.

sections. Trabaccolos are usually 50 to 70 feet long, but are sometimes found in smaller sizes around 40 feet with a single masted lug rig. (See Figures 4-26 and 4-27.)

A typical, ancient decoration found on small indigenous craft in almost all parts of the world is the "oculus." This often painted, sometimes carved, eye in the bows of boats was first used in the ancient Mediterranean. (See the Greek fifth-century-BC trireme.) It was common as early as the middle of the first millennium BC, and is evident on pottery decorations showing Greek ships of this time. On the trabaccolo, the oculus serves as a functional part of the boat as well. It is a carving now that surrounds the hawsehole in both sides of the bow, such as in Figure 4-27.

The trabaccolo, if any still survive, even under power, is a trading boat that is sometimes found outside of the Adriatic sailing into Malta, Sicily, or the eastern ports. However, its own locale was the upper Adriatic near Venice and Ancona. It is unmistakable with its colorful, full-ended hull and high bows pushing a white bow wave down the Adriatic.

An Adriatic lugger more trim in line and rig than the trabaccolo is more frequently encountered today. This traditional fishing lugger of the upper Adriatic is 45 to 50 feet long, though sometimes larger, with a lively but not excessive sheer. It has two masts; the forward one is slightly taller and carries the larger sail. These boats are typical of the Adriatic with their high narrow

*Figure 4-27. A well-worn trabaccolo with a
shortened rig. (Galvani di A. Marchi)*

Figure 4-28. Three double-ended fishing luggers typical of the Adriatic. Similar to the trabaccolo in rig, they have more practical sailing hulls with finer lines. (Galvani di A. Marchi)

Figure 4-29. The small craft of the Adriatic, as elsewhere, reflect much of the character of their larger contemporaries. The extended side washboards are an influence of boats from the Aegean and Ionian seas. (Galvani di A. Marchi)

Figure 4-30. The trabaccolos of more than a century and a half ago, as illustrated by Antoine Roux, are similar to the craft in Figure 4-28. The rig and general character have hardly changed. (Peabody Museum, Salem)

rudders, broad rudderheads, deep gunwales, and boomed lugsails of the eastern Mediterranean. Like the larger trabaccolos, they are planked and framed in oak with decks of pine, but they are proportionately deeper, not as beamy, and have a much finer entrance and run.

It is curious that this lugger is very much the same boat as that illustrated by the great marine artist Antoine Roux in 1816, which he identifies as "Trabacolo" (see Figure 4-30). This sort of boat is undoubtedly the trabaccolo type used by Commodore Preble in 1804. It is doubtful that the American commodore would use a boat as unlikely to sail well as is a twentieth-century survivor by the same name. It is a reasonable speculation, in any case, that the handsome eighteenth-century lugger, as painted by Roux, was the ancestor of these later Adriatic

luggers. It should also be pointed out that the larger, fuller, bluff-bowed trabaccolo is a trading vessel carrying lumber and stone about the coastal ports while the early version was more diversified. There is often such a distinction in a basic type of workboat, but seldom is there so great a difference in form.

In the lagoons of Venice there still may be seen an occasional sailing barge called a bragozzo, which when under sail is distinctive in its sail decoration. It has a large main lugsail and a very small one on a short mast well forward, with no other headsail. The bragozzo is a clumsy flat-bottomed bargelike vessel. (See Figure 4-31).

In any discussion such as this of indigenous watercraft, it would be a slight to the Venetians to ignore the most familiar of all indigenous boats. The gondola of Venice is at once a taxi, a ferry, a light freight transport, and a family vehicle, and varies in appearance from humble to luxurious. As of this writing its future is threatened, as it has been on many other occasions. However, this current threat may be of more serious consequence. The ancient craft of gondola building tends to be dying for want of young appren-

Figure 4-31. The bragozzo of Venice is the traditional sailing barge of the lagoons of the North Adriatic. It is a hard-working, ungainly craft.

tices. None of these graceful, unique, beautifully built little canoelike hulls are of recent construction. A century ago there were in Venice ten thousand of these boats; only a few hundred remain today.

The Venetian gondola is a very special watercraft whose qualities and employment are in most respects not comparable to the other boats discussed in this book. (See Figures 4-32, 4-33, and 4-34.) It is, however, nothing if not indigenous to its locale. It is a craft rigorously bound by tradition. It has had only a few changes in its design and styling perhaps in five hundred years. Its light canoe-like hull may vary in length from 30 to 50 feet, though the standard gondola of today is 36 feet. Always painted black, its graceful hull is sheathed with several strakes of thin planking over approximately 40 delicately sawn frames. It is open for two-thirds of its length, but there is a deck aft of its canopy that forms a platform for the gondolier and his single sweep. The starboard side of the boat is eight inches shorter than the port side to offset the drag of the oar and to provide the added asymmetrical buoyancy for the gondolier, whose oar-sweep works in a raised carved oarlock on the starboard side. This allows him to row and steer simultaneously from his standing position to port. The ends rise steeply, with the stem carrying the traditional gondola-identifying decoration, which consists of a number of spiked projections turned forward, reminiscent of old galley rams, and one turned aft. The graceful stern is often unnoticed because it is overshadowed by the ostentatious bow. The gondola is simply the basic unit or common denominator of transportation

in Venice, where the waters once swarmed with glittering varieties of more elaborate, oared, galleylike transports. Some of these are still floated out on ceremonial occasions.

Before this discussion of watercraft in the Adriatic is ended, it should be reemphasized that the existing craft today are reflections and remnants of a comparatively recent domination by a great variety of sailing craft. This is true not only of the Adriatic but also in a less concentrated way of the entire eastern Mediterranean. There was a marked similarity in all the sailing workboats with their sweeping, often exaggerated sheerlines and high ends, their weather cloths or raised bulwarks protecting the amidships waists, the high-aspect rudders, and, most of all, the popular balanced-lugsail rig.

This lugsail, which carries a boom on its foot unlike the northern lug of the British and French coasts, is similar and, some say, related to the oriental version of the lug rig. It is my belief that this rig evolved as a result of a gradual development of the lateen rig—a rig that was indigenous to the eastern Mediterranean. There is no objective evidence that is specific enough to indicate the real origin of either the lug rig or the lateen. The classic Greek and subsequent Roman sail of the pre-Christian era was the basic squaresail and, in some occasional instances, a spritsail, apparently on small craft. Sometime in the years following classic Rome, the lateen and lugsails appeared. They could most logically have originated very simply by experimentation and adaptation of the squaresail to other than downwind sailing, as on the Nile. It was proved a practical option in sailing the *Kyrenia II*. Such experimentation would most likely take place in the smaller craft, which were undermanned and could not conveniently rely on oars. Large vessels, except for the independent traders, were basically galleys or oar-powered boats, because the Mediterranean is a sea of light and unreliable winds, varied by sudden and violent weather in the winter months. It is not a sea to encourage development of large, complex sailing rigs. The lugsail was a natural development and was still the basic sail of the Aegean and Adriatic when working sail was used, even as an auxiliary. In the western Mediterranean, there is no compromise with the lateen.

Figure 4-33. Though gondolas are similar in style and form, they differ in decoration. Notice the forward deck ornamentation on these two gondolas. (Italian Government Tourist Office)

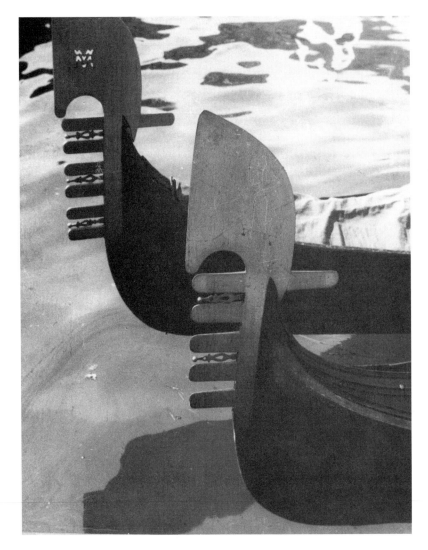

Figure 4-34. The bow ornament that is standard on most gondolas has its origin in the postmedieval era. Its meaning is controversial, but certainly the horizontal bars under the upper hornlike profile are variable, which may or may not be accidental. (Italian Government Tourist Office)

MALTESE CRAFT

The geographical center of the Mediterranean is very close to the islands of Malta, and it is in this British bastion that there is to be found a style of watercraft combining the nautical practices and heritages of the sea's East and West. There are two distinctive types of craft still evident and indigenous to Malta. One is a combination fishing and transport boat; the other is essentially for harbor transport and is propelled only by a single oarsman.

This latter harbor boat, the Maltese dghaisa used in Grand Harbor, Malta, is not unrelated in character and utility to the Venetian gondola. In

Figure 4-35. The Maltese dghaisa, like the Venetian gondola, is an all-purpose harbor craft. The differences in configuration, however, are as readily apparent as the similarities. The high ends of the Maltese boat are like great scimitars. The boatman stands and rows facing forward with crossed oar looms.

Figure 4-36. The Maltese dghaisa-tal-pass is a colorful inter-island carrier and harbor boat. Though each boat is decorated differently, they all share certain features. For example, there is always on each bow a small but distinctive oculus. The traditional washrail is removable in sections, a practice that began at least a century and a half ago from the evidence in Antoine Roux's record of these boats. The distinctive shape of this boat is its most immediate identification. It has a steep forward sheer and high, broad extended stem; it is somewhat related to the boats of the Adriatic. (David Scott)

Figure 4-37. *This painting by Antoine Roux in 1826 shows a Maltese taffarel under sail and oars (in light air). She carries a sprit rig, which several centuries ago was a popular rig in the Ionian Sea. Note the removable bulwark panels still in use today as a spray shield. (Peabody Museum, Salem)*

structure and appearance, however, there is a difference. (See Figure 4-35.) The dghaisa (sometimes called draissa) is a heavier, fuller boat than the gondola. The oarsman stands well amidships and faces forward and with crossed oar looms propels the boat with short even strokes. Surrounding the central open area of this boat there is a raised rail and seats along the side for passengers. There is often a higher carved backrest in the after end. The stem and stern posts are high, nearly vertical, but with a slight inward rake and with the greatest width at the top. The stempost is nicely scimitar-shaped in the Turkish fashion, while the sternpost is cut off horizontally. The boats are generally from 20 to 25 feet long with a beam of about 6 feet. They are nicely cared for, generally painted brightly with a white waterline boottop and natural varnished sheer plank and end posts.

For transport between the islands, particularly between Malta and Gozo, and sometimes for fishing, there is a larger, more capable boat. This boat, called by the more awkward title dghaisa-tal-pass, is quite shapely and is heavily constructed in the manner of all Mediterranean beach boats. (See Figure 4-36.) This craft, also sometimes called a taffarel, is distinctive with an upswept bow and high stem characteristic of Malta. It has a deep waist with a high protective gunwale in the fashion of the Turkish and Aegean boats. This gunwale, however, is arranged in removable flat panels, originally to accommodate oars and for more convenient loading in harbor. On the forward rail there are king posts, which rise above the rail panels and provide a base of attachment for them. These contemporary boats are all motor-powered today but formerly carried a sprit rig and long bowsprit, as can be seen in a most charming watercolor by the celebrated French artist Antoine Roux in 1826 (see Figure 4-37). Their hulls have lost none of their color or charm and are brightly painted in several colors, often in blues that match the sea, with yellow and red trim. The oculus in the bows of the dghaisa-tal-pass is ever-present.

The largest typically Maltese workboat is the present-day version of the old speronara. This boat today is very like the dghaisa-tal-pass but is larger, heavier, and carries an auxiliary sail, although it is basically a powered craft. The sail is a high-peaked lateen or a settee on a short mast. The hull is beamy, about 14 feet wide to an overall length of 45 feet, with fine ends. It has the characteristic Maltese upswept bow with a high stem forward, rail posts, and paneled gunwale washrail. The rudder is deep, has a high-aspect ratio, and rises slightly above the sternpost aft. This is a handsome, capable seaboat in the best tradition of the Mediterranean. The Maltese can be justly proud of all their well-kept indigenous boats, but mostly of this lateener.

SICILIAN CRAFT

Although Malta is at the center of the Mediterranean and has been for centuries a military bastion commanding the comings and goings of commerce between the East and West, it has not been a site for the development of a separate culture. But just to the north of Malta is the historic land of Sicily—a large, fertile, and beautiful island. The fine arts to be found in Sicily, the great Greek temples with handsome columns still standing, the decorataive arts of the people reflecting Norman establishments, the Byzantine architecture and mosaics, and the medieval cloisters and baroque cathedrals all testify that here the West and the Near East fell in together. The situation suggests that whatever indigenous watercraft are built and used here might also show some evidence of a blending of such mixed cultures. Unfortunately, there is little left but traces.

In Sicily, the indigenous horse- and donkey-drawn carts are colorfully decorated with scenes of Sicilian history, much of it with medieval themes. The indigenous art is populated with knights on horseback, fourteenth-century towers, and fanciful designs; much of it suggests that the Normans were once here, and they were. These decorations are occasionally carried over to small fishing boats and harbor craft (see Figure 4-38). But the more basic features of Sicilian boats are found in their shape and construction. One's very first impression is that they are heavy and rugged; their stem and stern posts are similar to Maltese boats, but their hull shape is more like western Mediterranean craft. Figure 4-39 is a sketch made in Palermo harbor of a typical shapely but shabby little harbor boat about 18 feet long.

The larger fishing boats, which engage in a community endeavor common among Sicilian fishermen called trap net fishing, are similar in general construction to the harbor boat. They are not as deep in hull, however, and are narrower and flatter of sheer in proportion. The dimensions of an average trap net boat are 32 feet overall, 30 feet waterline, 8½ feet beam, and 1½ feet draft (light). As is evident from the profile in Figure 4-40, these boats carry a large raking lateen sail and a deep rudder. They are fitted also for from six to eight oars. These lateen-rigged boats work in conjunction with

Figure 4-38. Bow decoration on a Sicilian fishing boat. (Fenno Jacobs)

Figure 4-39. This little harbor boat of Palermo is the rugged common denominator of native Sicilian craft. The boats of Sicily show a greater similarity to the boats of Malta and the Adriatic than to those of the western Mediterranean. This is no doubt because of the ancient ties of Sicily to the lands of the Aegean and the Levant.

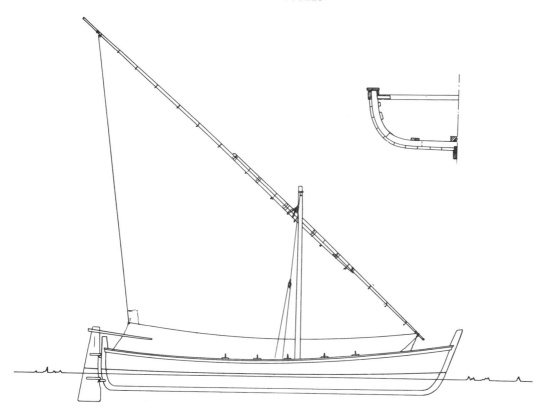

Figure 4-40. A Sicilian trap-net boat. The fishermen of southern Siciliy are slowly converting to powercraft, but this sailing boat still prevails as a workboat. It is typical of the double-enders working the coastal fisheries in the past.

a larger bargelike craft of 55 feet or so in length, which carries and works the heavy nets. Much of the fishing in Sicily is carried on this way, today without lateen rig. Fishing craft are powered now with diesel engines, and after postwar recovery, the fishing boats have become predominantly modern twentieth century.

A Sicilian boat that was well known because of its unique appearance, which evolved because of its special employment as a harpoon boat, is the swordfishing craft working in the Strait of Messina. When working, this swordfish catcher is rigged with a very long bowsprit pulpit platform, which is approximately as long as or slightly longer than the boat itself. This long pulpit is supported by heavy stays from a tall mast. The hull of this boat is shown in the profile sketch in Figure 4-41. The smaller swordfish

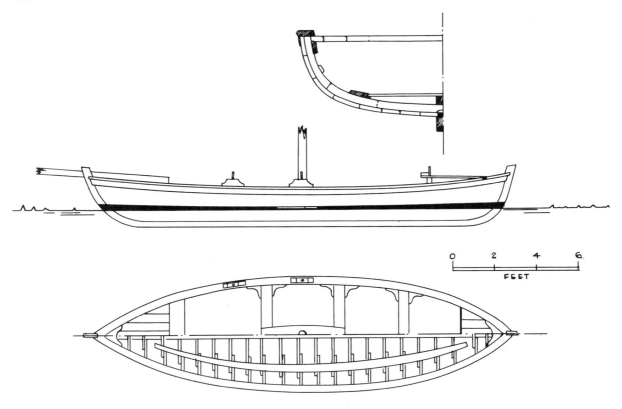

Figure 4-41. An old-style Messina swordfishing boat—a low, graceful double-ender. Boats of this type are generally rigged with a long bow platform and a harpoon pulpit. In the past, they approached their quarry under oars.

boat is a shapely double-ender propelled by oars and also steered by oar, not too unlike an old American whaleboat. It is about 20 feet in length on a beam of 6 feet with a 2-foot depth from gunwale to keel. It is almost completely open, with three thwarts and short decks forward and aft. It has short projecting stem and stern posts and a gentle, natural sheer, but such features are more restrained in this Sicilian boat than in most other Mediterranean boats.

In recent years a new and larger type of harpoon boat has been introduced to Sicily. The larger boat is still changing and developing, but its features, designed to improve fishing techniques, include a longer pulpit platform which, added to the increased size of the boat, allows the harpooner to be over the fish when the stern of the boat is 80 to 100 feet away (see Figure 4-42).

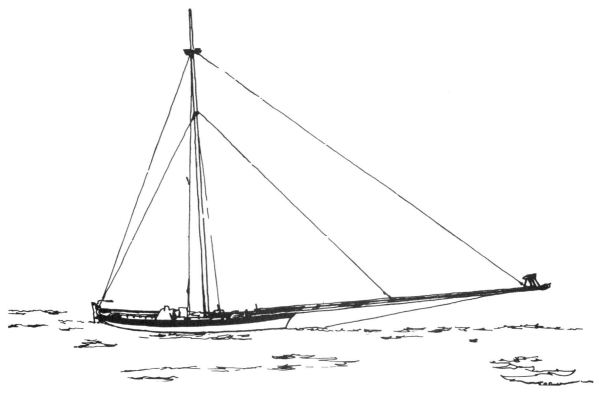

Figure 4-42. *This type of large swordfishing boat with a greater pulpit extension and mechanical power is replacing the older harpoon boats.*

Figure 4-43. *A Sardinian workboat. The boats of Sardinia are distinctly western Mediterranean in character. Unlike Sicilian boats, these are the same types of boats found along the Ligurian coast (the water between the southern French coast and the northwest coast of Italy), the southern French coast, and the Spanish coast as far west as Malaga. Because the island of Sardinia is fairly isolated, the local boats are preserved and maintained well and still carry a single lateen sail for prime propulsion.*

This distance makes motor power possible. By rigging-in the pulpit platform, this larger boat is capable of hunting swordfish farther at sea. The smaller boat, while fishing less efficiently, will remain unimproved and unchanged. Hopefully it will still be used by a few fisherman. Swordfishing is a seasonal operation and the boats must remain versatile for other modes of fishing.

While the western shores of Italy are not particularly distinguished for their characteristic watercraft today, the colorful boats that were there in abundance a century or more ago may still be seen in Sardinia. Many of these Sardinian craft still carry sail (the pure lateen) and are typical of larger craft formerly used in the Ligurian and Tyrrhenian seas.

THE LIGURIAN COAST

Of the larger working craft, a rare occasional vessel remains from the expired era of sail. Rightfully these demasted but identifiable sailing workboats could be passed by as obsolete, but some old instruments of our past die very hard. The people who own and sail such surviving workboats live as marginally as do their boats. The ancient mariners of Sardinia cling to the older ways tenaciously. They may have preserved for a few to see and still fewer to appreciate a very occasional ancient and deteriorated sailing coaster. Such typical craft were found here or there around the Ligurian Sea, in some out-of-the-way port of Corsica, or even out in the Gulf of Lyon. These coasters could be related to the Spanish feluccas used by Moorish pirates, which were related to the old galleys of Genoa, which in turn were perhaps related to the ships of the classical Mediterranean.

I remember quite vividly being anchored many years ago in a small harbor on the Ligurian coast. It was a foul, cold night with a penetrating misty rain and a wind off the Maritime Alps that whipped across the harbor in sporadic blasts. It was sometime during the midwatch at an in-between hour when all of the lights of yesterday had been extinguished ashore and none of the lights of tomorrow had yet been struck. The boatswain of my watch reported a dim light making into the anchorage. We identified it when it was finally within about a hundred yards as a fishing vessel or coastwise boat of some local type. At about this point, the rattle of anchor chain was heard and the lone light was extinguished. The event was logged and forgotten momentarily. About a half hour later the boatswain reported that this craft was dragging anchor and was very close to colliding with us along our starboard side as we swung on our mooring. We attempted to hail her skipper but could not rouse him. I lit one of our large searchlights and told one of the seamen on watch to drop down from a boat boom onto the deck of the old two-master. There was now a little dog running about creating his own confusion. At about this same time, the old boat's companion hatch squeaked open and a weathered face peered up with wide eyes staring in dis-

Figure 4-44. A navicello sketched in 1937 when the type was fairly common. Now there are none left.

belief at the gray steel wall and forbidding naval guns beside and above him. The whole scene was illuminated by the blue glare of the searchlight beam on the black water around us. In another instant a young sailor joined his master on this slippery old wood deck below us and with an expressive stream of Italian oaths they got up their anchor, started a loud, one-cylinder auxiliary, and disappeared quickly into the black wetness of the night.

It was not until this experience was over that I began to reflect that the boat of this encounter was unlike any boat in my limited knowledge. Having been at that time in the Mediterranean

Figure 4-45. A sailor-made model of a navicello. These vessels were classic and most favored merchant vessels of the Ligurian Sea, where they sailed. Navicellos once carried the famous marble fresh from the quarries of the Carrara hills north of Pisa. This was the source of the stone from which Michelangelo and Leonardo carved their great sculptures. (George Woodside)

only a few months, I had not yet become very aware of the Mediterranean look in boats. I had never heard of a navicello of the Ligurian coast; and when, as on this craft, I observed the foremast on a two-masted boat raking sharply forward, my first impression was that there had been an accident. With the coming of the clear, crisp morning this Italian navicello was revealed in all of her worn and mellowed glory, having anchored about a half mile away in the inner harbor beyond the mole. Later that day I went ashore and sketched as accurately as I could the impression of this boat which appears in Figure 4-44.

A navicello was most notable for its unusual rig. It formerly, perhaps two centuries ago, was a lateener. The sails of the latter-day navicello are similar, but not intentionally, to those of a staysail schooner, with two staysails between the masts set on upper and intermediate stays, a jib, set flying, and a large gaff mainsail. This boat also carries a large triangular topsail in light weather. The hull is comparatively large—65 to 70 feet long. Navicellos once were used largely for transporting fine Italian marble from the ports near the Tuscan hills of Carrara. It must have been easy to carry her lofty rig with such ballast as Carrara marble. It is doubtful that any navicellos remain today.

Another coastwise boat of this region, which together with the navicello grew from a common ancestor, is the tartane (*tartana* in Italian). We find in Chapman's *Architectura Navalis* a most graceful little Italian coaster of the eighteenth

Figure 4-46. The tartane originated from this small vessel of the Ligurian coast in the sixteeenth century. It has a classic Mediterranean profile with its deep sheer, waist rail, and curving stem carrying a beaklike appendage.

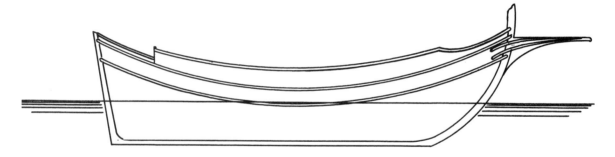

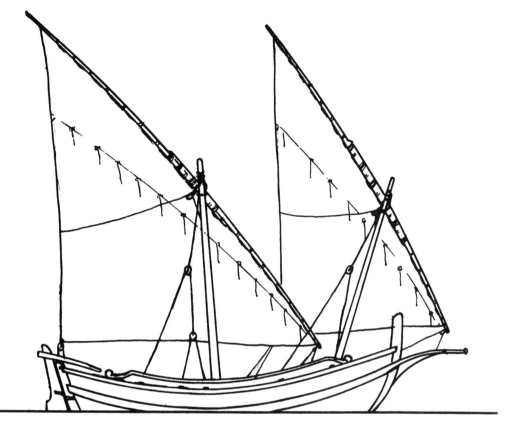

Figure 4-47. The Italian tartana of the mid-seventeenth century traded throughout the Ligurian Sea and was the ancestor of the nineteenth- and twentieth-century grande tartanes of the French and Italian coasts.

century identified as a tartana, with two masts carrying lateen sails and the foremast raked sharply forward. (See Figure 4-47.) This foremast is not uncommon for the old lateeners, but it is a characteristic that was employed primarily by the larger fellucas, chebecs, and provincial barques. The profile of Chapman's tartana is very interesting in other respects, because the boat is so thoroughly Mediterranean in character and detail. In Figure 4-46, notice the raised washboard gunwale in the low sweep of her waist, the broad low rubwale, the rising stem-

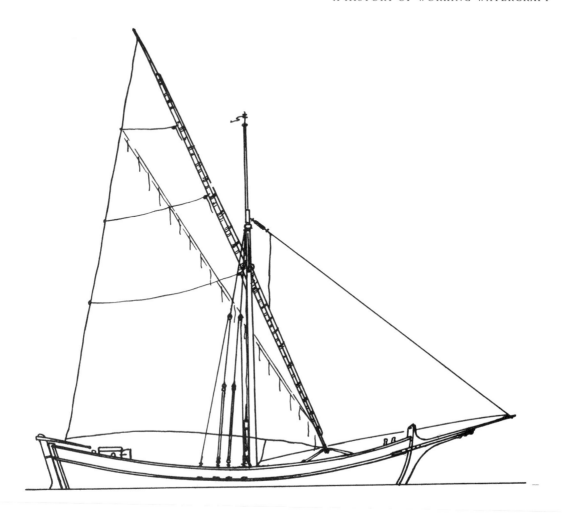

Figure 4-48. *The grande tartane of southern France was a noble and proud boat. Its lofty lateen sail and large headsail (set flying) gave its sail plan a most pleasing and modern distribution. This is a profile of the boat at the beginning of the nineteenth century, but it remained the same for more than a century.*

post, and finally the projecting beak head. Only three centuries ago, this pretty little lateener, perhaps no more than 40 feet long, if that, was a prototype for an innumerable generation of coasters and traders of the western Mediterranean. The tartana was the forerunner of boats to come after the Renaissance and before the Age of Enlightenment had developed into the Industrial Revolution.

Small coasters such as the tartana could only grow larger and, in the process, experiment with mast and rig. One became a navicello or another

Figure 4-49. Antoine Roux recorded two types of tartanes in 1816. The one on the left is a trader; the one on the right is a fisherman. The spinnaker set of the large headsails should be noted, as well as the versatile use of water sails and topsails. (Peabody Museum, Salem)

chebec; another became a more efficient single-masted lateener and was refined along the southern French coast to be the *grande tartane* of Provence. Figure 4-48 shows the profile of this handsome type at the apex of its development about 1800. The accompanying reproduction of Antoine Roux's watercolor of two tartanes, Figure 4-49, preserves his accurate impression of them under sail. A fishing tartane and and a trading tartane demonstrate here the great versatility of their sails in good weather. Clearly shown here is a new refinement of the western Mediterranean lateen sail. From this painting it seems obvious that the sail and yard are held within tacking control on the *inside* of the running shrouds.

The tartane of the twentieth century was further refined and Westernized to become a cutter-like lateener, with two headsails and a topsail set on the upper half of the lateen yard, as in the navicello. (See Figure 4-50.)

The tartane was of course a victim of her own affluence and impressive nineteenth-century grandeur. In an age of commerce under sail, she

had no peer in coastwise trade in the western Mediterranean. Sailing under French, Spanish, and Italian flags, and with small ethnic differences, she was a dominant type for nearly two centuries. But now she is gone except perhaps for an occasional isolated remnant or mastless hull. I saw two under sail in 1939 near Genoa and made the hasty sketch shown in Figure 4-50. Two or three may have survived after World War II.

Besides the tartane, there was a smaller, poorer type of lateener in the Ligurian region. Normally just called a Tuscan coaster, she carries a single, heavy, forward-raked mast in the ancient manner

Figure 4-50. The twentieth-century tartane developed into a poor, modified lateener that expired during World War II. Today it is essentially extinct. The sketch of one of the last few in the 1930s shows a topsail over the lateen main and several triangular headsails to the bowsprit.

with a heavy lateen yard. There is usually a long bowsprit that pushes forward a large triangular headsail set flying from a toggle on a masthead halyard. The Tuscan coaster has a shapely, beamy hull with deep gunwales and a raised, capped stempost. The outboard rudder is swung on a nearly vertical sternpost with a tiller crossing above. She makes a very pleasing picture with her nicely proportioned rig and stained sails pushing down the coast with a northwesterly kicking up a sea behind her and the mountainous coast ahead. Such boats are 45 to 50 feet in length and are built according to the rules of tradition and their builder's critical eye. A very similar boat found in the Gulf of Lyon is a fishing lateener called a bateau boeuf. Originally this boat was a poor man's tartane and was used in the coastwise trade. It is today almost obsolete.

Farther to the west, beyond the Gulf of Lyon, large lateen fishing boats indigenous to the coast of Catalonia are still in use. This coast has few natural harbors, aside from the great port of Barcelona, and for the most part is a rocky coastline that is punctured by small sandy coves that lend themselves well to beaching boats. There are great stretches of beach strands as well, and for centuries the Catalonian fishermen have been hauling their boats up these sunny, sandy shelves. The boats here are of several sizes, the largest being 35 to 40 feet in length. The style is one of ruggedness, generally with a forward-raking mast and a single lateen sail. The boats today are also motorized and all have a large, protected propeller aperture. Figure 4-54 shows one of these hulls stripped down for painting, with a nice but patched job of carvel planking exposed. The smaller Catalonian boats are about 15 to 17 feet long and are generally rowed. All are open with only partial decks and deep gunwales. They always have heavy, bilge keels for beaching, which,

Figure 4-51. The lateen-rigged vessels out of the southern French coast and the general traffic in that area were most numerous in the early nineteenth century. They have left their mark in ship design and excellent sailing form though none exist today. This handsome painting by Antoine Roux in the second decade of the nineteenth century shows the typical chebec in the foreground, often armed and used by the Tripolitan pirates as well as the French and Italians as gunboats. The vessel in the distance to the right is called a pinque, an unarmed merchant type. (Peabody Museum, Salem)

together with the structural keel, are on the same horizontal plane.

The boats of Valencia and the Balearic Islands to the south of Catalonia are of similar style, but of an intermediate size, between 25 and 30 feet. Figure 4-53 shows a typical motorized fishing boat of Majorca entering Puerto Sóller.

The boats that have occupied our attention for the past several pages are of a most typical western Mediterranean model. With only slight regional variations, most of the boats of all types from Tunis to Gibraltar are of this same form and style. Besides the characteristic double-ended form, the most common element of this Middle Sea style is the raised stempost with a decorative cap. In some regions, such as in the vicinity of Genoa, the stempost and the sternpost are turned sharply inward. (See Figure 4-56.) Occasionally on some small beach craft or harbor craft one may encounter a very curious and useless remnant of ancient Mediterranean ship construction—the forward-thrusting beakhead (see Figure 4-55). This remnant is not confined to the western Mediterranean alone and was mentioned in connection with the Turkish taka. The beakhead is apparently a hangover from the days when it was the forward-jutting stem platform of Venetian galleys or fifteenth-century naos (medieval Mediterranean trading ships). It was used on the early Renaissance tartana, and in the last tartanes

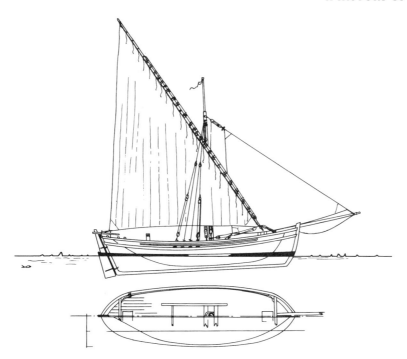

Figure 4-52. The bateau-boeuf still may survive, one or two in the same area that was once dominated by the tartane. This is perhaps because the bateau-boeuf has always been a similar but poor copy of a tartane and consequently cheaper to build and maintain.

Figure 4-53. Balearic Island fishing craft are typical western Mediterranean boats with a few local variations. Their stems are vertical and without curvature. Their keels have little rocker and there is a bit more flare in their bow sections. The acetylene stern lantern for night fishing is standard equipment on coastal boats from Italy, France, and Spain.

Figure 4-54. The hull of a Catalonian beach-operated lateener, a boat that strictly follows the tradition of the western Mediterranean. This is a rugged but shapely double-ender, heavily built with a flush deck below her deep gunwales. Note the heavy beaching keels. The sailing rig is a single lateen without headsail on a mast raked forward in the centuries-old style. Most of this type of boat depend nowadays on heavy semi-diesel or gasoline engines only.

Figure 4-55. This beach boat of southern France has a "chicken beak," a form found throughout the ages on Mediterranean craft.

Figure 4-56. The Genoese utility harbor boat and beach craft is typified by the inward curve of the stemposts and sternposts. The boat in the foreground is overshadowed by the great industrial harbor of Genoa. (David Scott)

Figure 4-57. Beach boats of the French Mediterranean coast.

became a type of clipper bow. It is not, however, a clipper bow, at least not the American-type clipper. There is strong evidence to warrant belief that this forward-raking stem on the old galleys of Venice was adopted from the classic triremes of Rome and ancient Greece where this structure was truly a beak. As a ram, it was an effective weapon. It originated in the early centuries of the first milennium BC.

The ubiquitous, graceful little beach boats are the smallest and most purely Mediterranean of all of the indigenous boats in this great blue sea. They come in many sizes and colors. Some are bright and new, others are old and shabby, and all suggest styles of centuries past

There are few if any boats on the North African side of the Mediterranean that have any indigenous quality not already noted as a general Mediterranean quality. The boats of Morocco are mostly Spanish-Mediterranean. The boats of

Algeria are very like the French beach boats of the Riviera, to be described below, except they are not maintained as well. The boats of Tunisia are largely Italian in form and structure. There is, however, in Tunis an interesting small beach boat of Italian origin that is no longer to be found in Italy. It is called a martiquiana and was used in the lower Adriatic region as far up as Brindisi. The boats were not too long ago quite capable sailboats of the indigenous Adriatic lugger type.

The boats are generally under 30 feet in length, but some have been built up to 40 feet. They have the typical deep, narrow rudder of the trabaccolo and are of similar shallow construc-

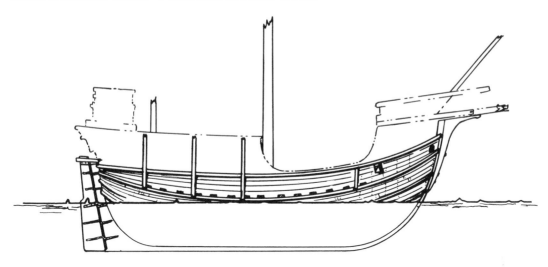

Figure 4-58. While the false stem knee of Figure 4-55 may have some remote connection to an ancient ram, it is more likely a holdover from medieval ships. This profile of a fifteenth-century nao shows the clear and functional use of the stem knee that later evolved into a type of "clipper" bow (as it became known in America).

Figure 4-59. The smallest beach boats are very much like Maine peapods, with a few distinctive Mediterranean touches. The boats are seldom more than 12 feet long. They are in their own way the classic essence of carvel boat form, as is the Norway skiff of the north.

Figure 4-60. The Marseille dory with its straight sections stands out from the other Mediterranean craft in this photograph. These dories, with their original lateen rigs, are the boats of van Gogh's famous painting of the beach of Saintes Maries.

tion. The comparative lightness of the boats is essential because of the beach operations. The most identifiable feature is the distinctive raked-out "clipper"-type stem knee. This feature, which is noted elsewhere in this chapter on Turkish, Greek, and French boats, is unique on a boat originating in the Adriatic.

Among the great works of art, there are many contemporary representations of small workboats. Few are painted with technical accuracy. Because many of these artists were of Mediterranean heritage, there are many scenes that include local Mediterranean watercraft. However, it is unusual to find an indigenous Mediterranean boat painted by an artist who is not from the Mediterranean, who is an impressionist, and whose drawing in this context is fairly accurate in detail and form. The color, composition, and grace of the boats in Vincent van Gogh's well-known *Beach of Saintes Maries* contribute altogether to the total aesthetic quality of the painting. The execution of the boats in this painting, when they are examined closely, reveals the artist's competent eye for detail. He certainly did not make these boats out of his imagination. He painted them from life. The unstudied but natural placement of an oar or casually dropped coil of line, the inside of the transom, the curve of plank and frame are all very real in this painting. Yet the bright colors and slightly exaggerated forms of the boats create an otherworld unreality, causing some knowledgeable people to dismiss the boats as figments of van Gogh's mind.

It is quite true that boats like these rendered by van Gogh in the 1870s no longer exist on the beaches of Saintes Maries, France, or anywhere for that matter. They did, however, exist there at one time, among these beaches near the Rhone estuary west of Marseille. The beaches are wide and flat in this delta land, and the boats undoubtedly had to be flat and keelless like a dory. They were definitely large, colorfully painted sailing craft with

Figure 4-61. The Valencia lake barge, which is less a barge than it is a graceful double-ender, is a classic lateener carrying a typical forward-raking mast and single sail. Its work is mainly transporting oranges from the groves across Lake Albufera.

Figure 4-62. The Tunisian lateen-rigged coaster has a square-transom stern, a ketch-type sail arrangement, and a large headsail.

single lateen sails on long willowy yards. Today, there is nothing left of such boats, except for a very few power fishing and harbor craft around Marseille. These boats are similar to an American dory in hull form but without the tombstone transom. They are quite like the boats of van Gogh's beach scene but without the mast and sail. One of these boats can be seen among others tied up in the inner harbor quay of Marseille (see Figure 4-60). "Marseille dories" are about 18 feet in length and 6 feet in beam. They have the natural sweep of sheer created by the flat, flaring sides of this elemental boat form. The ends are double and the bottom is flat, with the gentle fore-and-aft rocker of all dories. The freeboard is increased by a raised gunwale plank with tumblehome, which is tapered off at the ends. Except for its dory form, the Marseille boat is thoroughly Mediterranean in construction. Without doubt it is the rare existing relative of the brightly colored boats painted by van Gogh on the beach of Les Saintes Maries one hundred years ago.

It must be apparent at this point that in the Mediterranean there are different forces at work that shape the boats and preserve them. There is very little economic incentive to support or encourage new construction. Where truly indigenous qualities were observed (aside from Turkey), they appeared most predominantly in the smallest craft. In the Mediterranean, existing watercraft are simply a manifestation of historic truths. The political and cultural conditions of communities are reflected in the arts and crafts of their working people and are generally an indication of their national progress.

The Mediterranean Sea is bordered by many countries of various and conflicting political persuasions. The former coastwise trade has in this century been supplanted by international and intercontinental trade carried by many other more efficient transporters. With modern trucks, cargo planes, railways, and large freighters in use, there is little need for small coastwise cargo

Figure 4-63. Fishing boats of the Catalonian coast of Spain are heavy, rigged, sail-motor combinations. Some still carry large lateen yards as shown in this photo taken in 1980 on a beach near the Costa Brava east of Barcelona. The larger boats are sardine seiners. The smaller craft are pot haulers.

vessels. The fisheries of the Mediterranean are limited, indeed, and can support only local markets and limited numbers of independent fishermen—hence the concentration on small fishing boats and beach craft. There is no demand for great numbers of herring trawlers or drifters on this sea like those supporting large industries in many northern countries.

This is the picture of today's workboats in a sea where once there was a proliferation of indigenous craft both large and small engaged in all types of water commerce. The Mediterranean has not lost its historic significance as a stage for the flexing of international sea power. It has simply moved to a dependency on participants who are not of the Mediterranean world and on vessels far too large and complex to have been developed in any one locality.

THE
IBERIAN INFLUENCE

IT IS NOT KNOWN DEFINITELY which civilization was the first to settle on the shores of the Iberian Peninsula. The Phoenicians early in the first millennium, possibly the Aegeans, and later the Carthaginians established outposts on the Spanish Mediterranean coast as well as the Atlantic coast of Portugal. It is a reasonable conclusion from this that the early boat-building practices of this entire region were first derived from the eastern Mediterranean.

EARLY BOATS OF THE ATLANTIC COAST

Let us imagine a scene three thousand years ago of a Phoenician trading boat drawn up high on a sunny, sandy shore of the Iberian coast. Her very few crewmembers are, in their self-sufficient fashion, restoring a sick bottom plank and tightening the caulking between others, having scraped clean the entire barnacled surface. The boat itself is nicely constructed with smoothly worn planks held together by tenons in mortises. She has high ends with a dominant stempost rising at the bow and graceful inward-curving sternpost. Her forefoot and keel are of heavy timber, nicely scarfed to shape a fine entrance. Her deck is set from stem to stern on beams that notch through the side planks. (This practice began with the ancient Egyptians and persisted in both southern and northern European boats for nearly thirty centuries.) The old boat's deck is well below the sheerline, making a deep, protective gunwale, and she may very likely have an open area in the waist for cargo space that is most accessible. She carries double kingposts at the bow on both sides of the stem. Her single mast, normally stepped amidships, has been lowered and is temporarily serving as a ridgepole for a striped awning. This fabric that provides protection against the burning Mediterranean sun is normally the single sail and is nicely sewn and roped. It is adequate in area to cover most of the boat's deck. Her cargo has been unloaded

Figure 5-1. This scene shows a perception of a Phoenician trading vessel hauled out on a beach of the Iberian Peninsula, probably the southern coast of Portugal. The date is approximately the beginning of the first millennium BC, or about three thousand years ago. The scene follows the approximate layout by the renowned artist-historian Björn Landström in his work Quest for India. *The boat and its repair work are different, however. We reject his horse-head figure on the stem, which has sparse archaeological support, and liken the boat to a poor trading vessel of modest appearance similar to* Kyrenia II *(Chapter Four). The two crewmen of this boat are puzzled over how to best restore a mortise-and-tenon plank. The real point of this illustration is to note the early arrival of eastern Mediterranean traders and their subsequent contribution to the maritime arts in the land near the outlet of the Mediterranean. (Tom Price, after Björn Landström)*

on the beach. With an assortment of rope, line, and other gear strewn at random on the sand, the men work leisurely at the task of getting out and fitting a new plank while the master checks his valuable items of trade for restowage. This shipwright's tools that are skillfully turned to the repair work are the basic adze, the caulking tool made of bronze (a precursor of a caulking iron), the mallet, the bow saw, the draw knife, chisels, and the block plane. The entire scene, with the exception of the language and the dress of the people, is timeless on these Iberian shores.

The detailed shape of the boat and her protruding deck beam structure has, during the millennia, been refined. The boat's cargo and freight have been replaced with traditional fishing gear, but the boats of today on all coasts of the Iberian Peninsula have the same basic characteristics of the ancient boat just described. The high stempost still dominates the sweeping sheerline; the sternpost still curves inward; the sides and bot-

Figure 5-2. A well-worn small craft pulled out on an Iberian beach in the late twentieth century. This small four-oared inshore beach craft shows vague but positive remnants relating to the boats of millennia past: the raised plank on the gunwale, extended stempost, smooth planking. It is an ancient boat of the Iberian shores.

toms are smoothly planked and caulked where repaired. This nearly three thousand-year-old trading boat is much like the Kyrenia ship described in Chapter Four. The fishing boats of southern Spain and Portugal are still built in the open, most frequently on a sandy beachfront using the same basic tools. The rugged keel and scarfed stem are shaped into an easy, fine entrance. This bow form, and all the rest, so fundamental, yet with so many variations, originated in the eastern Mediterranean.(See Figure 5-1.)

The Iberian Peninsula's sea frontiers, which comprise the Spanish Mediterranean coast as well as its Atlantic coast and the entire Portuguese coast, are discussed in this chapter as a separate maritime entity. This is done because of the richness of the maritime heritage along these seafronts. The beaches, the harbors, the estuaries, the rocky promontories—all of these have been visited by sailors and their ships and have been departed from by tens of centuries of mariners, many of whom have made world history. The watercraft used by these mariners have left their mark on boats along the shores and among the many craft that still work commercially today.

Spain and Portugal continue very much as maritime nations, although not as great and powerful as they once were. But the legacy of their maritime past is still their greatest legacy. The inhabitants of their past, from the early landings of sailors from the eastern Mediterranean to the shipbuilders of Vasco da Gama's fleets, are still reflected in the wooden watercraft along these coasts.

There are odd-shaped boats along Portugal's Atlantic beaches that are still called "Phoenicians." There are boats that until very recently brought cargos of wine down the Douro River to Oporto. These graceful single-squaresail craft have the inexplicable profile of Egyptian riverboats of the

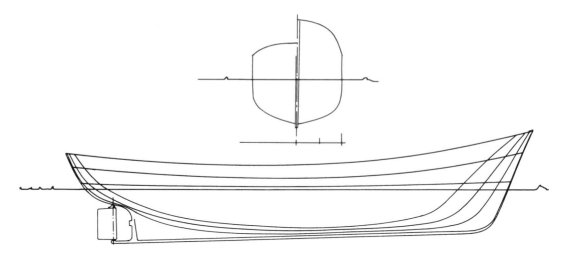

Figure 5-3. *The hull form of this Spanish trawler makes her suitable for extended operations. Her design is undoubtedly influenced by other seagoing trawlers as well as the universal requirements of trawling itself. The heavy trawler stern and forward-raking stempost are characteristics of Spanish and Portuguese construction and are found in some of the largest vessels still being built of wood.*

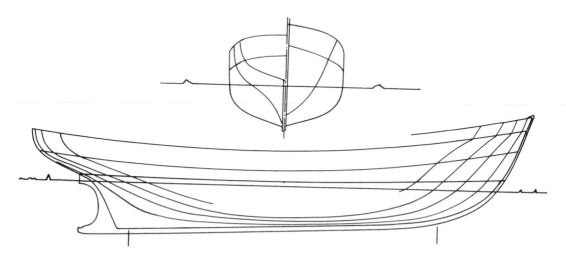

Figure 5-4. *Italian seiners and trawlers are similar in style to the Spanish boats but generally show more grace and lift of line. This seiner has the customary Italian counter stern instead of a trawler stern.*

pharaohs' dynastic periods. And some of the boats along the Spanish beaches have the ancient look of pre-Renaissance watercraft. (See Figure 5-2.) These relics are rapidly disappearing now, but here or there a rare one may be found in a sparsely populated place. We will discuss these and others a bit on the following pages of this chapter.

The boats built today along the southern shores of Spain are larger than the boats of the Catalonian coast, and are used for the sardine fisheries. These boats are built mainly to the south of the Gulf of Valencia in the region of Alicante. They are fairly large craft designed for seining with heavy, large nets. The shape of these boats is a departure from the classic Mediterranean style just described only in that the modern boats have a broad, overhanging counter stern to provide a good working platform. The stem rakes sharply forward and the bows show a great flare in the forward sections. The boats measure generally 60 to 65 feet in length with a beam of approximately 20 feet. This type of boat will be further described on subsequent pages on the boats of Portugal, where sardine seiners of the same identity are built. The boat as built and working in Spain is the most substantial of all contemporary working boats built in the western Mediterranean, and its likeness to the Portuguese sardine boats points up the common motivations, historical forces, and traditions that appear in all the Iberian boats. Typical hull lines are shown in Figure 5-3. The same build is evident in the boats on the Bay of Biscay. The most characteristic feature is the flaring bow section above the deck level (see Figure 5-5).

Fine sardine seiners are built, and have been built in the past, in Spain and Italy. However, because these two countries are more diversified industrial countries with comparatively minor fishing industries, more interesting boats are found along the Portuguese coast.

Since the first sea trade routes were extended from the Mediterranean to northern Europe without interruption for some three thousand or more years, the Atlantic coast of Portugal has offered its natural harbors, its pro-

Figure 5-5. Small Spanish tuna boats. These are really combination boats, because when tuna are scarce fishermen turn to sardines, squid, and bottomfish. (Richard H. Philips)

tected beaches, and its great river estuaries to countless laden boats and ships. The Romans called this land Lusitania and claimed it as part of their colonial empire. It was colonized before the Romans by Greeks and Carthaginians, who found Phoenician outposts already there. The Phoenicians likely followed the Minoans, first through the Straits of Gibraltar, in search of tin and copper. But not until comparatively recent centuries did Portugal become the crossroads between northern and southern Europe, or a point of departure for exploration to the south and the west. At the mouth of the great Tagus River, where there is a broad, protected estuary, the Romans built their town, which is now called Lisbon. The river flows down from far across central Spain, bisecting Portugal, and at last falling into the great harbor basin of Lisbon, where the current just before the river joins the ocean is nearly nine knots.

It is here in this magnificent natural harbor, which attracts ships of all flags, that there has long been a use for harbor lighters and small cargo-transfer craft. The Tagus River sailing barges, relative to the harbor craft and barges of other great world seaports, have been the most colorful, carefully constructed, and well maintained of them all. The sampans of Shanghai, the caiques of Istanbul, the gaiassas of Cairo, and the Thames sailing barges of London cannot stand up to the active Tagus River craft in character and capability.

There are two distinctive types of sailing lighters that were most predominant on the Tagus estuary. Basically, one is heavier, with a transom stern, and the other is a bit smaller and double-ended. The names are not descriptive, only generic, but they are more useful identifying labels than the words *barge* or *lighter*. These boats are not lighters or barges in the conventionally accepted meaning, which usually indicates large, flat-bottom, scow-like vessels for carrying bulk cargo, often with no means of self-propulsion. On the contrary, while these harbor boats of the Tagus carry all types of cargo, they have shapely and finely constructed hulls propelled by handsome spreads of sail from single masts.

The first type, called a frigata, is the heavier and fuller; it is some 68 to 69 feet in length and 18 to 19 feet in beam. (See Figure 5-7.) The hull is heavily constructed against the hard usage she suffers amidst the crowding of the harbor. She has heavy double kingposts on her bow rails and similar square pollards on the stern rails; she also has a very steep but natural sheerline that drops from her stem, tends to flatten amidships, and rises only slightly at the stern. Her hold area extends throughout the waist and is entirely open with only flat removable flooring in the bottom. The stempost rises vertically and straight and projects in the Mediterranean manner, while the stern has a broad transom with an outboard rudder. The rudder has a high, painted head, and the tiller passes inboard above a broad quarterdeck. Below this deck is a small unlighted cabin area. The raking mast just forward of amidships hoists a well-cut gaff mainsail on a fairly long gaff and loose

Figure 5-6. A canqueiro, a Tagus River lighter, whose extreme raking mast, shorter gaff, and carved and curving stempost set it apart from a frigata.

Figure 5-7. The sailing lighters of Lisbon were a most familiar sight, but few visitors looked closely at them. The tradition of their colorful decoration goes back thousands of years. This boat is a frigata, distinguished by its severe lines, plumb stem, and broad transom stern.

foot. While the sail is hooped to the mast, it is seldom lowered but rather brailed in. There is a single staysail and no bowsprit. This boat makes leeway in a manner that would not delight a yachtsman, but when beating across the Tagus's current on a brisk onshore breeze, this can be an advantage. The boat is characteristically decorated in many colors, often in shades of blue with details painted in yellow, red, and black, and bordered in white. The rudderhead and interior main deck beam facings are always carved and painted in intricate floral designs. The frigata's most impressive feature is her broad, powerful bow, which most certainly was developed to counter the steep chop in the Tagus's mouth when the wind and current cross.

The canqueiro, the other harbor type, is about 10 feet shorter than the frigata and is generally not as broad or heavy, although heavy enough for its rough employment. The general appearance of this boat is more suggestive of Portuguese antiquity than is that of the frigata (see Figure 5-6). The single-masted rig is very similar to the frigata's, except that it sometimes carries two headsails, both from inboard headstays with no bowsprit. The mainsail, also set on an aft-raking mast, often has a shorter gaff reminiscent

of the Dutch bezan rig. Many of these Lisbon harbor boats were originally lateen-rigged, but in this century, the Lisbon sailors have apparently become convinced that for working in crowded harbor conditions with much tacking, the all-inboard gaff rig is more accommodating and workable.

The bow construction of the boat is most curious (see Figure 5-8). The stem profile is rounded in a near semicircle from the keel to the upper terminus. The sheerline rises sharply in an

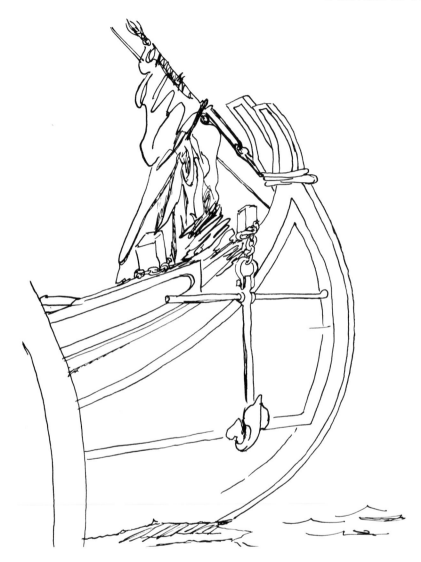

Figure 5-8. The double-carved stem of a canqueiro boat. It is as though the heavy sheer rail is trying to combine with the extended stempost. This same style is repeated in several other old Portuguese boats.

upcurve, with its heavy gunwale timber continuing over the stempost and up its forward face. The profile of this whole upper structure curves back on an inward slope. The resulting assembly is one that has not been seen on a boat since the Greek boats of the third century BC sailed from the Aegean. The most puzzling thing about this similar profile on Greek boats is that it was a feature of their sterns, not their bows. It is consequently difficult to speculate about the origin of the Portuguese bow. We know that Greeks and Carthaginians voyaged, traded, and settled on the Tagus before the Romans. The appearance of the rising ends of their boats may have made a very strong

Figure 5-9. A most startling sail plan on any Portuguese-Iberian boat is that on a muleta. Not now in active use, it passed from the scene in the early 1930s, but it is still discussed, and one or two have been restored. The muleta's sail plan has a proper explanation. It sets its drift net and then its broad sailing rig and drifts down to leeward and broad-side-to hauling its net with it. Its keel is also built up to not interfere with her leeway. She sails under the regular lateen sail on her traditional Mediterranean forward-raked mast. She fished out of the Tagus estuary. (Museu Marinha, Lisbon)

and lasting impression on the inhabitants. If this stem were used only on the boat in the Tagus River, it could be passed off as a local aberration. This is not the case, however, for there are other boats in the northern part of Portugal on the Atlantic coast with the same feature in decoration. These boats work from the beaches and lagoons of Aveiro and will be described in fuller detail later.

On the coast north of Lisbon, the shores are inhospitable with high rocky cliffs and open beaches. The Atlantic Ocean waves have a fetch of three thousand miles before they beat upon this coast. Yet there are many fishing villages, and the fishing industry contributes greatly to the Portuguese economy. Needless to say, the fishermen are a tough breed, their boats are strong and well adapted, and their wives frequently wear black. Many vacationers can be found in the summertime in these fishing ports along the fine sandy beaches below the dark cliffs. This is not surprising because the surf is generally up, the sand is white and fine, and the sun shines warmly. But still the sea is the Atlantic and not the Mediterranean; the Portuguese fishing villages of Nazare, Peniche, and Ericeira are not Riviera towns like Saint-Tropez, Antibes, or Portofino. The best boats grow on the most rugged seacoasts and, unlike garden vegetables, are nurtured in the most unkindly weather. In the worst months of the winter in Portugal, during the great Atlantic storms, the boats are drawn up high on the beaches, or where the beaches are inadequate, they are sweated up steep ramps to clifftops or even, as in Nazare, drawn up on the streets of the town.

One cannot look at any Portuguese working boats and not be strongly impressed with their ruggedness and fine maintenance. Especially impressive is the efficient performance of the fishermen with their boats.

On the beaches of the fishing village of Peniche, sardine seiners can be found that are very similar in style and appearance to the Spanish seiners described previously in this chapter. They are slightly smaller than the Spanish seiners and sometimes feature a broader elliptical stern. Figure 5-10 illustrates the lines and form of these seiners. These boats, like their Spanish

Figure 5-10. The Peniche sardine carrier is identified by its unusually long counter stern. This broad overhang makes a convenient net-handling platform for the fishermen to work from at sea. It also contributes to dryness where the boat is stern-launched from the beach.

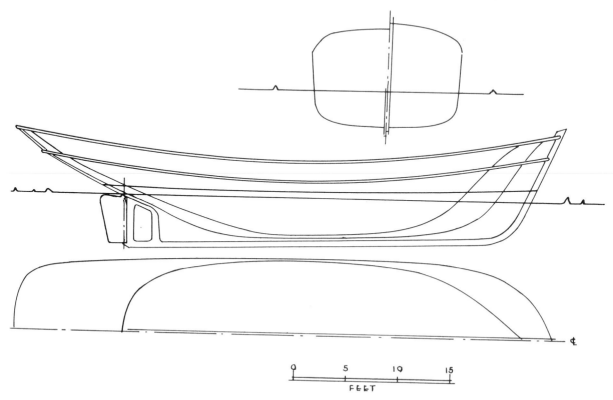

relatives, and, for that matter, all of the working boats of Portugal, are built in the open, often on the beach, sometimes with a temporary canvas shelter providing shade from the sun. The builders work, as is common in southern Europe, from experience and by eye, using knowledge that is centuries old and is passed on to them by their elders. Their creativity and imagination, however, are not totally overshadowed by traditional methods. The sardine seiners of Peniche and Sesimbra are boats of relatively modern configuration and have evolved as power-driven boats with very little suggestion of their sailing ancestors.

Figure 5-11 shows one of these seiners being constructed near Setúbal, south of Libson. The heavy, closely spaced frames can be seen above the deck level, where they are not doubled as they are in the body of the hull below. The forward-raking stem is characteristic of these boats, as is the broad, overhanging elliptical stern. The boat under construction here is typical and measures about 55 feet overall length, 15 feet beam, and 4.5 feet mean draft. It is typical not only of this region of Portugal but of the sardine seiners of the whole southern coast of

Iberia. These boats in Portugal alone were responsible for landing about 150,000 tons of sardines annually during the post-war period, worth as much as twenty million dollars to the nation's economy, and likely more today.

While these sardine seiners are typical of Iberia and are hard-working, excellent seaboats, they are contemporary boats that do not have the traditional heritage and character of most of the rest of the small Portuguese workboats.

On the Atlantic coast near the town of Aveiro, the sandy beaches flatten out to form broad, protected lagoons. Because of the proximity of the sea, there are large accumulations of seaweed in these lagoons, which are of considerable value in agriculture. The collection and transportation of the seaweed is accomplished by boats, and these boats are perhaps the most unusually formed and decorated class of sailing workboats in use in the Western world. They are called moliceiros because of their employment in

Figure 5-12. A stem of a moliceiro is elegantly decorated with scenes of medieval conquests.

Figure 5-13. A pair of moliceiros work the lagoon gathering seaweed. These unique boats are reminiscent of large gondolas with the swept-up bows and stern.

transporting *molicos* (seaweed). Their movement about the lagoons and canals reminds one of Holland and Venice. Aveiro itself resembles a Dutch city with canals, houses, and waterfront stores of Dutch facade.

The moliceiros are basically shallow-draft, lug-rigged lighters from 50 to 60 feet in length. They are open in the waist and seem nearly awash when loaded. Their most astonishing and perhaps most handsome feature is their upswept ends and "backswept" decorated bow and stem. From a distance there is no doubt that a moliceiro is a very graceful and well-proportioned craft (see Figure 5-13). Most of them are single-masted, but the larger ones are two-masted, with the fore being the smaller. The rig is somewhat like the bragozzo of Venice, with the smaller of the two lugsails being forward and without any staysail or headsails of any kind. It is a basic lug-rig form, similar to the rig of eastern Mediterranean craft three millennia ago.

The stem form of the moliceiro sketched in Figure 5-12 is reminiscent of the after end of a gondola, but it is my conviction that its origin is far, far older. The combination of stem and sheer plank extension that was noted in the boats of Tagus is apparent. On the sides of each bow extending four or five feet abaft the stemhead, there is an area of detailed pictorial decoration. The style of figures, both human and animal, is medieval in technique and style. The abstract figures of the border of these decorations seem to be older and, while documentation is not possible, there is an obvious similarity to eastern Mediterranean decorations originating on the Phoenician and Syrian coasts at the end of the second pre-Christian millennium.

It is most curious that the cut and set of the lugsails on the moliceiros are a combination of the northern and southern lug. The sail is boomless at the foot and tacked down at the mast. The sail is not dipped around the mast in tacking. The large, high rudder is most impressive, but the skippers are most casual about using it, staying at the helm only when maneuvering in

Figure 5-14. A small saveiro. This flat-bottomed boat with exaggerated sheer is launched into the surf. It exists in several sizes. See Figures 5-15 and 5-16.

Figure 5-15. This is the dramatic controlled surf launching on the Aveiro beach of a large saveiro, approximately 60 feet, with twenty-four men aboard. Note the bowman throwing off the antibroaching lines at the moment he feels broaching is no longer a danger. (David Goddard)

Figure 5-16. A large saveiro launching with the beach crew controlling the broach problem. (Museu Marinha, Lisbon)

canals. The moliceiro is an old, useful, and handsome boat and most functional. Its light and simple flat-bottomed structure, however, eliminates it from any work beyond canals and lagoons.

Near this same region, at Costa Nova, there is a seaboat that has much of the form and decoration of the moliceiro. The nearest thing that I could learn from a fisherman for a name to call them sounded much like "pirogue." They are perhaps similar to a French sailor's fancy of a great canoe. But there is a better name for them locally and it is saveiro. They are worked from the beach. These boats are of far stronger construction than the lagoon boats, but they are also flat-bottomed with high ends, actually a much higher bow than the moliceiro. The saveiro is perhaps the most unusual working boat among the whole list of Portuguese working boats. It is not a harbor craft—it works from the unprotected ocean beach, and the launching of one is a maritime scene that has surely developed from ancient roots. When the surf is up on the Atlantic coast below the lagoons of Aveiro these great open craft of near 60 feet in length are launched into the breaking waves. The operation depends in part on the buoyancy of the bow, the beach incline, some crude timber-rollers over the wet sand, and a final push with a crotched pole on the sternpost. There are four long oars for the fishermen aboard to use to pick up momentum and move out beyond the surf line.

Surf launching is the general custom along this Portuguese coast, and the boat's excessive sheer is no doubt the result of this requirement. Even so, the sheer is definitely exaggerated when compared to other boats of similar requirements. It is my conviction that because the boats are economically built and flat on the bottom for standing up on the hard sand, their quarter-moon sheer profile fulfills the demand for a form of natural strength. The characteristic shape can be seen in Figure 5-14.

Figure 5-17. To appreciate the diversity of boat decorative art, examine the port bow painting on this saveiro model. This boat is also the length of each of the four great oars, generally manned by four oarsmen each to ensure safe passage across the surf line after launching. See Figures 5-15 and 5-16. (Museu Marinha, Lisbon)

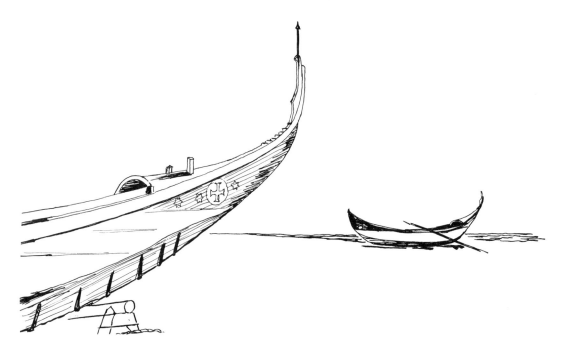

Figure 5-18. The stemhead of a saveiro shows the persistent ancient practice of lapping the sheer wale and the stempost as observed in the canqueiro and the moliceiro, Figures 5-8 and 5-12. The harpoonlike spike at the summit is a curious and diverse terminal but not as elaborate as the anchor-trident form at the end of the saveiro in Figure 5-16 and the curious cross symbol in Figure 5-15.

Figure 5-18 is fairly representative of surf boats' bows. While the sheer curvature is unusual, the general profile of these boats shows they are well suited for their use. They may be near 60 feet in length overall, but no more than 27 on the waterline. The bow is far higher than the stern, which is an obvious indication of their daily engagement with the nearly ever-present surf. But beyond the mere loftiness of the stem, the saveiro also has, like the moliceiro of the lagoons and the canqeiro of the Tagus, the curious extension of stem and sheer wale. And also, as though more is needed at this extremity, the stemhead, which is perhaps 12 feet above the water, is surmounted by a harpoonlike pole. This latter appendage is for the showing of a signal, the purpose of which, as far as I am aware, is known only to the sailors of Costa Nova. One might wonder from the description and sketch of this high-ended boat how a man could manage to get out on this stem if he must set this "signal," work a net, or scan the sea for fish. There is indeed a series of small steps fashioned as though an afterthought into the upper and outermost end of the stem where the short forward deck blends into it.

The decoration of the saveiro seems less lavish and a bit cruder than those of the lagoon boats; the old Maltese and medieval cross forms with six-pointed and five-pointed stars are often used.

There is nothing lost in colorful, compassionate, and reassuring names used for these and other beach boats. Generally throughout all fishing communities, the boats' names are quite naturally genuine statements of some affection to either person or deity. The Portuguese sailors are often more involved than most in such traditions—perhaps rightly so because of their complete and constant devotion to church and the elemental sea. However, two examples of typical boat names that were seen on the Costa Nova strand, rather directly translated, are: *Day-after-day-life-goes-off* and *God-help-him-who-has-to-work*. These are both literal translations. Such names contrast with a less reverent *Linda Darnell*, seen on a small beach boat some hundred miles along the shore to the south.

Both the lagoon boats of Aveiro and the nearby high-ended surf boats are from the same heritage, preserved through the years by the same traditions, economic fortunes and failures, and historic events that came and went. They are living, moving, solid monuments to an age that never was, as they combine so many mixed ages in their unique forms and decorations. They are suggestions of both the recent past and dim antiquity. We can say now that they have been successful, because they are still graceful and functional forms.

Down the coast from the beaches of Aveiro, there is an impressive, rocky promontory rising four hundred feet above the sandy beach and jutting out into the sea like a great, ancient, crumbling jetty of a race of giants. Immediately under the protection of this promontory on the south spreads one of the loveliest beaches of all Portugal and the fishing community of Nazare. But because the wind is generally from the west, this natural barrier to the northerlies does not prevent surf.

Along these beaches there is a special breed of fishermen and likewise special breeds of boats. The assortment of boat types in use at Nazare is sur-

Figure 5-19. The beach boats of Nazare are smaller than those of Aveiro but more varied. This heavy double-ended boat is much like a large whaleboat with a full body. The thwarts and transverse deck members are brought through the planking and pinned on the outside.

prising; there are normally to be seen, either on the beach, coming or going, or lying offshore, five identifiable styles of indigenous watercraft. Again, launching operations are off the open beach and the largest craft here is not more than 50 feet in length. Boats this size are frequently launched with the help of tractors to move them into position. In earlier years oxen were employed for launching and beaching, and sometimes a single ox or a team may still be seen. Altogether, there are about two hundred boats operating from this beach during the season.

The sardine seiners are the largest boats and are the same as those described earlier as coming from Peniche, which lies only about twenty-five miles down the coast to the south from Nazare.

The larger type boat is open and pulled by eight oars (Figure 5-20). It is high-ended, has a round bilge, and has a forward-raking stem. The boats of this type vary in size from 30 to 40 feet, and are used for managing long drift nets in conjunction with other boats. At first glance it seems to be only a heavily constructed large surf boat of graceful line that features a swept-up sheerline forward and a projecting stempost. There is present in some of these boats a curious and provocative construction detail that is apparent to those who look a second time and have an eye for ancient details. Some of these boats stand alone with a basic part of their structure apparently the same as that of the most ancient of all wood-planked boats. In the ancient Egyptian temple of Deir el Bahari in the Nile valley there is a row of stone reliefs dating from 1500 BC showing clearly the boats of Queen Hatshepsut with the great detail that the Egyptian artists liked to show in profile. Among other details in the construction of these boats, there is the depiction of projecting beam heads along the sheer at about the level of the deck. These are obviously the ends of deck beams projecting through the side planking, where, being securely pinned, they held together the boat's skin and kept it from spreading and sagging. These beam ends are also apparent in frescoes and reliefs showing Phoenician ships of the same period. They are very evident in the war boats of Pharaoh Ramses III as pictured in his tomb of 1200 BC as well as the ancient Egyptian boat of Figure 1-20. This type of construction, however, was not to be abandoned easily, because it is later apparent in the paintings of the galleys of classic Greece and still later in the bronze reliefs showing Roman war galleys as well as merchant vessels from the pre-Christian era through the third century AD.

This structural feature must have been a very fundamental doctrine of shipbuilding—not just of the ancient Mediterranean world—because it spread to the medieval ships of northern Europe which were planked Nordic fashion, with lapped strakes. This construction is evident in the thirteenth century English ships and the Hanseatic cogs, as shown on the official seals of the Cinque Ports and Hanseatic League cities. Most ships' structures continued to be held by these externally-pinned-through beams until the sixteenth century, when the great carracks and caravels finally added outside

Figure 5-20. A medium-size beach-launch boat at Nazare. This boat has three oars per side, and its high but not excessive sheer indicates a more manageable craft in the surf than the flat-bottom saveiro.

Figure 5-21. This scene of the fishing craft on the beach at Nazare is typical, or was in 1970. Unhappily, the tourist industry has moved in during the last two decades and the beach has been taken over by bathers and sun seekers. The fishing boats, those that remain, have moved south several hundred yards. The boats here were originally hauled about the beach by oxen—now by small tractors.

wales and massive hanging knees that tied the deck beams to the frames internally. Since that time ships and boats built of wood have, in the Western and Eastern worlds (as far as we can tell), adopted this far more logical, completely internal frame structure with only minor local variations—but not some of the large, surf-launched fishing boats of Nazare. The *Maria Eulalia* in Figure 5-19 was observed in the spring of 1970. The projecting beam ends with through pins are unmistakable along the white gunwale.

The boat in Figure 5-20 is of the same type, but the beam ends discussed above are not visible because they are covered by discarded auto tires as fenders along her side. The open, oar-propelled, surf-launched fishing boat of Nazare is unique to these central fishing beaches of Portugal. It is not found elsewhere, and only rarely beyond twenty kilometers north or south of Nazare. These are keel hulls and not flat-bottomed as are the saveiros of the beaches to the north. On the beach here below the rocky promontory there can be counted perhaps ten to fifteen of this design. Like all Portuguese boats, their hulls are brightly painted in reds, blues, yellows, and other colors, often with a contrasting sheer stripe. There is often a wedge-shaped area of color at both forward and after ends running up from the waterline and sloping away to the underside of the rubwale. This same form of decoration and style of painting is used in the boats of Malta. There are other decorations both on boats and ashore, such as the similarity of the crosses, that reflect the historic relationship between Portugal and Malta. The beach boats of Portugal, such as those in Nazare, have no Maltese counterpart however, for there is no Atlantic surf in Malta nor great open beaches of sand to draw up on. One of these boats, with seven or eight men at the oars and an additional nine or ten fishermen embarked, pointing its rising bow at a cresting breaker, is an image of everlasting seamanship.

There are two other types of smaller boats operated off Nazare's beach; one is unique. Both boats are of heavy, flat-bottom construction, but the xavega, which is 15 to 18 feet long with high freeboard, has a most surprising stem form. Figure 5-22 shows this type, and Figure 5-23 shows its structural section. The boat is referred to by the local fishermen as the "Phoenician," but the reason for this name is elusive and speculative. It most obviously must be because of the steeply rising bow and stemline, which rises at its extremity in a vertical line to a sharp point, which is some seven to eight feet above the keel. But how are these unschooled fishermen to know that Phoenician boats of three thousand years ago had vertically rising, extremely high stems? Or do they think about it at all?

Figure 5-22. A Nazare xavega, known locally as the "Phoenician." It is distinguished by its excessively high stem form, which terminates in a sharp apex.

The other of these two flat-bottomed beach boats, called a candil, has the less extreme, more conventional bow of the larger surf boat previously described. Both boats have broad transom sterns.

The remaining type of boat seen at Nazare is a powerboat of heavy construction. This type is not peculiar to these beaches but is entirely indigenous to Portugal. It is of a style that is much more common in fishing harbors and ports to the south. Since it is heavily built, 22 to 35 feet in length, and fully decked with a heavy diesel engine below, it is not an easy boat to drag out on the beach—but it is often done, sometimes by as many as twenty oxen. The boats are smaller variations of the Peniche-type seiner. They are in truth one step along in the development from the old lateen-rigged double-enders, which were very similar to the boats of the Spanish Mediterranean coast westward of Catalonia. The sterns, while still basically a double-ender form, have become broad and rounded. Some still retain the straight outboard sternpost with the rudder hung on it, but the tendency in similar hulls of recent years is toward a rounded, trawler stern. (See Figure 5-24.) These boats are used for lobstering. Typical dimensions are: length, 28 feet; beam, 9.5 feet; and gross tonnage, 4.5.

South of Lisbon a most active boatbuilding and fishing center is located in and about the well-protected harbors and beaches of Sesimbra and Setúbal. The boats of this vicinity include the sardine seiners previously discussed and the small lobsterboats above, but the most typical and graceful craft of this coast relate very closely to the lateen-rigged sailing double-enders of recent Mediterranean heritage. Figure 5-26 shows the hull lines of one of these boats, typical of many built in Sesimbra. This boat, about 23

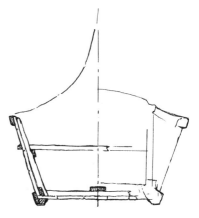

Figure 5-23. The unique keel-less construction of the flat-bottomed "Phoenician" is shown in this sketch, which represents the cross section amidships. The heavy beaching skids on the outer edges of the bilge perform the double function of providing strength and beaching support. The boats have bottoms curved up at both ends and transoms nearly as broad as the maximum beam amidships.

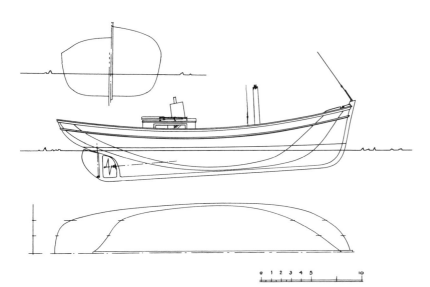

Figure 5-24. The typical Peniche lobsterboat is as nicely formed a boat of contemporary construction as one can find. These boats, like other Portuguese fishing boats, are measured and recorded officially from a builder's model made after the boat has been built. This boat's waterline aft shows an excessive hollow that mars the overall good lines.

Figure 5-25. Peniche lobsterboats are commonly beached as shown here because of the lack of well-protected harbors on the exposed Atlantic coast of Portugal. The boats are ruggedly built to withstand this service.

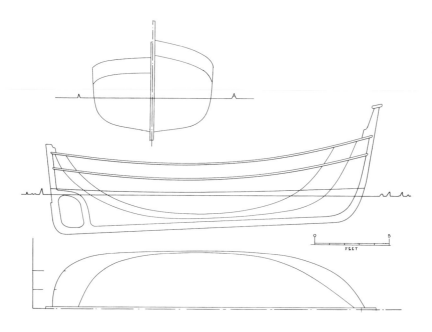

Figure 5-26. The hull form of the small seiners of the Sesimbra region have much of the same shape and construction as those of the Spanish coast.

Figure 5-27. These Sesimbra seiners are hauled out regularly on a ramp. Note the Mediterranean-style stem extension. Boats north of the Tagus River in Portugal do not have this feature.

Figure 5-28. The Mediterranean influence of bow decorations on these boats moored in Sesimbra is typical of the southern, more protected region of Portugal. The elaborate cross and the oculus are common in Iberian boat decor.

Figure 5-29. *A small fish-landing boat being pulled up on the beach stern first.*

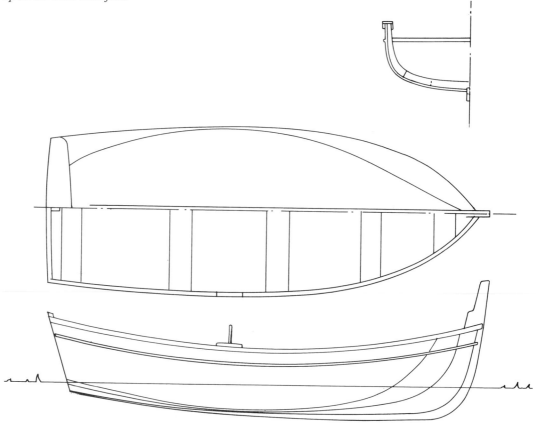

Figure 5-30. *The small fish-landing beach boat used south of the Tagus estuary is a graceful round-bottomed, surf-adapted boat. It is relatively light and easily handled by one or two fishermen and has an excellent capacity for its length.*

feet long and 8 feet in beam, is very similar to the Catalonian beach boats east of Barcelona, which still carry their lateen rig. These boats of Portugal have simply been adapted to power, carrying a small wheelhouse and sometimes a diesel stack. They are always multicolored. Figure 5-27 shows a number of these boats drawn up on the ramp in Sesimbra. Their identity is most immediately revealed by their extended stemposts with caps in the true Mediterranean style. In Figure 5-28 the several boats of this Sesimbra type on moorings show the owners' variable tastes in bow decorations, such as an oculus, a mermaid, and a Portuguese cross.

A very small but handsome relative to these "longliners" of Sesimbra is a rather diminutive, one-man pulling boat. In general profile this boat is reminiscent of the candil of Nazare, but she is a more graceful creature. She is lighter, a little smaller in dimension, round on the bottom, and has a deep transom stern. The hull lines of this boat, shown in Figure 5-30, do not reveal its grace adequately. It is necessary to see one hauled out on the beach or ramp with its stem pointing toward the sea in the misty light of a waxing sun (Figure 5-29) to appreciate the rocker keel and arrogant sheer that both blend into the raked stem. They are nice little boats, averaging 14 to 16 feet in length, and are used as fish transporters from the larger boats.

All but a very few Portuguese fishermen have given up using sail, as other workboat sailors have. On the most southerly coast of Portugal, where the harbors and the people are almost as Spanish as they are Portuguese, there is an exciting tuna industry. Here, out of Faro, Tavira, and other harbors along the Algarve coast, is a style of tuna-fishing boat that was still gracefully pro-

Figure 5-31. A tuna-fishing lateener of Tavira is very much a Mediterranean type of boat. Its lateen yard is long and its single sail is of the same cut as that of the Catalonian boats on the Spanish Mediterranean. The primary difference in the Portuguese boats is a plumb mast and a square stern.

pelled by a single, great lateen sail. This boat, again, is very similar to the Mediterranean Catalonian boat, except that it has a square, transom stern, rather than being double-ended. Her lines are very similar to those of the Sesimbra boats, combined with the transom of the smaller boat. The sailing rig was purely Spanish lateen with a single, long yard that was even longer than any used on the Spanish coast. For a boat of 30 feet, the lateen yard was no less than 45 feet long. Figure 5-31 presents the general character of one of these lateen-rigged tuna boats of the Algarve only thirty years ago.

THE REMARKABLE PORTUGUESE RABELO

As have most of the working boats of continental Europe, the boats of Portugal and southern Spain have been slowly dragged into the twentieth century. Powercraft are almost universally used, and sails are very rare. Even the old square-sailed Douro wine boat of the Oporto region is now finally gone—as a regular working boat.

This boat deserves a special page, not only in this treatise but in the history of boats. It is a special and unique boat. And it is recognized as much for its uniqueness as for its grace. For my own belief it is a graphic link to an ancient inheritance.

This Douro wine boat of Oporto is actually the larger and senior member of a like family of boats of Oporto and near region. Individually it is called by the Portuguese the *barco rabelo*. Of the other and lesser boats of this family of the Douro River, some are called *barquinha rabela* and *rubao de apegadas*. These boats are all very similar in hull structure and differ primarily in size. I will discuss only the rabelo, which is the largest and is worked only in the Douro. The smaller rivers north of the Douro have similar but smaller boats.

This rabelo boat, whose antiquity stands out in its appearance and profile, was part of an enduring trade in wine. It brought the great casks of unaged port wine from the vineyards down the long Douro River. The use of the boat as regular wine transports died sometime in the 1960s. It is tempting to compare the usage and style of this old boat to very ancient riverboats in both occupation and appearance. The old Egyptian boats of the Nile sailed upriver with great square-sails and long steering sweeps to guide them through quick turns of the river's bed. The rabelo of the Douro River has and uses identically the same long, balanced, and stern-mounted steering sweep and tall, large squaresail. The hull, like the Nile boats, is the simple form of a melon slice. But the heritage isn't all that simple and straight down the line.

Occasionally too, at Oporto, the cut of the old wine boat's squaresail is seen on smaller harbor craft. But the sail on the rabelo is suspended by a typical old-style yardarm made up of two spars doubled and lashed in the middle. It has but this single halyard on a long mast. The sail hoisted to the masthead has no lifts on the yard and no reef points on the sail. The sail has brail lines that can be handled by the helmsman and manipulated to give him the sail area with wind or without it to suit his needs. The brails are also critically useful in lifting the sail at the foot to see ahead. The helmsman stands on a built-up platform aft holding the long, heavy sweep that is balanced on a sternpost pivot. The rudder-oar at its forward end has several vertical wooden pins for the helmsman's grip. From his lofty platform he can see well over the cargo of wine casks to the river's bends and shallows, although the river's bottom must be nearly visible, for his boat's draft is very little.

The hull of the rabelo is as unusual in structure as is its rig. It is a flat-bottomed hull without a keel. The sides are built up in lapstrakes, or clinker style, that extend the ends fore and aft in upswept sheer to fitted wood blocks at both ends that take whatever place there is for the missing stem and stern posts. The hull is open and has

Figure 5-32. This is the famous wine-cask boat of Oporto, the barco rabelo. Up until the 1960s, these boats carried the unaged wine in casks in their open holds down the Douro River from the wine country. Since then, with the newly constructed dams to tame the wild river and the more efficient road transport, these boats have become notable for their strange beauty. New rabelos have been built, and they survive because of their unique attractiveness as well as their employment in local cargo transport around the Oporto estuary and nearby rivers. Sometimes their sails carry outlandish advertisements such as "Pepsi Cola." (Museu Marinha, Lisbon)

Figure 5-33. This handsome model of a rabelo shows the rare quality of beauty of the boats and their ancient roots. Compare the profile here to the profile of the Thera ship in Chapter One. (William Wiseman, Nautical Research Guild)

Figure 5-34. *This rabelo model is in the Museo Marinha, Lisbon, Portugal. It shows much the same vessel as Figure 5-33, without the live quality.*

raised bulwark weather rails along the sides. The wine casks rest on and between rails fitted fore and aft on top of the floor frames. The casks are generally stowed four abreast in the bottom and above in two levels of three and two.

It is worth some additional space here to recount the further unique structure of the hull. The bottom is laid out in longitudinal planking on flat and horizontal ground and in the plan form of the hull that will rise above. The transverse floors are fastened in and their spacing is determined by the number of wine casks the boat will carry. The master shipwright carries the measurements in his head and the whole design as well. The dimensions of the hull are all basic to the purpose of wine transportation, as they should be, and this is perhaps the last as well as one of the few vessels that exclusively defines the meaning of tonnage. The ton, or as it was in medieval English-French-Spanish, the *tun*, was

the standard wine cask itself. The number of tuns the ship could carry was its capacity—its literal useful volume of tunnage, now tonnage. The capacity of a rabelo of customary dimensions was 50 tuns. Figure 5-33 shows a typical cross section of the vessel with a tier of wine casks.

The hull dimensions of a rabelo have not been revealed in the nautical literature available, but based on the size and number of casks of port wine for which they were designed, the computation should come close enough. The length, accounting for cargoless overhangs, would be 64.9 feet, and the maximum beam, 15.1 feet.

The sides are planked up clinker-fashion from the ends of the floor timbers on both sides of the flat bottom with the shape and flare being strictly controlled by the builder. The ends are brought together forward and aft in a way that is difficult to describe because there are no true stem and stern posts for attachment. The terminus ends of the planking are brought together and with the aid of fastening blocks are lapped edge over edge alternately, one strake to starboard, the next above to port, and so on. As the planking is

Figure 5-35. This blocked-up exhibit of a genuine rabelo in the same maritime museum is much less convincing. These vessels are not built to a fixed standard size, but they generally exist according to the number of wine barrels they can handle in their holds. This is a small twelve-barrel vessel without a sail. The largest boats carry twenty-four barrels with sail. Sailing was done on an upriver voyage with the general prevailing westerlies. It was the downriver passage with the crooked river's turns, areas of rapids, and shallows that made a wild ride. It may have done something for the flavor of port wine, and certainly for its price. (Museo Marinha, Lisbon)

finally finished off, the lack of posts is not noticed and both bow and stern have steep rises; the bow form as well as stern form is a spoonlike shape. Whether this old technique of structuring determined the ultimate ancient rising ends form, or whether the form was deliberately traditional and laboriously held to over the years—centuries or possibly millennia—is a question for speculation. It *is* an ancient form. There are learned Portuguese historians who have labored on this question most diligently. The barco's genealogy is about as foggy as it gets, yet its obvious antiquity creates temptations toward speculation. I have read long papers that recite all of the ethnic diversity of Portugal, especially the coming and going of the invaders: the Moors, the Franks, the Normans, the Celts, and before that, the Romans followed by the Goths. These invaders and plunderers and settlers seldom experienced peaceful periods long enough to set up and develop successful water and sea transport and trade. I do not believe that the Normans contributed the clinker-planked sides as some scholars claim. It is not accomplished in the same technique in Portugal. The basic hulls are built in the pure age-old shell-first system, as are several other large craft of similar shape in this region. The boats are built by people familiar with seacraft rather than warcraft—their development is not an ethno-anthropological development. I believe that through all the mist-shrouded centuries of Portuguese finesterre existence we might very well have an element of heritage left on the beaches by that Phoenician crew and their friends so long ago.

It is tempting, and I must submit to it, not to leave the barco rabelo yet until we have said a final word about its configuration, upturned like a sweeping crescent. The nautical historians and archaeologists bend themselves out of shape attempting to explain it. They compare the shape to ancient Egyptian boats evident in clearly recorded reliefs and votive ship models from dynastic tombs of pharaohs such as Tutankhamen. All of the ancient graphic art from the prehistoric eras of the eastern Mediterranean recorded their watercraft with upturned ends, the most refined example being the Thera ship discussed in Chapter One. The nautical historians seem to make much of this style and talk about its mystery. It is *not* really a mystery—I believe it is simply the result of primitive shell-first building before the discovery of the advantages of starting the structure with a keel and shaped stem and stern posts. The building process of the barco rabelo is the living demonstration of the swept-up ends without keel or end posts.

The boats of the Douro are built by skillful hands guided by experienced eyes and very long memories. But all other Portuguese boats, however, built under 25 tons and engaged in the fisheries, must conform to government standards of safety and performance. They must all have a stability analysis, requiring cross-curves of stability derived from accurate hull drawings. The builders of these, therefore, build models of their craft and deliver them to the naval architect of their choice for the required computations. This represents a rare example of marriage between science and native art, and a very useful one. It is a pragmatic means of preservation of whatever valid and confirmed qualities are inherent in the traditional types.

The great old Portuguese flotilla of sailing fishing craft has undergone a transformation to contemporary technology—one of the last to do so on the European continent. Before World War II, I cruised south from the English Channel and made a landfall in the very early morning on the southwest Portuguese coast. I recall counting more than one hundred sails of lateen-rigged sardine boats. As I remember these sails, they were of a variety of weather-stained pastels against a distant hazy and fog-banked coastline. It was a thrilling introduction to the great Mediterranean, which lay another day away and beyond. Forty years later, Portugal is modernizing and rejuvenating its fishing fleets. I am sure that much traditional construction has prevailed.

Iberian culture exists in the Atlantic islands of Madeira, the Canaries, and the Azores. Much of the Madeira islanders' diet is seafood, and the fish caught here are much the same as those of the off-shore and inshore fisheries of Portugal. The smaller boats, however, while operating under oars or with sail, are obviously much less refined. They are open, with beamy, shallow hulls of most graceful proportions, but they do not have the steeply rising ends so often found on the inshore boats of Portugal. Their characteristic feature is the nicely rounded profile of the stempost. Beginning at the keel with a gentle continuous arc, the stem projects upward and forward to its simple and undecorated terminal some two feet above the sheerline. The sternpost is only slightly lower and similarly curved. The external keel, as well as the stem and stern posts, are notable in the extent of their sided external dimensions beyond the planking at the rabbet. This characteristic feature creates an old and primitive appearance in all these boats. All of the boats are fitted with heavy bilge keels for hauling out on a rugged shingle beach, much of which is heavy cobblestone. There are basically two sizes of these craft; the smaller are approximately 18 feet to perhaps 20 feet in length overall, while the larger are about 35 feet in length. The larger boats are partially decked and most are motorized. The hull forms

Figure 5-36. Whaling in the Portuguese Azores had been an age-old tradition, which international law now prohibits, thus these whaleboats are less visible. The boat in this illustration is or was a typical whaleboat that operated from the beaches of Fayal. It is very reminiscent of the old whaleboats used in the American industry launched from whale ships more than one hundred years ago, even to the wooded bow chock for the harpoon line and the wild ride behind a harpooned whale. It appears to be an excellent boat under sail.

of both types are nearly identical, and the predominant choice of color is green with a yellow sheerstrake above the rubwale.

The most predominant boat in the Azores, and the only indigenous type, was used for pursuing whales. (See Figure 5-36.) This type was adopted almost without change from the conventional shipboard whaleboats of more than a century ago. Whaling was a proud and significant industry in the Azores, with the boats operating together in a working federation. The boats were launched from the beach in protected coves and sailed after a pod of whales under a short sprit or gaff rig. The sails and masts were dropped for the final approach before striking. The entire whale hunt, including the type of boat used, was nearly identical to the much-documented technique of the nineteenth-century New England whaling industry. It is interesting that this part of a great nautical tradition had been preserved in a remote showcase in an insular world until recent international agreement ended it all. Whaling as a way of life has mercifully ended.

There is perhaps no other region in the Western world that has generated a greater variety of indigenous working boats than the Iberian coasts. This chapter reflects this variety and abundance of both sailing and power craft. There are still some types and variants of types in Portugal that have not been mentioned. The descriptions of the boats of Portugal, while not complete, are, however, perhaps as comprehensive as those in any contemporary survey. The fishing industry in Portugal is, like Norway's, a significant national industry. Unlike Norway's, the techniques of fishing and the types of fish caught are of a great variety, and this difference leads to more numerous types and styles of boats. This, together with the different climate and coastal geography, accounts for greater numbers of smaller craft operating from beaches. The same factors largely account for the existence of the smaller fishing

craft in the Mediterranean and the larger more powerful craft in northern Europe.

Portugal is a unique country of contrasts laced with the millennia of Europe's history, and her boats reflect this. The climate is normally delightful and sunny, but storm clouds often threaten just offshore on the horizon. There are formidable rocky headlands, where enormous Atlantic seas beat continuously. But these same rocky headlands shelter the inviting white sand beaches between them. The people, too, are full of contrasts, sad and smiling, proud and humble—their heritage is a strange mixture from the centuries-long Moorish occupation and the struggles of European Christians to regain their lands. The Iberian Peninsula, because of its central location, has been the intermediate land between the European north and the Mediterranean south. It also leads to the East and to the Western hemisphere. On these old and still contemporary trade routes, it is genuinely the crossroads of the Western world.

With these conflicting mixtures of tradition, which most likely began when the first Phoenician stopped to beach his boat or when some unrecorded earlier civilized sailors visited in search of trade, the Iberian boatbuilders have persisted in their craft. Boatbuilding continues in the traditional manner in the many such small fishing ports as Sesimbra. The methods and tools of the builders even now are very old. Building always takes place in the open—sometimes on the beach or beside the road, where the planks and timbers can be transported. There are other building locations where timbers are still handcut in open saw pits. Despite such seemingly primitive habits, Iberian boats are exquisitely modeled, and Iberian sailors are as skilled as the best of any country in the basic arts of seamanship. It is only reasonable that this should be so, because these people have been practicing their crafts for about three thousand years.

THE
NORTH AMERICAN
MARITIME HERITAGE

THE ORIGINAL EDITION of this book was not so much involved in the origins of native craft or prehistoric roots of maritime culture. While the former, writing on North American craft began with boats of the Northeast coast and boats of the European inheritance, we are now aware that there were indigenous American maritime people whose watercraft considerably predated those and should be described. There were more than one people because the Native Americans were not of one interconnected nation. There were many, and unhappily, because of a scarcity of recorded genealogy, the great diversification of the people, and the geographical distribution, the maritime life must be regionally and separately distinguished.

PREHISTORY OF DUGOUT
CRAFT BOTH PACIFIC AND ATLANTIC

There are those who deserve some particular attention because of their proximity to the earliest of human habitations on the western continents. The archaeologists and anthropologists specializing in prehistory are not in agreement on the earliest evidence of human inhabitants on the western continents. They are all satisfied, however, that there was a land bridge from eastern Asia that was the logical route for the first migration. These people, who were likely following the migrating animal herds and seeking a temperate and livable region, must have soon found the islands along the northwest coast of North America. It is still a place of more or less abundant sea life—fish and sea mammals, a place of nutritious plant growth and seasonal temperance.

I can recall my first visit to Oregon and Washington, and my amazement at the great size of the trees. Not that I had been raised in a region of no trees—in Ohio and Pennsylvania, Maryland and Virginia, which I knew, there were the great pasture oaks, tall loblolly pines, and the enormous shade

Figure 6-1. The original inhabitants of the North American continent most certainly used watercraft of hollowed logs. No one knows how long ago that was. However, on the northwest coast in the islands of Vancouver and to the north the Native American inhabitants are still there, and their native watercraft are of hollow logs. The Salish tribe's canoe is distinguished not so much by its decoration as its exceptional extended ends. It shows the complete use of a very large tree trunk. And the trunks of trees in the Northwest are the largest on the continent. (Burke Museum, University of Washington)

tree elms that hung over the town's streets. These trees would be dwarfed when compared to the trees of the Northwest. This does not include the sequoia giant redwoods. The size of the pines and firs and cedars in Oregon was astonishing—I hope there are some remaining.

The early people to arrive in this Northwest land were apparently also impressed by the great arboreal domain. It was the red cedar tree that they selected to be the logs for carving out their watercraft. During the period of stone and bone tools the carving was necessarily slow and very plain. When metal tools first became available is not very precisely known. According to the archaeological reports and the historians at the University of Washington's Burke Museum in Seattle, there is evidence of dugout log boats more than ten thousand years past. This is remarkable, and could well predate any records of watercraft in the old world of the Mideast.

This discussion must confine itself to the more recent watercraft that are sculpted and decorated and of which we have examples and images in the recent centuries. These craft are the heritage and inheritance of the peoples still living among the Northwest islands. These islands and territories extend from the southern shores of Alaska south below the Puget Sound. This region contains many Native American tribes who used the dugout canoes and are still building a few. Some were used in protected waters among the islands and riverine areas and others were used in ocean waters. The Tlingit in the lower Alaskan Peninsula used both. The Haida Islanders in their larger, more separate islands to the southwest were responsible for the large Haida canoe with its rising handsome bow. This was an ocean-type canoe. To the east of Haida is the Tsimshian land with its large riverine canoe, steered by a large stern paddle. To the south of this is the Kwakiutl and Salish habitat

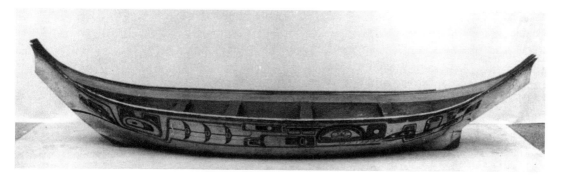

Figure 6-2. The Haida-type canoe is the most beautifully shaped canoe and the largest of all. It is also the most decorated. It has a rising bow and stern and finely cut concave waterlines. This illustration is an example of the Haida canoe that existed in the eighteenth and early nineteenth century in the offshore large island of the Queen Charlotte group. It was an oceangoing canoe. (Burke Museum, University of Washington)

with their respective types and styles. The large ocean canoe of the Kwakiutl was highly decorated and in the late nineteenth century carried sail as well as the paddlers. This was a type of war canoe, extending between both ends up to 60 feet, and carrying fifty warriors. Salish canoes included the shovel-nose shape, similar to some found on the Atlantic coast. In this region also were the Nootka with their ocean canoe, also with short spritsails and a high decorated end.

Most of these canoes were carved from red cedar; however, the low density and strength of Sitka spruce were appreciated and adapted for smaller riverine canoes of the Tlingit region.

It is difficult, if not impossible, to assign a time when the Northwestern American aboriginal people began to carve out or hollow the log to make the first boat. Some of the dedicated historians of Northwest culture seem willing to believe that the hollow log canoes began simultaneously with the earliest archaeological period they have identified—sometime around eleven thousand years ago. This is much too early, I believe, for the adaptability of stone tools. There are many questions of anthropological development, as well as developing lifestyle. Considering it in the basic arena of the natural habitat, when the earliest migrants arrived in the Northwest it

was a veritable garden with abundance of good life resources. There were fish and game everywhere within reach. There were unlimited choices for shelter, and furs for clothing. In fact, it was probably many centuries of adaptation to this environment before these early Americans thought of looking elsewhere than the land and rivers about them for other sources of sustenance. It was more likely curiosity plus the need to move out that caused them to reflect on how to get afloat. In the meantime they were also probably feeling a bit crowded. Nothing attracts migration and interest in a new settlement more than good life resources. The Smithsonian researchers tell us that their best estimate of population for this prehistoric culture in the Northwest extending along the Northwest islands to Oregon's southern line was 200,000 people. The logical extrapolation of this, according to an expert from the area, is 20,000 dugout log canoes. This when the first European explorers arrived.

When bronze and iron tools arrived, the canoe-making industry certainly experienced a great expansion, not only in quality and quantity, but in canoe size. I will not speculate on how the great trees were felled that were hewn into the larger war canoes and the ocean fishing canoes. We can only describe what we see today in terms that we understand in the absence of literate documents. But the native peoples' record of their past is in the oral tradition, and we have a record of the first Tlingit encounter with a ship from the east. They were alarmed when they first saw the ship, and described the strange sight on the horizon as "all white. His wings turn this way and that as he moves across the water.... This strange vision turned slightly and headed directly across the water, toward them. When well into the harbor . . . wings were folded, a harsh grating sound drove terror into the hearts. . . . " This was in 1786. This description indicates that Native Americans at this time were unfamiliar with sails.

By this time the native log canoes were sophisticated and elegantly carved and decorated. Illustrated here are examples of log canoes of the Northwest in model form from The Burke Museum of the University of Washington. Figure 6-1 shows the Salish canoe with its distinguishing style of bow. In Figure 6-2 we see the canoe from Haida (now the Queen Charlotte Islands, well off the mainland). Notice the flaring bow and sharp waterline form of this ocean canoe. Finally, the elegantly carved eagle head of the ocean Kwakiutl canoe is depicted in Figure 6-3.

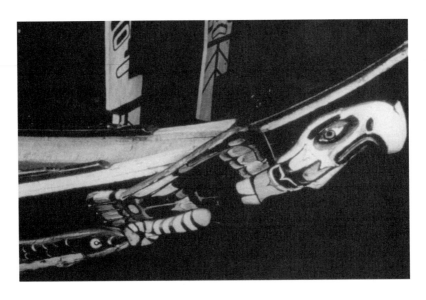

Figure 6-3. Some of the Northwest coastal log canoes were decorated with carvings similar to those on the native totem poles. This bow decoration is a true and ancient eagle figurehead. This figure is spread on both sides of the bow of a Kwakiutl ocean canoe. (Edwardo Calderon)

The shape of the Salish canoe suggests a similar characteristic in an Atlantic coast native canoe. One of the five nations of the Iroquois culture in the area that is now New York were exploiting the estuarine waters of the Hudson River, Long Island Sound, and environs. We only have the scarcest evidence of these watercraft because of lack of documentation. There is one source, however, that carries some evidence of these native watercraft, and that is the early descriptive and illustrated maps of regional America in the early sixteenth century. One that recently came to light in Amsterdam shows Manhattan, New York, at the southern end of which was the new colony then called New Amsterdam. On that rather explicit map is drawn or engraved a number of native canoes together with the contemporary sailing ships of the Dutch settlers as well as a small Dutch open boat. The artist was aware of watercraft and he drew the European ships and boats so accurately that it is reasonable to believe that the native canoes were correctly drawn. The date of this drawing was 1655.

An old contemporary wood cut, unfortunately unavailable, of the New Amsterdam scene of mid-seventeenth century includes the profile of the eastern American native log canoe. Its ends, both bow and stern, exhibit the extended characteristic known as the "shovel nose." This similar form existed in the Salish canoe of the Northwest except it was predominant only at the forward end. I believe that this form was the natural result of the cylindrical form of the large logs used. The central broad surface of the log was preserved as a useful extension for stepping ashore or as a platform for fish spearing. It could have simply been decorative. The New Amsterdam canoes show a rather bulbous terminal on the nose but that was likely an identity characteristic.

Farther south in the Chesapeake Bay, the American natives found the ideal fishing ground, a great sunken estuary extending nearly two hundred miles from its northern limits to the ocean. It was and is a broad estuarine sanctuary, an incubator and hatchery of ocean fish, wintering marshes for migrating waterfowl, abounding with oyster beds and clams and the ubiquitous blue crab. The watercraft here were simpler and smaller log canoes. Yet these log canoes were the first watercraft for the white European colonists when they later arrived.

The log canoe, as I said in Chapter One, continues in this world to be the most prolific and overwhelmingly abundant type of watercraft. It is used on all of the world's continents and islands—wherever trees grow and primitive tools are at hand. Where axes and adzes are or were not available, the tree trunk is burned hollow by controlled fire. The shapes of the finished canoes are nearly limitless. Presently the most graceful shapes of hollowed-log indigenous watercraft are in Asia and the Caspian Sea's marsh region as well as Indonesia, Vietnam, and Thailand. These regions fall outside of the prescribed limits of this book's discussion. It is also a subject that requires another volume.

There is only one other significant Native American watercraft besides the dugout log. While similar in its material source, it was unique on the North American continent and most probably anywhere. It is a true shell-first–built boat, and shaped in an ideal hydro-geometry. Its basic shell is taken from the white (paper-bark) birch tree. The bark is taken in as large lengths as possible from a single tree. The sheet of bark is laid on the ground and worked by spreading and folding into the shell form of the canoe. Heavy rocks on the shell's inside and stakes driven into the ground on the outside hold the form in place as the work progresses. Clamps and wedges are used to shape and hold longitudinal strips as the thwarts, gunwales, and strength structure are worked into place. Broad, flat frame strips are heated and steamed to place thin, wide frames close together throughout the bottom. The inevitable outside cracks and splits in the bark shell are patched with resin and pitch. The two sides are held together at both sharp ends by stitching. This strong lashing-stitching is most important for overall strength as well as local strength where the boat is most vulnerable. The stitching is of a fiber from the roots of spruce trees. The finished canoe is a very remarkable watercraft. It is light enough for one man to carry on his back while portaging between lakes and rivers in the north woods. The canoe can be repaired from natural materials at hand in the forest, and it can be paddled swiftly and silently on expeditions requiring it. It has a capacity to carry together with the hunter's own needs the carcasses of two deers. It is an existing example of original American watercraft of a natural and efficient waterborne shape that allows for little improvement.

The Native American watercraft on the Atlantic coast below the Chesapeake Bay was much the same as that in the Chesapeake. The lack of large birch trees in the south and gulf coasts as well as the multitude of small lakes and riverine geology resulted in less need for water transport. The consequence was fewer watercraft and the dependance on a few great log canoes. The slowness of construction or the hollowing of logs by controlled burning resulted in the larger but fewer canoes.

There is evidence of some offshore canoe use in the Northeast region of North America near and about the estuary of the St. Lawrence River. The native tribe called Micmacs, living in the region of Newfoundland, New Brunswick, and Nova Scotia, now the Maritime Provinces of Canada, found their protean needs in the fishing among the semiprotected islands and coasts in the Gulf of St. Lawrence. Little is known about the style or structure of their watercraft, but present knowledge of the rigors of the sea in this region would indicate something stouter than a birch-bark canoe.

The single most ubiquitous, most adaptable, and enduring watercraft among the Native Americans—the birch-bark canoe—must be acknowledged.

Later the settlers from Europe brought their own European boats, their shallops, their pinnaces, their skiffs, their schooners and various types that they developed into the "American boats."

These American types are discussed on the following pages according to their region of development and where they are used or were recently used. Most of our sailing workboats are now history. Where they are still significant or where existing examples still exist, they will be described.

In my concern with the small indigenous workboats of North America, it is necessary to be discriminating. In the wide scope of present-day working craft along the thousands of miles of North America's coastline and within the boundaries of maritime provinces and coastwise states, there are some craft that are copies of Old World boats or directly reflect such heritage. These European adaptations cannot reasonably be included as true American craft. Such examples may be noted briefly, but their truer and less adulterated ancestors are still likely to exist and most probably have been described in their original environment in the previous chapters.

It would be unwise and unfair to plunge directly into descriptions of existing American boats without first paying respects to those most worthy craft that have passed into extinction with the days of sail. Along the eastern seacoast of North America, from the Canadian provinces to the Gulf of Mexico, during the nineteenth century, large numbers of sailing workboat types were in use. Most of these craft were American derivatives in design and construction. Many survived into the early twentieth century, but almost all have gone today. The causes of their extinction are obvious and well documented. For the most part, the advantages and attractions of mechanical propulsion made sail uneconomical. The expansion of the American economy and the technologies of mechanical refrigeration, rapid transportation, and urbanization of society were also equal contributors to the extinction of these fine old sailing craft.

Many truly American working sailing craft were significant and deserve mention. The early colonial and Revolutionary War sloops and shallops developed and evolved into schooner types. Some of the most notable were built in Chesapeake Bay and loosely referred to as Baltimore schooners. On the New England coast the old heel-tapper fishing schooners gave way to the faster and seaworthy pinky schooners and larger Banks schooners as fishing grounds were extended. The Virginia pilot schooners and New York pilot schooners of the nineteenth century became the models for later ships and yachts. The smaller double-ended schooners, such as the Block Island boats and the Chebacco boats, were fine seakeeping models. The oyster industry of the Delaware and Chesapeake Bays developed unique craft, such as the Delaware sloop and the Chesapeake oyster sloop. An early nineteenth century schooner called a pungy had the sleekness of a Baltimore clipper's hull. Later the Chesapeake bugeye and skipjack dominated the oyster fishery, numbering into thousands.

The smaller sloops of note along the New England coast were the double-ended Quoddy boat and the Friendship and Muscongus sloops. There were catboats developed for the scallop fisheries of the sounds, and the Noank sloop mainly for lobstering in Long Island Sound. Farther south, there were the sprit-rigged sloops of the North Carolina sounds, which were finely modeled hulls for shoal-water fishing. There were the beamy sponge

Figure 6-4. The unique form and lapstrake hulls of Nova Scotian boats reflect the ancestry of northern Europe. This boat on the beach at Sydney, Nova Scotia, is used by independent fishermen in the local lobster industry.

sloops and smacks of Key West carrying great spreads of sail. (These should not be confused with the Greek sponge boats that later dominated this Florida fishery.) In the Gulf of Mexico there were the Louisiana oyster sloops, Biloxi schooners and catboats for shrimp fishing, and the New Orleans lugger, which was said to be fast and weatherly and the only American working boat using the lug rig.

On the Pacific coast the boats of the Columbia River and Puget Sound were smaller than the eastern boats, were double-ended, often undecked, and carried a single spritsail. Some of these boats were used in the gill net and salmon fisheries until very recently. The sailing workboats in the San Francisco area were direct copies of Mediterranean craft, identical in rig and hull to those of Italy and Spain. They were called by the likely but incorrect name *feluccas*. A genuine felucca was a Mediterranean boat of the Algerian coast during the eighteenth and early nineteenth centuries. It was often used in the pirate business, hence its name, to Americans, became notoriously linked with the Mediterranean.

The culmination in performance, grace, and fishing capacity of sailing workboats was finally reached in the great schooners sailing out of Boston, Gloucester, and Nova Scotia. The racing competition between these boats became so heated that the last ones were designed by well-known yacht designers.

However gracefully these boats may have expired, they are gone and have settled for their spot in American maritime history with one or two replicas. However profitable they may have been in their time, they could not have continued or existed in today's economy. The work of a dozen sailing lobsterboats is done by one today. A fishing schooner from the Banks often arrived with rotted fish in her holds—today's modern boats do not. Today's scallop dragger can take in one haul of her dredge two days' catch for a scallop boat under sail. And most modern shrimp boats are part of multimillion-dollar fleets and industries owned by very large companies. The best thing to say now about sailing fishing boats is they were kind to the maritime ecology!

What still attracts the individual sailor in his own small boat to the sea? There is little question that the fisherman of today in his small powerboat has faced the same diminishing opportunities as the fisherman of the past with his sailing boat. The expedience and reliability of the contemporary motor-powered workboat in some environments, however, does allow the continuance of small, individually operated craft in a competitive market.

The coasts of northeastern America used to abound with types of small craft that were unique and indigenous to their regions. The majority of these types have not been replaced after they deteriorated and consequently today only a few remain. However, as written in previous chapters, a few indigenous craft stubbornly survive and prevail in the more isolated communities, especially those with significant fishing industries or, as the Chesapeake skipjack, with the state's regulatory help.

On the farther east coasts of the North American continent, which include the maritime provinces of Canada, the native boats are ruggedly distinguished and flavored by their North European heritage. Yet this is mainly just a flavor. The boats are reminiscent of Scottish and Scandinavian craft in their structure, which is predominantly lapstrake, but their styles are creatively American–Nova Scotian. The general style, rather than the design, of these boats is the indigenous factor. There are long, slim clinker-built lobsterboats with broad transom sterns that appear to be second cousins of the Jonesport boat (the well-known Maine lobsterboat type to be discussed in this chapter). There are double-ended lapstrake pulling boats whose form is like the timeless Norway skiffs. There are canoe-sterned, clinker-built powerboats that are obviously descended from the nineteenth century small double-ended Tancook whalers or Hampton whalers, and many others. The nineteenth century ancestors of these boats can be examined only through their drawings and illustrations; the present-day versions are still on beaches and in harbors of Prince Edward Island and Nova Scotia.

When I was a boy of twelve, an old and skilled boatbuilder friend of mine created a 14-foot sloop for me, which he built entirely by an instinctive hand. He was from Prince Edward Island, and he built from memory a handsome little lapstrake boat with steam-bent frames and a Scottish-Norse stem on molds shaped entirely by his inner eye. This boat followed me for more than twenty years, and I well remember how she was built, how I learned to sail in her, and how she responded better than many boats I have owned since.

NEW ENGLAND WATERCRAFT

Much has been written of the New England dory and the famous Banks dory of the same mold and origin. Most observers would say that the dory is an indigenous New England type, and so it is in a way. But in another sense, a dory is built on a model that is so fundamental and natural that it is hard for any age to claim it. The first planked boats of ancient Egypt were built to the same basic sectional form. Boats in Scotland and in southern France identified with the Middle Ages have been of this form. There is a Marseille dory still in limited use almost identical to the New England dory except for the latter's "tombstone

Figure 6-5. A well-worn dory resting at her mooring in a Maine harbor.

stern." A log dugout canoe used by the fishermen of the coast of Senegal in West Africa has the same basic shape. A dory form is popular and basic beyond a doubt, and it is easily identified. Its popularity stems from its natural simplicity. The sides of dory-type boats are essentially "developable," that is, they can be sprung to shape from a flat surface. A straight plank bent in an arch and set on an angle can become a dory side. The most common and simple dory can be built with one-piece sides. The bottom is flat with a slight rocker, and the number of frames is minimal, perhaps only four. A more shaped and refined dory may have as many as five or six planks per side.

The dory is, to use a New Englander's description, "cranky" when light, but gains in stability as she is loaded. It established a reputation for seaworthiness as a line-trawling boat for the old Banks schooners of the nineteenth

Figure 6-6. Shooting a seine from a dory. Dories are rowed from either the seated or the standing position. (National Fisherman)

Figure 6-7. A typically shaped Maine peapod. This indigenous double-ender is quite similar to some Mediterranean beach boats.

century. Quantities of dories could be carried compactly on deck in a "nest" when the thwarts were removed. These boats averaged about 18 feet in length on the American schooners. The dory is in use today in seining operations. A smaller, one-man dory is used by the contemporary Portuguese craft fishing the Grand Banks.

Another well-known and efficient little boat of New England still surviving with some vigor is the Maine peapod. This little double-ender is smaller and more refined than a dory. The peapod was originally designed for sailing with a small spritsail. The entire rig with mast and sprit was easily put up or down and stowed in the boat. A peapod is similar in form and size to some French Mediterranean beach boats, but without extended stem and stern posts (see Figure 6-7).

One theory is that the Maine peapod originated in the Penobscot Bay region of Maine sometime in the middle of the nineteenth century. Another theory is that these little double-enders are related to or inspired by the Native American's canoe. Both of these theories are dubious. There has always been an abundance of small double-ended hull forms in the "Down East" region, which includes especially the Maritime Provinces of Canada and the Cape Breton area. These hull forms are many and varied: deep and full, shallow and light, either plumb-ended or with raking ends, and either smooth-planked or clinker-planked. The contemporary Maine peapod also shows many of these variations in form and structure. If there is any single regional source of these double-enders, it is more likely some part of Nova Scotia. The Scots centuries ago learned to appreciate double-ended craft from the Norse.

At any rate, the Maine peapod is a serviceable little utility boat that became popular a century ago as an able little lobster-pot hauler for a single

Figure 6-8. The capacity of a dory is surprising. The more weight she takes on, the more she will resist immersing her hull and the greater her stability will be. This one has a load of wet nets that weighs nearly half a ton.

lobsterman in the Penobscot region. Peapods are still popular and can be found in various sizes, shapes, and construction forms. On several stretches of the northeast American coast, there are small double-ended utility boats from 10 to 15 feet in length. They are ideal beach boats, simple harbor boats, or tenders.

Along the coast of northeast United States and the Maritime Provinces of Canada, there is a strong seagoing heritage. Sailboats of the past and powerboats of the present have always been built with a keen eye to both performance and ruggedness. They have been crewed and owned by discriminating sailors and fishermen with demanding requirements. These boats have been built in an area that is near inshore and offshore fishing grounds that produce premium seafood products: lobster, scallops, and some shrimp. This area is dotted with naturally protected harbors and coves and is blessed with indigenous boatbuilding woods in fair supply. In just such an environment, boats of strong regional influence are developed. Boats built here have had a considerable influence on uncounted pleasure and working craft along the entire eastern seaboard.

As the old pinky schooners and the excellent smaller sailing craft, such as the Friendship and Muscongus Bay sloops, ended their working days, a powerboat was developed for lobster fishing in Nova Scotia that became a basic model for various similar types in both Canada and Maine. In Down East Maine this boat was known as the Jonesport boat (see Figure 6-9). Her typical dimensions were length from 32 to 45 feet, beam 10 to 12 feet, and draft (light) 2½ feet. With her converted automobile engine she made speeds up to 16 knots. She had, as her present-day versions have, a fine,

Figure 6-9. The lines of an early Jonesport boat.

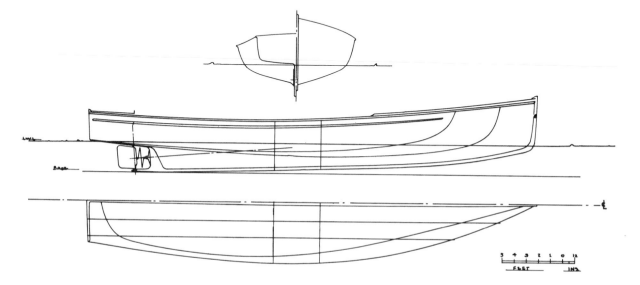

sharp entrance with a long, flat run of underbody terminating in a broad, flat transom. Originally, the Jonesport boat had a forefoot cut away, raking up at about 15 degrees from the straight keel line to the stern. This made beaching easier where docking facilities or piers were not available. The construction was of light, steam-bent frames of oak or ash, closely spaced and of rather flat section aft of midships. The Jonesport boat was, as most are today, planked with white cedar or sometimes clear-grade pine about 1 to 1½ inches thick.

There was generally a low cuddy cabin forward on these partially decked boats, and today invariably a steering shelter house, open on the back and at least one side, for tending the lobster haul. This shelter is often fitted with side curtains rigged for inclemencies.

In Nova Scotia, similar boats can be found that relate more closely to older sailing models with double-ended form or canoe-type sterns. The Canadian boats are sometimes undecked without any shelter.

There is no such thing as a single, stereotyped design for lobsterboats any more than there is one for most other indigenous boat types.

The contemporary Maine lobsterboats exist

Figure 6-10. A lobsterboat of the Penobscot. This boat is not far removed from the earliest Jonesport, or Cape Island, boat. Note her side sheathing for protection where the pots are hauled aboard and the open section of her wheelhouse on the working side.

Figure 6-11. A wide variety of styles is evident in these lobsterboats at anchor. (Mike Brown)

in many models and a variety of sizes. They reflect, to a great extent, the affluence (or lack of it) of their owners. Some are apt to be rather "hand-hammered" looking. On the other end of the scale, there are those of most modern construction and professional finish including, currently, one well-respected builder's product in fiberglass. A selection of this variety in finish and taste can be seen in Figures 6-10, 6-11, and 6-12. While these boats show individuality—they vary in size, equipment, construction quality, and in some cases hull form—they exhibit a definite overall similarity that unmistakably stamps them as a native type.

Having described the older Jonesport models, it is useful to describe similarly a very recent boat built in Blue Hill, Maine. This boat is a most excellent example of modern working-boat design in this locality. Even though the more conservative fishermen may still distrust her fiberglass hull, she is

Figure 6-12. A newly built lobsterboat on the ways. (Anchor Light Studio)

Figure 6-13. The modern lobsterman, if he is affluent enough, can work from a fiber-glass, yachtlike work-boat. The hull of this model in molded plastic was originally designed for the U.S. Coast Guard even though it was based on a lobsterboat model. (W.H. Ballard)

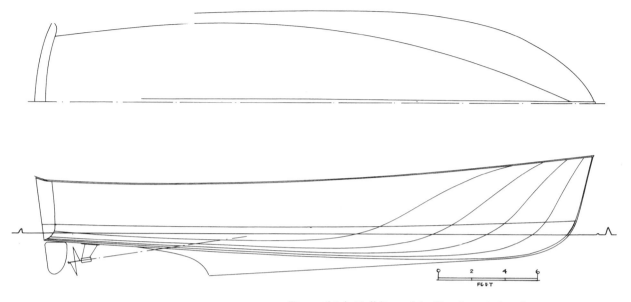

Figure 6-14. Hull lines of the fiberglass-reinforced plastic lobsterboat shown in Figure 6-13.

a respectable example of the best in lobsterboats. (The boat is illustrated in Figure 6-13 and her lines are shown in Figure 6-14).

First, it is only fair to say that this boat was not designed in Maine but in Maryland. However, her designer was strongly influenced by the Maine model and the requirements there, and the boat does not depart from the New England form. She cannot be identified as anything other than a Maine lobsterboat. The hull is 33'10" in length, 11'0" in beam, and 2'6" in draft. Her light displacement is about 7,500 pounds and she has a top speed of about 21 knots with a 170-h.p. diesel. The photograph shows her rigged for dragging, which is the off-season employment of some lobsterboats from November through March. While this model has an excellent hull form, which is quite adaptable to the requirements of the industry, she is not typical of the higher-performance lobsterboats. She is not particularly fine at the waterline: her half-entrance

angle is approximately 25 degrees, while 10 to 15 degrees is more common in the older boats and certainly permits a more easily driven hull. In addition, this hull, following the more recent tendency, shows a greater immersion at the transom. These fuller-bodied characteristics undoubtedly provide a more stable working platform and one that can carry a greater range of loads with less change in power requirements.

Leaving this analysis, it is appropriate to look briefly at some characteristics of a lobster hull model from the Portland, Maine, area. The lines of this boat are shown in Figure 6-15 and a photograph of her test model in Figure 6-16. This boat, according to her builder, was "one of several to the same molds." She "made a clean natural drift" according to one expert observer, averaging about 13 knots with a 100-h.p. converted gas engine. She shows the slack bilges of the Jonesport model and a very fine entrance with a half angle of about 10 degrees, essentially a hollow

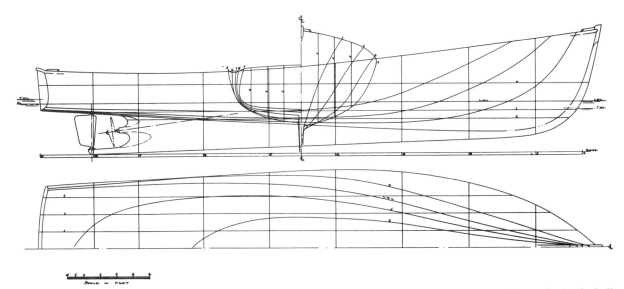

SCALE IN FEET

waterline. Her length is the same as the fiberglass model described above, but
she is less beamy. She is deeper in the forefoot and should be easier in a seaway. Her sections forward show a nice flare. This hull was tested, together
with a number of other models of Maine lobsterboats and Chesapeake crabbing and oyster launches of similar dimensions, in the U.S. Naval Academy
model basin in 1960. This model of a Portland-built boat exhibited a clear
superiority over the others as being the most easily driven. On a per-pound
basis of boat weight, she showed the lowest power requirement over the complete displacement speed range. In tank tests among waves in a head-sea condition, this model again showed a definite superiority over the other models.

*Figure 6-15. The hull
lines of a highly effi-
cient lobsterboat built
in Portland, Maine.*

*Figure 6-16. The
tank model of a Maine
lobsterboat undergoing
tests for research in the
comparative efficiencies
of small fishing craft of
the North American
coast. This model,
whose lines appear in
Figure 6-15, proved
superior to several
Maine and Chesa-
peake Bay fishing
launches. (Model by
John Gardner)*

While the tank tests described above were limited to specific designs under specific comparative powers and sea-state test conditions, the Portland model's design was exceptionally good. The characteristics were chosen so they could be used under difficult and demanding operating conditions that require optimum hull performance.

There is no excess weight on a good lobsterboat hull. There are no concessions or compromises in design or construction to provide roomy accommodations, or, as in many fishing craft, large fish holds, or auxiliary machinery for refrigeration. The primary employment of a lobsterboat is quite different from other fishing craft. The greatest load one must carry is a deckload of lightweight lobster pots, and even that is only

intermittent. The catch of lobsters may on a very good day run to three hundred pounds, but not very often. It is not surprising, then, that the performance qualities of a lobsterboat, developed in an excellent testing environment, have attracted the attention of many small-boat designers. Lobsterboat hull forms and dimensions have been widely adapted and imitated—sometimes successfully, but often with indifferent or even poor results. Where the employment of such hull types is in pleasure-craft use, there should be considerable attention given to weight limitation. Such lightweight hulls with slack bilges do not respond to great changes of displacement. Fuller entrances, greater immersions aft, higher freeboards, and harder bilges are generally the

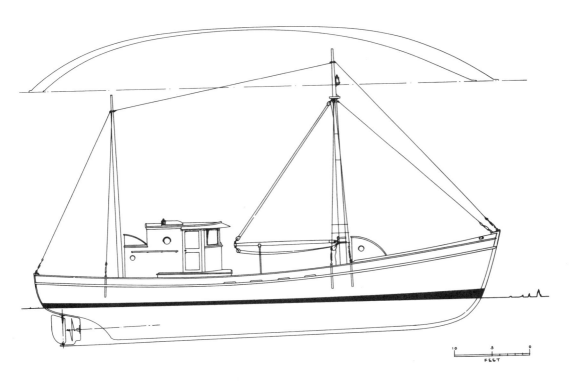

Figure 6-17. The profile and waterline form of a Maine sardine carrier.

features found in the modifications to the original forms. These are all concessions for comfort, carrying capacity, and certain aspects of stability and steering.

There is also on the coast of Maine a boat that is characteristic of a broader spectrum of New England working boats of the fisheries. This boat, while it appears from not too far a distance to be a New England–type dragger (to be discussed immediately below), is not a dragger or even a fishing boat. It is actually a fish carrier, specifically a sardine carrier. Because of its employ, it is not, nor need it be, built as ruggedly or heavily as a real working "dragger" or trawler. The Maine sardine carrier transports the produce of the fishermen to the buyers and packers. It is essentially a coastwise boat, but since it works off a northern, rugged coast from early spring to December, it is a boat built to exacting specifications to provide substantial seakeeping ability.

On the average, these boats are 55 to 60 feet in length, with a beam of nearly 15 feet and a draft of about 5 feet. While there are some with transom or squared-off sterns, the more typical stern form is the canoe or trawler type. The profile and waterline form of a typical sardine carrier are shown in Figure 6-17. The strong characteristics of a high bow with an easy entrance and a dragged keel line are evident in this boat. This style of fish carrier is also seen in Figure 6-18, which shows one working out of Rockland, Maine.

Sardine carriers have especially strong bottom construction because of the concentrated loads from their built-in concrete fish tanks, whose typical capacity runs to about one thousand bushels of sardines. Separated fish tanks in the larger of these boats provide some additional advantages to the owners and packers. For instance, the catches of different fishermen can be separated; entire loads are seldom lost or condemned because of a few bad fish; and partial loads may be carried without involving the labor of cleaning the single large fish hold. The engine power installed in these boats varies, but 150 h.p. in a diesel is considered quite ample.

In character the sardine carrier of Maine is most traditionally "Down East." While the illustrations shown are of a type, the boats vary in size and stern form, a few even in hull form. There is still, however, strong adherence to a singleness of character and style. This style is of New England. It will be seen again in the appearance and character of the dragger, a description of which follows.

The New England dragger is perhaps more indigenous to New England as a tradition than as a specific type of boat. The modern New England dragger is essentially a heavily powered fishing trawler, distinguished by its ruggedness as necessitated by its all-season operation on the exposed Georges Bank one hundred miles or more beyond Cape Cod. Its design follows the modern concept of a motor trawler (a typical one being about 80 feet in length), and this concept is not indigenous to New England. Today's new boats are the sophisticated products of competent naval architects specializing in fishing-boat design. However, there may be a few of the older, smaller draggers still about New Bedford, Stonington, Gloucester, and other harbors of southern New England. These draggers reflected at least some of

Figure 6-19. An eastern-rigged New England dragger. The masts can carry steadying sails. The eastern dragger, and her western sister, almost always carries at least one dory on top of, or near, the wheelhouse. (Ivan Flye)

*Figure 6-20. This western-rigged New England dragger is actually a combination boat. Her bow pulpit may be used for sword-fishing. (*National Fisherman*)*

the characteristics of their local sailing ancestors, notably the Cape Cod cat-boat, Noank sloop, and Gloucester sloop boat.

There were originally two types (and many still are working) of New England draggers, the "eastern" and the "western." The essential difference in style aside from minor variations in form is the location of the deckhouse and the number of masts and their locations. The western style dragger has the deckhouse and accommodations, including the engine space, forward, and the fish hold aft. It also has a squared-off stern and a single mast. The

Figure 6-21. A large, modern steel dragger. She still bears a strong resemblance to the original eastern type. (Ivan Flye)

Figure 6-22. A Gloucester fishing schooner that has been converted to a dragger. (National Fisherman)

eastern model is opposite in respect to the location of the deckhouse and the fish hold. It has two masts in a cut-down schooner arrangement.

The boats are very heavily built, with sawn frames on heavy keels and keelsons, inner and outer stems, and heavy planking. This construction closely follows nineteenth-century New England shipbuilding practice, which is most commendable. When such construction is used on craft smaller than the great clippers, packets, or Gloucester schooners, the boats seem to be overscaled and overweight. However, it is difficult to argue

Figure 6-23. The lines form of the Sea Bright skiff. This lapstrake boat evolved into the powerful sportfishing pleasure craft that are all loosely labeled "sea skiffs." Note the box keel.

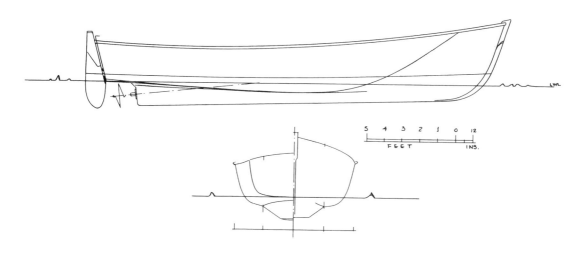

against success, and these boats have been successful. I have not seen any recorded loss of one of these draggers that was due to failure of her basic structure. They are stable and most seakindly.

Figures 6-19 and 6-20 show two typical New England draggers of the eastern and western styles respectively. These boats represent an intermediate stage in the evolution of the modern steel trawler (see Figure 6-21). They represent the classic mental picture conjured up when the term *New England dragger* is used on the eastern seaboard.

Along the coast between New England and the Chesapeake Bay, there are few surviving boat types that are uniform either in style or in performance. Descendants of a type known as the Jersey sea skiff, however, do operate from the various inlets along the New Jersey shore. The present-day models of this type have many of the qualities of good Maine lobsterboats. They have a lively sheer, flaring bow, a forward-reaching stem, and slack bilges. They are also of lightweight, but strong, construction. They generally have lapstrake planking and greater beam than lobsterboats.

A special form of boat, called the Sea Bright skiff, can be seen occasionally along the Jersey shore. This boat is identified by its unusual bottom construction. It is essentially a round or sometimes V-bottom hull with a hollow box-type keel. This is apparent in the simple hull-form sketch of Figure 6-23. The true purpose of this appendage or distended bottom configuration is elusive. Some observers contend it allows a flat bottom surface to keep the boat upright when it is beached. Others feel it provides added bottom strength without too much added weight. It also provides a more accessible bilge under the engine, by acting as a bilge sump.

The box-keel form similar to that of the Sea Bright skiff is, from the hydrodynamic point of view, a poor idea. It is simply an additional small hull carried below the main hull. In addition to the frictional and eddy drag it adds, the box keel is close enough to the surface to contribute to the wave drag as well. In towing-tank tests I undertook several years ago on several models of this type, it was most evident that this type of configuration suffered an added drag of approximately 20 to 25 percent over hulls of similar shape but without boxed keel forms. The effect on both maneuverability and power expended is nearly that to be expected if a beer keg were attached to the boat's bottom.

It is this sort of individual expression in locally conceived boats that sometimes contributes to their early extinction. The survival of Sea Bright skiffs for their fifty years or more is undoubtedly due to other qualities. Their lightness and strength, as well as comparative dryness, are important factors. However, I suspect that some of the larger models, which were highly powered during the Prohibition Era of the 1920s, earned an exaggerated reputation for evasiveness in a sub-rosa world.

THE CHESAPEAKE INFLUENCE AND THE ALL-AMERICAN BOAT

The Chesapeake Bay area is a unique body of tidal water. Its ecology nurtures a great abundance and variety of seafood. Its channels and tributaries lead close to many large urban areas. Quite naturally the Bay has large numbers of workboats working profitably between its shores.

None of the Chesapeake Bay boats of considerable distinction in the days of sail exist any longer. A small number of sailing workboats still exists, however, that is notable—more notable perhaps for the unique survivability of the small fleet than for the qualities of the individual boats.

Before describing these sailing workboats, it may be pertinent to note briefly the employment of these working boats of Chesapeake Bay.

The fisheries in temperate zones generally provide a seasonal industry. The Chesapeake is a good example of this natural cyclic employment. There is a variety of seafood usually available for harvesting, and the employment seasons also extend themselves nearly throughout the year. In the summer months, from early May through September, the crabbing season is in force. Beginning in October and extending through April, the oyster season goes on. Clams are taken by hydraulic dredge throughout the year but are better during the colder seasons. There is presently (1993-94) a disease that is destroying the Chesapeake oyster fisheries, with no evidence for an optimistic future.

In addition to the fisheries, there is a certain amount of cargo and produce still moved on the water by small carriers. Some of these carriers serve the fisheries and other commercial and farm needs.

It is remarkable that in this industrial, agricultural, and maritime region there are no more indigenous boat types than there are. This is true perhaps because the watermen and owners of working boats employ themselves in more than a single industry and use the same boats for more than a single purpose.

The most common type of boat construction in the Chesapeake Bay is the shoal V-bottom hull known locally as a *deadrise*. This term is a generic one and does not adequately describe any boat. It is perhaps better to briefly describe a typical Chesapeake fishing launch as a chine-built boat of from 30 to 45 feet in length, 8½ to 11 feet in beam, and 3 to 4 feet in draft, with a shallow V-bottom ending on a chine slightly below the waterline. The chine is low and flat throughout, rising only slightly forward sometimes above the waterline. The stem is generally plumb or raked a little forward, but almost always has a straight stempost. The sterns are round with a graceful rake aft

Figure 6-24. A Chesapeake Bay "buy boat" loaded down with a deck load of oysters. This fine photo was taken in 1970. It is not typical of the present situation in the oyster industry. (Robert de Gast)

or have a flat transom with little or no rake. The round-stern boats are generally the larger ones and are used most frequently as oyster tongers with patent tongs. They are often called Crisfield-built. The smaller square-stern boats are used in shallower waters, and during the oyster season they are operated by one person with the old-style hand tongs.

Actually, the powered launches of the upper and lower Bay are all variations on a single theme. They vary primarily in size and in regional and seasonal employment. As the old sailing brogans were smaller, open editions of the bugeyes, the small power launches are similar to the large ones and, even in basic form, to the larger light-freight carriers and many "buy boats." They may rig clam dredges in spring and summer, and then rig the mast-boom rig for lifting the heavy patent tongs in the fall and winter. A buy boat is a large deadrise 50 to 70 feet long that is capable of carrying upwards of 25 tons of oysters, which are bought from the oystermen in the Bay or before the oystermen return to port (see Figure 6-24). This scenario is true only in good oystering seasons. Unhappily oystering presently is a fast deteriorating industry. In addition to pollution, a new imported disease is destroying live oysters in their beds. At the present rate, the Chesapeake oyster will not survive further.

Figure 6-25 shows the lines of a typical round-stern launch, and Figure 6-26 shows those of a smaller square-stern model. The form of this latter boat indicates a lighter, more easily driven boat. However, her low forward chine and full entrance do not indicate that she would be very competitive among the finer hulls of the New England coast. In spite of her clean run

Figure 6-25. The hull form of a typical Chesapeake round-stern deadrise. This type of boat may be seen in Maryland and Virginia waters of the Bay in many sizes and occupations, from small oyster-tonging boats to large buy boats.

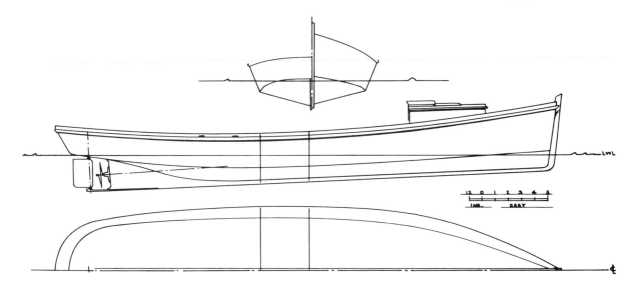

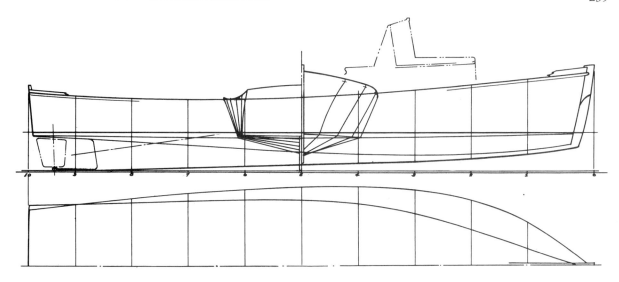

Figure 6-26. There are many variations of the square-, or transom-, stern deadrise, but this hull form shows a typical one. The boat is generally smaller than the round-stern deadrise and is used for crabbing and oystering. When used for oystering in the winter, this boat's two-man crew tongs the hard way, with hand tongs.

aft, her low chine forward creates a shoulder wave that is inefficient and awkward. Some similar models are even fuller than this one in the forward chine.

It is in the afterbody and run of some of the larger boats that the most serious difficulties lie. The boats when under construction are set up with the keel laid horizontally along the ground blocks and the chine carried aft paralleling this horizontal keel line until (at approximately three-quarters of the waterline length) it is turned back up toward the stern waterline. This sort of chine curvature creates a full body too far aft and generates a form that is most inefficient. The distribution of displacement is such that about 60 percent of it is confined at only 20 percent of the length of the hull, which is too far aft. This displacement distribution is most evident when the curve of the sectional areas, as shown in Figure 6-27, is examined. A curve such as this simply shows the areas of the hull's cross sections below the waterline at any indicated station along the length of the hull. A hull whose characteristics are of this nature tends to have a great eddy drag as well as a considerable wave resistance.

Not all of the Chesapeake-type hulls have this extreme chine curvature. There are many that show a cleaner or flatter run, particularly the smaller craft, and these are probably the present-day descendants of the once popular and fast crabbing launch known as the Hooper's Island boat. The original Hooper's Island craft were characterized by a long, rather narrow hull of light weight and draft. They frequently had a rounded fantail stern with a reverse rake and a chine that followed the waterline throughout the length of the boat. The deeper sections, with sharper V's, were forward of amidships, which produced a clean, flat hull run to the transom; some boats even showed a slight hollow in the run. These boats, developed more than eighty years ago, were modeled on an early racing motorboat that appeared about 1905. This

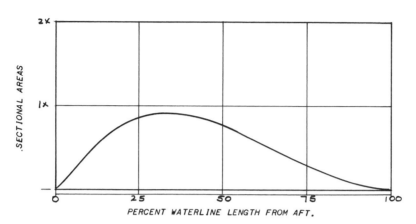

SECTIONAL AREA CURVE FOR CHESAPEAKE
ROUND STERN "DEADRISE" BOAT

Figure 6-27. This curve indicates the distribution of hull volume for a typical deadrise boat. The greatest volume occurs at about 35 percent of the boat's length from the stern.

Figure 6-28. The smaller hand-tonging boats are all deadrise but more individualized by their owners.

motorboat undoubtedly made a considerable impression among the Chesapeake watermen and set a style that, with further development and better engines, became a type. A typical Hooper's Island boat, sometimes called a "draketail," is shown in Figures 6-30 and 6-31; her dimensions are 35'6" length, 6'5" beam, and 2'0" draft. The boats of this early type were often narrow with breadths at the waterline less than one-sixth of their lengths. They were consequently fast with the comparatively low-powered engines of sixty years or more ago. As they and similar early boats developed with

Figure 6-29. Hand tongers at work on a square-stern deadrise. (Robert de Gast)

higher engine power, they naturally grew in beam. Now the beam-length ratio is something more like 1 to 4 or 1 to 3.5. The chine lines are still low and flat, terminating in present-day boats at the outboard corners of a flat rectangular transom. The raked-transom type of deadrise boats are the older models, which are also narrower in beam. They have a short overhanging counter with a V-transom. They were built when engine power was much lower and squatting was not a problem. They are undoubtedly more comfortable in a Chesapeake chop, and although they are no longer being built, many are still on the contemporary scene. These boats are period-

Figure 6-30. The hull form of a Hooper's Island boat shows a narrow, fine-lined shape with the chine lying flat on the waterline from stem to stern. The boats are unquestionably fast and efficient in the short, choppy waves of the Chesapeake. This type is sometimes called a drake tail.

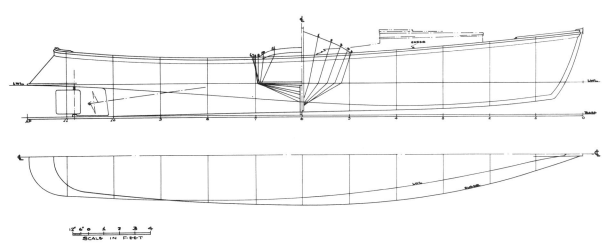

Figure 6-31. A Hooper's Island deadrise. Easily identified by its reverse-raked, rounded stern, this indigenous type is no longer being built. A subtantial but diminishing number still exists in Maryland and Virginia. This boat has been recently reinvented in fiberglass. It also has been replicated (by the author) for a social experiment in Bay ecology education. (David Q. Scott)

ically repowered with larger automobile engines and are thus forced to use "squat-boards," which effectively extend the waterline and prevent stern sinkage.

Generally the construction techniques of Chesapeake boats are similar and are motivated as much by simplicity as by tradition. There are some designers who will argue that V-bottom construction is as difficult and requires as much skill as round-bottom, steamed-frame construction. It is perhaps true that setting up the frame is comparable in the two methods, even granting the fact that the V-bottom or chine hull has five basic segments to a full frame plus its knees and gussets, while the round-bottom boat has only three. However, most Chesapeake chine boats, because of their sturdy cross-planked bottoms, find no need for bottom frames. The essential frames are heavy sawn timbers on the sides between chine and sheer clamp under the deck edge. While the bottom planking is set crosswise, often diagonally from the keel, the side is planked lengthwise in wide planks, about three to four strakes per side. In smaller craft as few as two or even one broad plank per side may be used. The comparative simplicity of planking in the Chesapeake manner is obviously more economical and adaptable in the Chesapeake, where the fishermen are frequently their own builders, than the careful fitting, spiling, and beveling of the many planks used in round-bottom boats. This fact is more evident in the comparative cost of the two types of boats.

The deadrise hull form could stand some improvement. It would be highly desirable to lift the chine line well above the forward waterline

Figure 6-32. "Patent" tonging is usually a small, two-man operation. Note the squat-board brackets at the stern of the boat in the foreground to adapt to the newer high-powered engines. (Robert de Gast)

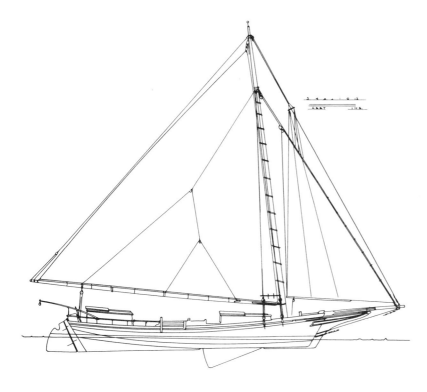

Figure 6-33. The outboard profile of a Chesapeake oyster dredger. Commonly referred to a a skipjack, this workboat is the last survivor of working sail in the waters of continental United States. There are less than a dozen still working because of the scarcity of viable oyster beds.

and rake the stem forward, which would produce a flaring section and a finer waterline. The chine knuckle now present in Chesapeake craft would be virtually lost.

Only two elements—size and speed—can be considered similar when comparing the New England indigenous craft to those of the Chesapeake Bay.

Both are medium-displacement hulls capable of length-speed ratios in the order of 2.8 at maximum power. Both types show strong local characteristics but, generally too, exhibit the individualities of their owners. Beyond this they are adapted to their own environments and employments as is proper.

In the Chesapeake boats, the individuality among oyster tongers may show in the location of the short, stubby mast: some are forward, some aft. In the small freight carriers and buy boats, the deckhouse is generally aft, but sometimes it is forward as is more prevalent in American boats elsewhere. There is occasionally no shelter or cuddy in the smaller hand-tonging boats. This is no doubt so because their owners are the children and grandchildren of watermen who in earlier years sailed in small, open crabbing skiffs.

The most unique working boat in the Chesapeake is the oyster dredger, pronounced "drudger" by the watermen. Because the law still permits limited or no dredging of oysters by powered vessels, the most distinctive of Chesapeake craft accordingly works under sail. Old documents and registrations officially refer to these boats as *bateaux*, their generic name. Now these craft, two-sail bateaux, are popularly known as skipjacks. The profile of a Chesapeake skipjack is shown in Figure 6-33.

Dredging for oysters by sail power is motivated by man-made laws for natural conservation, true, but also natural law and efficient practice support the use of sailing craft. It is a fact that an oyster boat, moved by sail, will haul a dredge over an oyster bed more gently and less destructively than will a powered dredge boat. The oysters gathered in this way may not taste better, but their shells will be less damaged and they will go to market fresh and "live." In addition, because the sailing craft cannot clean off an oyster bar so efficiently as can a powered craft, the crop will be conserved for the future. Unhappily the "greed" factor prevails and immediate quantity is more important with no regard to continued harvests next year.

Figure 6-34. A reefed oyster dredger working the beds. This is a working skipjack. (Everett C. Johnson)

In recent years, the conservation laws have been relaxed to allow two days per week when dredging can be assisted by the engine power of the "yawl" boats carried by each skipjack. This change in the rules is the result of an oyster blight and allows the oyster dredgers to receive a more steady profit from their rugged work. There is hardly any question that these sailing boats of the Chesapeake would not exist without the protection of state law. This artificial safeguard does account for the existence of a working fleet of sailing craft in a densely populated and highly industrialized region. The effectiveness of this type of preservation, coupled with the conservation of natural resources, could be a case for study. It has many facets to recommend it. It must be added in this 1994 revision that the con-servation of the Chesapeake's oyster resources has suffered over the last decade to some extent from the waterman's lobby in the State House. Also the oyster beds are nearly depleted, caused largely by an oyster blight, a larvae disease, as well as the increasing lack of restraint in the volume of oysters taken by oyster boats.

Not too long ago, there were other types of sailing craft in the oyster fleet, such as the finely modeled, round-bottom, two-masted bugeye and the round-bottom, gaff-headed oyster sloop. The skipjack in the late 1880s replaced these older boats because of her shoal V-bottom form and more economical construction. She is comparatively simple to build and operate. The dredging operation, as may be seen in Figures 6-34 and 6-35, is essentially the towing of a trian-

Figure 6-35. Two skipjacks dredging "arsters" in the Bay. (Robert de Gast)

gular steel frame with iron claws on the leading edge of a heavy iron-net
pocket over the oyster bed at four to five knots. This speed must be held
because a faster speed would merely bounce the dredge along over the high
spots of the bottom ineffectively, and a lower speed is less efficient in fill-
ing the dredge. Consequently, both jib and mainsail have three or four rows
of reef points, and most winter dredging is done with sails deeply reefed to
keep the dredge boat from going too fast.

The average skipjack is approximately 45 to 50 feet long with a beam of
16 or more feet. She has a shallow draft and carries a heavy centerboard. She
has a heavy, raked mast and the mainsail is hooped to it, except for the upper
portion between the headstay and the jibstay. The jib is on a partial club and
is self-tending. She has a substantial bowsprit above her clipper-type long
head set on a raked stem. All these boats, like their predecessors, the bugeyes,
oyster sloops, and pungys, carry decorated, painted, and carved headboards
and trail knees at the bow.

The bow form of today's skipjack is truly American in origin. It first
found favor in the Chesapeake on many of the fast Baltimore clippers. In the
early nineteenth century, it became a trademark on small, raked-mast
schooners and brigs sailing in the revenue service and the merchant trade to
the Caribbean, Mediterranean, and African coasts. It was later used on the
great Yankee clippers in a more restrained form and consequently is still
popularly referred to as a clipper bow. A similar bow form can be found on
some small craft in the Mediterranean today, but it is of a far older and different design. It is discussed in Chapter Four.

Skipjacks are characteristically fitted with taffrails and have stern davits
for their yawl boats. The rudder is generally hung outboard of the broad

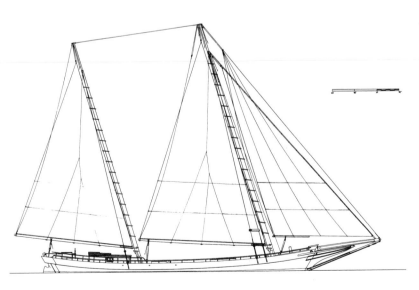

Figure 6-36. This is a typical outboard profile and sail plan (not ordinarily drafted) of a typical Chesapeake bugeye or three-sail bateau. The original bugeyes were built-up log bottoms. She has a nice sheerline and balance of rig. They were the swiftest working boats under sail on the Chesapeake. (Iver Franzen)

transom, but steering is through a linkage from the rudderhead to a steering wheel. These boats in their rig, construction, and overall appearance reflect the essential and inherent ruggedness of working sailing craft, but they have unfortunately diminished in number each year and new skipjacks are not being built. At this writing there are no more than ten still working, and they are marginally decreasing because of lack of oysters.

The skipjack is a unique American workboat. It is the only one under sail in the continental United States, or, as a recently cohesive fleet, in the Western world. As a sailing craft, its hull form is effective and practical, well adapted to its employment. It is stiff and able under sail; however, its flat, beamy hull of chine form leaves much to be desired when going to windward.

The skipjack, as a type, was developed only about one hundred years ago as a more economical fishing craft than the former sleeker, faster bugeye. The bugeye, with its two-masted ketch-type rig, is essentially a well-molded double-ender. She has a round-bottom hull framed and planked, or in the older boats built up, on a five-to-nine-log bottom in the manner of older and larger sailing vessels. The skipjack, with a V-bottom chine-form hull, is far more economical to build, and with her greater beam and flare of sides can carry more oysters. Skipjacks and bugeyes existed together for more than fifty years, but as replacements were made the owners naturally chose the skipjack. As a consequence there are no bugeyes in use today. The last bugeye is now a museum exhibit. The *Edna Lockwood*, Figure 6-37, exists and sails today in good health.

Figure 6-37. This is the only surviving bugeye in 1993. She is the handsome Edna Lockwood *owned by the Chesapeake Bay Maritime Museum. Built in 1889, she still has her nine-log bottom intact. She is nearly 55' in hull length, and 17'2" in beam. She was nominated to the National Register of Historic Places in 1986. It is very curious, but none of the museum's genealogical research has ever turned up any lady of 1889 or thereabouts named Edna Lockwood. (Charles Kepner, Chesapeake Bay Maritime Museum)*

The bugeye developed sometime after the Civil War to satisfy a growing demand for oysters. This demand, which from the early nineteenth century was quite brisk, was responsible for the early exploitation of oyster beds in the Chesapeake by smaller craft of the Chesapeake log-canoe type. The log canoes grew into the larger and similarly rigged brogans of approximately 25 to 30 feet. The brogan was actually a small bugeye. Both bugeyes and brogans were most efficient working craft under sail, but as commercial boats they inevitably and ultimately lost the race with economy of construction and engine-powered propulsion. The skipjack today is the slowly dying survivor of a once great industry.

The Chesapeake bugeye deserves a few more lines before leaving the Bay's boats. It is or was the "top of the line," as the term goes, and the ultimate development of the original log canoes. The Native American log canoes, of course, were here when the first European settlers arrived. That was in the early decades of the late seventeenth century. One of the first permanent English settlements, if not *the* first, was in Kent County on the upper eastern shore of what is now the "Shore" of Maryland. The establishment was on Kent Island, which is a rather large island in the upper Bay, separated from the main Delmarva Peninsula by only a narrow passage of water called Kent Narrows. As they came, the settlers here as well as to the south borrowed and exploited the basic design of the native dugout log, first combining two logs side by side, pinning them together by heavy iron rods, or earlier by wood "trunls" or wood cleats and/or mortises and tenons. At any rate, the purpose was enlargement, more capacity and ultimate seaworthiness. Washboards, the added plank on the sides, were for more freeboard and dryness. These canoes grew in size and shapes until the late eighteenth century and early nineteenth century. They were into the fishing industry—oysters, fish, and crabs. The two-log canoes by that time had sail and sailing shapes.

The requirements expanded as did the size of canoes into the nineteenth century. They had log bottoms of up to five logs, and the outboard logs were generally shaped in to above waterline. There were always an odd number of logs in order to provide a center log or "keel" log. This log often had the centerboard slot with a rim or bossing carved around it. The side planks were attached above the outboard logs and shaped to a sheerline established by eye and experience. Both stempost and sternpost were set in at the ends. The dimensions of such a fishing or oystering log boat would be nearly 35 feet length and 7 feet beam with five logs. The log racing canoes surviving and sailing in series competition today are direct descendants of these mid-nineteenth-century five-log canoes. The sailing rigs developed differently and the surviving rigs today are just two, one in Maryland with the standard three-sail, two-mast Tilghman rig, and the other in Virginia's eastern shore called the Pokomoke rig, which instead of the usual triangular jib on a bowsprit has a small spritsail on a forward-raking mast in the bow. By midcentury or before, it was only another short step to build a seven-log canoe, and the best existing example of such is an old crab dredger named *Old Point* surviving as an exhibit at the Chesapeake Maritime Museum. It is a motor-powered dredger built at Poquoson, Virginia, in 1909. Her dimensions are 52' length, 12'10" beam. Her hull is much like a small bugeye's, and so she may have begun her life, but there is no record.

The smaller rigged boats were generally one-masted but sometimes two, with seven logs sometimes but five other times. These were called brogans, and their lengths averaged between 40 and 45 feet. But the limits on log hulls had not been reached in the nineteenth century for sailing rigs until the nine-log hulls were built with a substantial two-masted, three-sail rig and a fully decked hull. The type of boat became known as a bugeye and no experts can agree on the origin of the name. I will not even

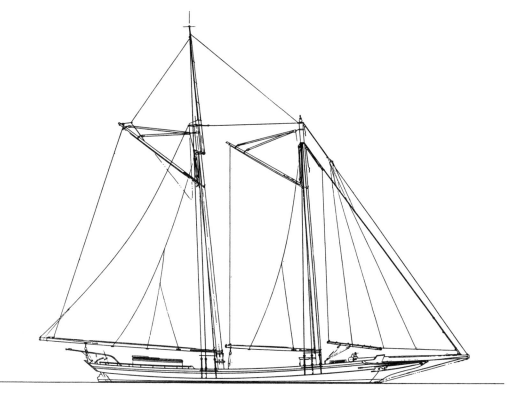

Figure 6-38. The larger typical working sail vessel was the Chesapeake schooner. The most significant and best-performing of these craft since the Baltimore clippers was the Chesapeake pungy schooner. The originals are all gone now—the last one destroyed by fire in Oxford, Maryland, in 1942. This profile is of a replica pungy built in 1986. Designed by the author, she is Lady Maryland *and is operated very successfully out of Baltimore as a "living classroom" for disadvantaged children.*

try—the stories go on and on. But a good well-built bugeye under sail is a handsome sight. There is just one left now in sailing condition. She is, as stated earlier, the *Edna Lockwood*, in good condition, having been restored in 1977, and belonging to the Chesapeake Bay Maritime Museum. Her photo under sail was supplied by the curatorial office there, to which we are grateful (Figure 6-37). *Lockwood* is close to 55 feet in length and 17 feet in beam. Her name, oddly enough, derives from her nine-log bottom. Apparently there was no person in the community named Edna Lockwood. She was built near Tilghman Island at Knapps Narrows in 1889 by John B. Harrison, an expert in log-built vessels. He also built the famous racing log canoes *Jay Dee* and *Flying Cloud*.

To briefly describe an oddity in her construction that relates to the same asymmetry in hull

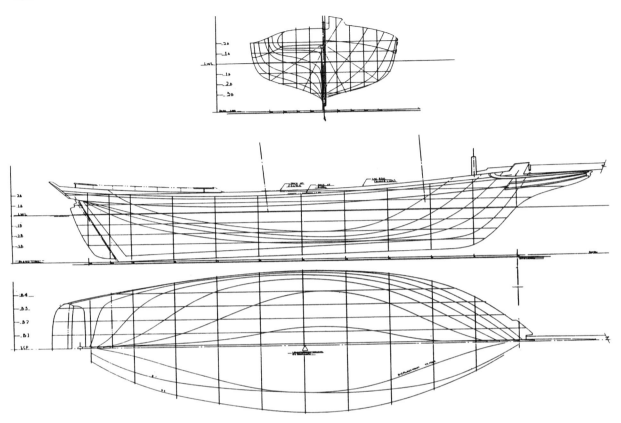

Figure 6-39. The lines plan of the Chesapeake pungy
Lady Maryland.

form as found in the Venetian gondola, the *Lock-wood* was built to sail closer to the wind on the port tack, and so is several inches beamier on the starboard side—it is shaped into the hull. This was because her owner, an oysterman, preferred to dredge on the port tack and to come about to starboard easier. She has the common double-ended hull with the so-called "patent stern" to lend her the broad platform aft and protect the rudderhead.

The *Edna Lockwood* is the last of a style of graceful, fast, and rugged American sailing workboats. Numbering into the hundreds, once, bugeyes were the great and efficient oyster boats that could sail the oysters to market faster than any other—even the pungys, which were larger, and the round-bottom sloops, which were heavier. The bugeyes were likely outnumbered by the oyster sloops, but both types prevailed for a while. When the market for oysters expanded together with better rail service to the West, there came a need for the industry to modernize: More dredge boats were needed but they had to be less costly to build and serviceable by big buy boats, which would purchase directly from the dredgers on the oyster beds. So then was invented the chine-bottom, simply built skipjack.

There is yet an even more noteworthy Chesapeake Bay vessel, larger, less numerous, but

Figure 6-40. The Lady Maryland *under construction in 1986 as the planking process began, at the Light Street Shipyard, Inner Harbor, Baltimore, where both Baltimore clippers* Pride of Baltimore *were built.*

more impressive than any of those previously described. It is the pungy schooner. Pungy schooners were not basically into the oyster or fisheries business. Their origins and heritage did not relate to log-bottom boats, even though the bugeyes toward the end of the nineteenth century were framed up from the keel in a conventional manner, like pungys. The pungy has an older heritage. We do not know exactly when they began or why they were so named, but it is fairly clear that their builders knew about fast schooners. It is likely that in the second or third decade of the nineteenth century when the demand for privateer schooners ended and the slave trade became restrictively unlawful and unappealing, the new commercial schooners on the Bay took on a new shape. They became sharper—as described in their certificate, "sharp-built"—with low freeboard, raked masts, and also a down rake to the keel. They were rather smaller editions of the famed privateer schooners out of Baltimore during the War of 1812. Their rigs were not as lofty, there were no square topsails, nor all the light-air kites. They were just very plain commercial schooners— poor cousins to the great topsail schooners that confounded British commerce between 1812 and 1815. It is most likely they were conceived

and built by the builders of the great privateer schooners and their descendants.

They began to be popular around 1835–40 and continued into the twentieth century—the last one expired in Oxford, Maryland, around 1940. Its name was *Wave*.

A fairly accurate replica pungy was built in Baltimore in 1986, named *Lady Maryland*. It has been sailing successfully every season since 1987 carrying and educating inner-city youth in the ways of sailing and the ecology of the Chesapeake. She is shown here under construction and in her design profiles (Figures 6-38, 6-39, and 6-40).

The Chesapeake pungy was a rather all-purpose freight hauler on the Bay. In my early life in and around Annapolis I remember seeing one or two. The summer season often brought them in, sometimes alternating with an ordinary schooner, selling fresh vegetables, especially watermelon, right from the boat. Their regular loadings for Baltimore's markets from the Eastern Shore farms was standard. In off-seasons they

Figure 6-41. Perhaps the smallest and most diversified of all the native watercraft of the Chesapeake Bay is the Chesapeake crabbing skiff. This is the outboard profile of a typical crabbing skiff of about 17-foot length. She was named Iree *and was carried aboard the Baltimore clipper* Pride of Baltimore *as the ship's boat and sank with her on her Atlantic passage from the Caribbean in 1986. Most of the skiffs were built with a beamy stern, two-planked sides, a shallow deadrise, and centerboard with a sprit rig or as this sail plan shows, a sliding gunter rig.*

Figure 6-42. A small Chesapeake racing log canoe, in 1975. The regattas of these boats are still carried on regularly every summer. They are fast with trained crews who provide live ballast on hiking boards run out on either side to windward. The boats are the last remnants of the original Chesapeake log canoes.

Figure 6-43. Beach repairs in the Bahamas, 1969. This out island has a heterogenous assortment of working sloops. The hull in the left foreground exhibits a typical underbody with some drag. (Skipper Publishing Co.)

hauled miscellaneous cargo. Their extra speed under sail made them especially attractive for perishable freight. But in poor times they were not too proud to haul lumber or cement. They are history now, and *Lady Maryland* has taken up the torch and sails with impressive speed with young people to teach the ways of the Chesapeake.

BOATS OF THE BAHAMAS AND THE CARIBBEAN

There is but one other purely indigenous sailing workboat type in the eastern coastal waters. In the Bahama Islands a distinctive, flourishing fleet of sloops and catboats still exists.

The Bahama sloop, like other sailing workboats, survives marginally. But there is in this environment an ideal combination of elements accounting for the natural survival of the sailing fleet. There is first the sailing breeze that blows consistently and reliably. Also, the waters are protected from the ocean by the natural ring of islands and the shallow Bahama banks. The islands are well off the paths of commerce, and their resources will support only a relatively small population. The population centers on the various islands are within comfortable sailing distances of each other.

Transportation is ideally by boat and preferably the leisurely sort provided by sail. The employment of the boats is in both fishing and light cargo

Figure 6-44. The classic lines of this Bahama sloop on a quay in Nassau reflect the colonial heritage of these boats. The square-tuck stern with a good flat run and sharp deadrise originated here in the eighteenth century. (Iver Franzen)

transport. The fishing is confined most profitably to gathering conchs and catching fish like groupers, and when these items are ready for market, they are generally transported to Nassau.

These sloops and catboats exist in an economic never-never land. They are a special case for survival, as are any sailing workboats surviving today. Here in the out islands, the true islanders are genuinely poor or else money is of far less importance to their natural way of life. Surrounded by rich, seasonal, off-island tourists and winter guests, whose money is also of some

Figure 6-45. This is an interesting square-tuck stern on a Bermuda sloop. It is a clear statement that its builder was not going to be completely bound by tradition. This is a Nassau sloop observed in 1993.(Iver Franzen)

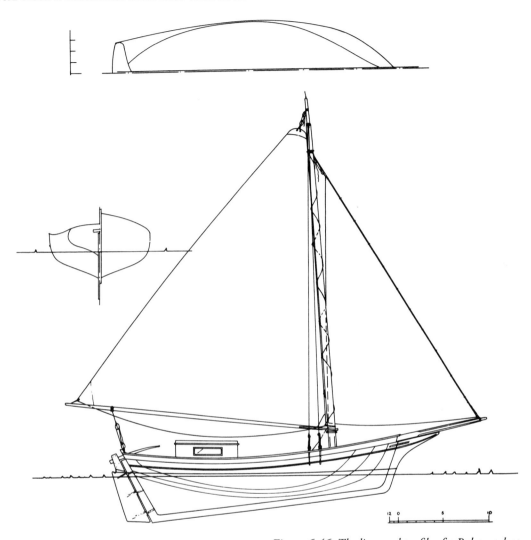

12   0   5   10

Figure 6-46. *The lines and profile of a Bahama sloop with a characteristic clipper stem form. Many of today's sloops have straight stems and no bowsprit. These craft are generally larger than and are related to the sharpshooter model, which carried only a mainsail on a mast stepped well forward.*

consequence to them, these boats continue to provision and supply transport. The Bahama sloops are a classic example of the parallel existence of a marginal economy and a commercially successful one.

Bahamian skippers, like all good seamen, try to pay attention to the maintenance of their boats. They are generally painted two or three times a year and are provided a new set of cotton sails every third year. The annual competition of the Out Island Regatta serves additionally to

Figure 6-47. Two sloops of the Bahamas in their best dress for the annual workboats regatta of the Out-Islands. Note the small club topsail, a nontraditional use of a main topsail with a jibheaded mainsail—a fairly common practice in the Bahamas. (Skipper Publishing Co.)

generate pride in and maintenance of these fine boats.

The Bahama sloops, like the now-obsolete Bermuda sloops, are descendants of the eighteenth-century English sloops and cutters. They still retain much of the original character, sometimes exaggerated in their configuration. However, the builders are presently not too restrained in their creativity (see Figure 6-45). The boats vary in size from 20 to as much as 40 feet in length. A typical lines form is shown in Figure 6-46. Construction is solid: heavy planks on sawn frames cut from native Caribbean mahoganylike wood, known as "horseflesh." The frames are often made from natural crooks. The hull is deep-heeled with a characteristic broad wineglass transom on which is hung an outboard rudder. The stem is usually straight and unadorned, but often is seen with a bowsprit over a clipper-profile stem knee.

It is worth emphasizing that the type of sail on the Bahama sloop is most distinctive. It is a living prototype of the earliest north European fore-and-aft sail. At the turn of the century, the Western world's sailing yachts carried the universally used gaff-rigged mainsails, generally with tall gaff topsails on additional spars above. Thus a large gaff-rigged racing sloop with her heavy gaff and a topsail on the topmast with two long clubs at its luff and foot had a very complex and top-heavy rig. There is little wonder that these Bahamian sailors in their poor economy set a simple triangular sail on a single but taller mast, which was gradually almost universally accepted after its introduction. Because of its similarity in shape to the sails of the Bermuda and Bahama sloops, it was often called the Bermudian rig and is still so referred to in England. Actually, the Bermudian rig, or, as it is more frequently referred to in the United States, the jibheaded or Marconi rig, is similar *only* in the triangular shape of its sail to that of a Bahama sloop and very approximately so at that. The Bahama sail is nearly as long on the boom as it is on the mast. It is loose-footed and fills with a very large draft, which gives it a baggy shape. The cloths of the sail are sewn parallel to the leech instead of "cross-cut" as are more conventional modern sails. The sail has a large headboard, or preferably a miniature gaff hoisted on a single halyard. This gaff is undoubtedly the surviving element of the original Dutch hooked gaff introduced in the early seventeenth century and adopted shortly after by the British in their American colonies. It could also be the reason for the vertical cloths in the sails. In any case, the sails appear consistently baggy and oversized.

South of the Bahamas in the Caribbean, the working boats almost defy clear indigenous classification. There are some exceptions, of course, such as the Belizean sloops, the Trinidad pirogues, the Martinique pirogues, the St. Kitts sailing lighters, and perhaps a characteristic trading sloop. However, the more important and overriding distinction of these vessels is what may be called their "Caribbean character."

The small, indigenous working boats of the Caribbean are still largely sailing craft, most frequently of the poorest and least adequately equipped sort. Their designs and rigs reflect the same ancestry as the boats of the Bahamas. They are not, however, as well preserved. They are most generally built by their owners on the banks of rivers or in the less active corners of small ports near the sources of an indifferent selection of boatbuilding timber. The hulls are old and patched even when they are first launched; their masts and spars are often selected from available trees with only the bark removed. These characteristics, as well as their basic inherited good form, identify them as indigenously Caribbean.

Some Caribbean craft do stand up better than others, reflecting a better economic life or consistent maintenance by their owners. This is true among the Leeward Islands and other islands where the tourist trade has lifted the economic status. Among these also are the sloops of Belize. These boats are 22 to 30 feet long with sturdy cedar-planked hulls on natural crook frames of Santa Maria (a type of hardwood similar in color to mahogany). The lines of a typical Belizean sloop are shown in Figure 6-48. While it is similar to the Bahama type, it is essentially shallower. The rig is also similar, except there is a stemhead balanced jibboom instead of a bowsprit. The boats are steered with a kind of yoke on the rudderhead in place of a tiller. (This yoke is taken along by the skipper whenever he leaves his boat.) The sloops are used for fishing, primarily, and some have live fish or bait wells cut and boxed into their bottom. When so fitted they are called "smacks" instead of sloops. There are perhaps thirty of these boats that continue to work in the waters off Belize.

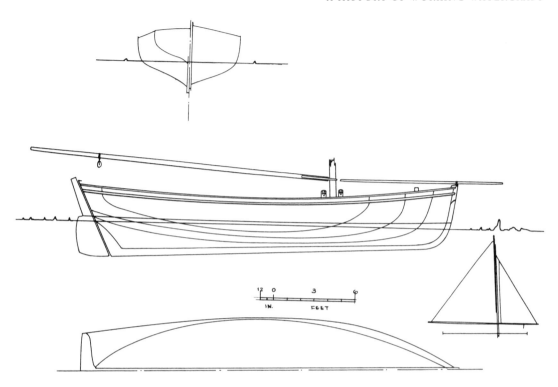

Figure 6-48. The hull lines of a typical Belizean sloop of Honduras show a nicely modeled, low-free-board hull. The sails are typical Caribbean sails except for the balanced jib with its club pivoted on the stemhead.

In the Virgin Islands there was until recently a kind of sailing workboat that was known as a St. Kitts or Nevis sailing lighter. These heavy, sloop-rigged craft had very full and deep-bodied hulls and were simply a larger, fuller version of the average interisland sloop, designed for cargo capacity consistent with their employment. They measured about 50 feet in length and nearly 20 feet in beam.

In the eastern Caribbean, in the area from Trinidad up through the Grenadines, the charac-ter of the boats shows a much greater variation. The boats reflect, more than other Caribbean boats, continental European influences rather than British. This is especially true of a small open boat, now powered, in Trinidad, called sim-ply a pirogue. Figure 6-49 shows the lines of one of these boats together with a section showing the typical structure. The boats vary between 20 and 24 feet in length and are often powered by out-board engines or low-horsepower inboard engines. They are generally fitted with a live fish well amidships. The construction of these craft is most interesting and relates closely to that of very early primitive craft. While they are essentially of lapstrake construction, the backbone is a hol-lowed log. This construction represents an evolu-tionary stage in boat development of primitive communities. It was originally used by the ancients when they first built planked-up hulls. It was also a stage in the development of Norse

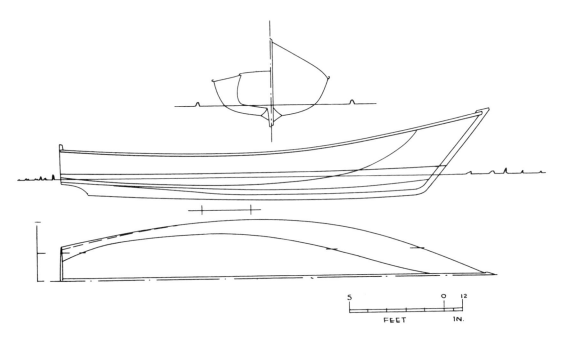

Figure 6-49. The lines of a Trinidad pirogue built with a dugout log in place of the keel. The rest of the hull is basically clinker-built.

boats after builders abandoned the most primitive frame-and-skin craft and built their early versions of lapstrake-planked hulls. It is a most logical process in the Caribbean because primitive log dugout boats have been used here for many centuries—no one knows exactly how long.

Pirogues are also still in use among the Antilles. They are particularly in evidence on Martinique and St. Lucia, where there are most colorful, trim-lined beach pirogues. These boats have a high freeboard with fine ends, and an unusual extended, sharp, bladelike bow skeg. The boats have as many as six to eight pairs of crooked kneelike frames to reinforce the sides and support the upper plank, which provides the necessary depth to the hull. These boats, together with the pirogues of Trinidad, are prime examples of true indigenous Carib craft, exhibiting, as they do, successive states of basic development.

Among the indigenous boat types of the world, there are a greater number of dugout-log craft than any other type of more sophisticated construction. There are more dugouts, also, that could be noted in the Caribbean region, and on the rivers of Central America, especially in Honduras. Also, others proliferate in South America, Africa, and many other regions of the world where there are people living in primitive or near-aboriginal environments. To avoid repetition, I have made no attempt to describe all of them. In Chapter One, however, where the structural development of boats is reviewed, the West African dugout-log fishing craft was selected as an existing prototype of all dugout boats.

The Caribbean sloop is most representative of the better small sailing craft of the area. It is a boat that has been described as a poor relative of the Bahama craft. Such an observation might

Figure 6-50. A St. Lucia canoe drawn up on shore, presenting a clear view of her unusual extended bladelike bow. (Reg. A. Calvert)

Figure 6-51. A St. Lucia canoe under a native spritsail rig. Her extended bow is just visible below the painted waterline. (Reg. A. Calvert)

seem unfair, but because of the proximity of these regions, comparisons are inevitable, and it is a broad generalization.

As the typical Caribbean sloop, one could do no better than to choose a boat frequently associated with the Leeward Islands of the Lesser Antilles. The hull lines and sail plan in Figures 6-52 and 6-53 illustrate a typical Antiguan sloop, which is 25 feet long, 8 feet in beam, and 4 feet in draft. Such boats are well built in St. Johns, Antigua, on plain but clean sailing lines showing a deep-heeled hull, broad transom stern, and low cutter-sloop rig. The rake of the transom and curve of the stempost may be slightly greater than the Bermuda model; otherwise the similar-

ity is close. The hull structure is framed in the same way from the same type of local woods, while the planking is pitch pine and must be imported. The builders, like most true indigenous boatbuilders, work by eye, experience, and simple traditional rules. For example, the depth of the hull is half of the extreme beam measured about one-third of the length from forward; the depth is taken from the deck edge to the top of the keel vertically. The rig is also constructed by rule of thumb, with both the boom and the mast height from deck to truck being the overall length on deck of the hull. These traditions after several generations have become almost superstitions and in many cases are inviolable. A recent

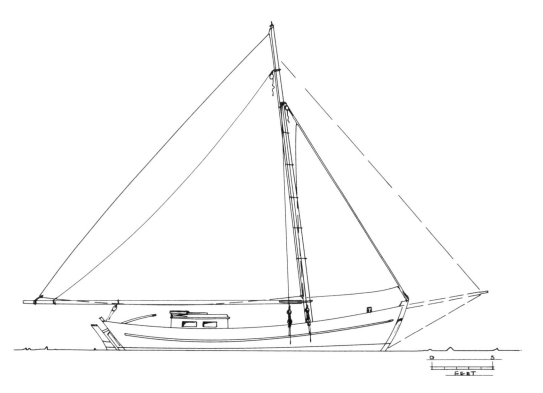

Figure 6-52. The profile of an Antilles fishing sloop. This boat, which was observed in Antigua, is well built of good materials, a practice that is to be commended in the Caribbean.

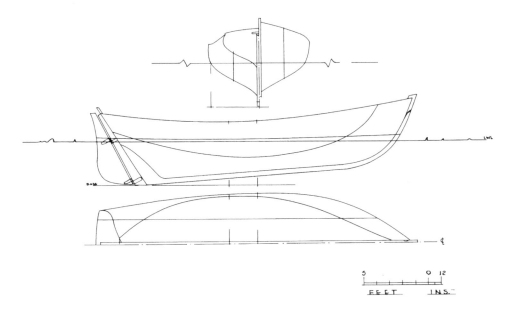

Figure 6-53. The hull lines of a typical, but not standard, Antilles fishing sloop.

effort has been made to teach the builders (who are in some respects receptive to ideas to improve their means and ways) how to build with steam-bent rather than sawn frames. Such a technique would allow faster construction and lighter, stronger hulls with more internal room. Unfortunately, this requires that builders be able to read plans in order to lay out the molds (see Chapter One). Many of the builders in this area have expressed the need for further help in training courses for shipwrights.

Regardless of their age and condition, which in some Caribbean regions is deplorable, Caribbean boats still provide needed lifelines among the native island population. They will for a long time to come. These boats, under sail, are impressive and handsome. Figure 6-54 shows an Antilles sloop moving out from an island in the Grenadines—a typical Caribbean sloop in a typical Caribbean setting.

One constant factor in the character of boats engaged in shrimp catching in the various regions of the world is their greatly varied designs. The designs vary largely because of the different techniques of harvesting the shellfish. In England until recently there were still some shrimp boats or "prawners" working under sail as small sloop-rigged boats. In Portugal the heavy little shrimp trawlers are operated from the beaches. But in the United States, where shrimping is one of the most profitable fisheries, the shrimp trawler has evolved in the last fifty years to become a most formidable boat. Originally developed in Florida, this indigenous design has spread throughout the Gulf Coast region even as far as Mexico, and the type can be identified in use along the east coast of South America.

The North American shrimper began as a variation of an improved powerboat based on the Greek sponge boat of the west coast of Florida. But unlike the sponge boat, which cannot be identified as an indigenous American craft because of its close relation to the Greek spongers of the Aegean, the Gulf shrimp trawler has become a true American boat common to the southern coast. After a relatively quick development period, it reached its present characteristic form and style about sixty-five years ago, though it was then a relatively small boat of 30 to 50 feet in length. This shrimper style is reminiscent of the old Greek boats in its full-bodied hull, sweeping sheerline, and fine entrance. It is otherwise purely a powerboat hull. It was perhaps the first type of powered fishing craft of any size to have the pilothouse located forward. This is possibly because the early boats had no power winches and the trawl was hauled by

Figure 6-54. A large working sloop of the Grenadines with double head-sails. A boat of this size and in such good condition is seldom found to the west of the Antilles and the southeastern portion of the Caribbean. (R.B. Mitchell)

*Figure 6-55. A traditional small Gulf Coast shrimper, now obsolete. (*National Fisherman*)*

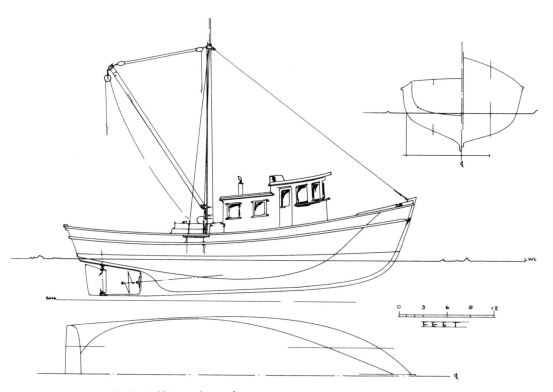

Figure 6-56. The old-style Gulf Coast shrimp boat shows its relationship to the old Greek spongers in its lively sheerline and full bow. The boat itself is a purely American development, and modern shrimpers with this basic configuration are built in lengths over 80 feet and are used in many fisheries of the Western Hemisphere.

hand. The modern crew want a maximum of free working deck area aft. So when most European and American trawlers were locating their deckhouses aft, these shrimp trawlers with forward deckhouses were unusual. The design has remained largely unchanged, and the present-day Gulf Coast shrimp boat continues to grow in both number and size. The lines form of a typical shrimper of the 1950s and 1960s appears in Figure 6-56. The most popular size is about 65 feet in length. Larger boats are built today, often to supply several fishing industries; built of steel, they are most sophisticated.

The old-type shrimper is heavily built of the best domestic woods and materials. The stem is of choice Appalachian white oak; the keel is a single unscarfed piece of Douglas fir; the planking from keel to waterline is of cypress and from waterline to deck is of Douglas fir. The frames are of steam-bent white oak, and the decks and transom are of yellow pine. The fastenings are of heavily galvanized steel bolts and boat nails.

The shrimp boat of today, while larger and more handsomely equipped than that of fifty years ago, hauls lighter trawls and so is rigged with twin outrigger booms in a double-rigged trawl arrangement. The boat's form provides a dry foredeck. This type of craft is becoming a modern fish-processing factory equipped with facilities for cleaning, flash-freezing, packaging, and delivering the shrimp to truckers ready to take them to market.

Old shrimpers were most rugged, capable smaller boats, and I can personally attest to their resistance to underwater damage. In the late 1940s a shipyard owner and I took a trip up the Chesapeake in a small retired Florida shrimper. We had four sailing craft in tow and were making a good seven knots when we struck an unmarked submerged foundation of an old lighthouse. The impact threw us off our feet and ripped off the propeller after moving the shaft out of its engine coupling. The boat was firmly aground on hard, jagged concrete, resting on her keel and bilge, and the tide was running out. The boat remained there without taking on any measurable amount of water. She remained until the

next high tide, when she was taken in tow. The damage proved to be confined to the propeller and the shaft, with only minor scuffing of the keel and bottom planking.

On the west coast of Mexico where the ancient Aztec culture flourished several hundred years before Columbus crossed the Atlantic, there is a type of fishing craft that is perhaps the last example of any working Native American boat. Aside from the large canoes of North American tribes described early in this chapter, there is no evidence of any watercraft of open-water ability before the arrival of the Europeans.

On the Pacific shores of Mexico, there are some dugout-log boats of interesting and sophisticated character undoubtedly related to the pre-Columbian cultures of this land. These boats today are abundant in the coastal regions beyond the Sierra Madre del Sur range. The hulls are adzed from single large logs of parota wood and may be as long as 28 to 30 feet, with a beam of 4 feet or slightly more. Their shapes vary slightly, but there is a consistency of form that distin-

Figure 6-57. Side view of an Acapulco dugout. Note the outboard bracket at the stern. (Capt. Richard Johns)

guishes these boats from the log canoes of river, jungle, and most tropical island regions. These boats are shaped with a graceful sheer curve that obviously adapts them to ocean beaches and surf launching. It is this characteristic more than any other that separates the canoes from other boats. The bow and stern forms of these Mexican boats also exhibit a utilitarian rake, which combined with the sheerline produces an overall pleasing functional seaboat shape. Figures 6-57 and 6-58 show fair examples of these boats along the Acapulco beaches. Like all dugout-log boats they must be protected from drying and cracking. A little water is always left in the bilges, and when the boats are hauled out they are covered with wetted canvas or, in the older manner, with palm fronds. Like most dugouts, these boats have long lives—generally more than fifty years and sometimes a century—and they are closely linked with the past. That these Mexican dugouts originated from the old Aztec culture is apparent in the reserved decorations and painted patterns on the hulls. These continuous abstract patterns encircling the hulls from end to end are the same patterns and styles used in the pictograms painted by the Mixtec people who lived in the Oaxaca valley about AD 1000. It is most likely that the Mixtecs fished from boats very much like today's—adzed out of parota wood, shaped with a graceful sheer and good freeboard to rise through a crest of surf, and painted with a bright edging border below the sheer with half a dozen of the brightest colors. Today these boats may work within sight of the glittering luxury hotels of Acapulco.

The working craft of the Pacific coast of the United States are nowadays highly systematized, mostly owned and operated by large and wealthy companies. The tuna-fishing industry now operates large, yachtlike, highly engineered and professionally designed vessels whose individual costs may

Figure 6-58. Bow view of an Acapulco dugout. The nets hung to dry are used for seining sardines off the beach. (Capt. Richard Johns)

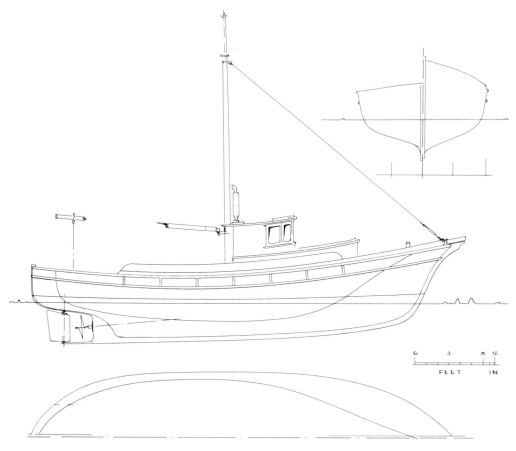

Figure 6-59. The hull configuration of a typical old-style Monterey boat. The original Mediterranean character and heritage are apparent in these basic lines.

exceed $2.5 million. These conditions are similar in the shrimping industry of the Atlantic and Gulf coasts. The systems approach is perhaps the most efficient way to supply the market demands for popular seafood products like tuna fish, but it has largely eliminated small owner-operated indigenous boats.

On the Pacific coast, however, a type of boat that has developed strong local character during the twentieth century can still be found. These boats are seen most frequently along the central California coast, but many may work farther north or south. They are known generally as the "Monterey boats." Their basic identifying features are a beamy round-bottom hull, a full double-ended form, and a type of clipper bow of Mediterranean origin. The bow form is generously flared and the stern is extended in a characteristic curving rake, giving the whole hull a pleasing and graceful line. Some more modern versions have a full, round stern eliminating the older double-ended form. Some still carry double rubwales along the side with vertical stiffeners, which make a very heavy and strong side structure reminiscent of the early fourteenth- and fifteenth-century caravel construction. These boats are heavily framed, sometimes with the older

type of sawn frames, more recently with heavy steamed frames. The entire form and structure strongly suggest a Latin European influence. This likeness is in no way the result of directly copying any Mediterranean craft, as were the earlier San Francisco "feluccas." It is, rather, the result of second- or third-generation traditional influences that have resulted in a healthy and thoroughly sea-capable form that embodies much Old World character. These contemporary Monterey boats can only be thought of as truly American types because they have no predecessors and have grown to suit their American environment and employment.

Monterey boats, as their name implies, are found in and around Monterey, California, and the San Francisco area. The simplified profile and plan of a typical Monterey boat are shown in Figure 6-59, and the individual variations in structure and details can readily be seen in Figure 6-60.

The dimensions of Monterey boats are represented by one example measuring 42 feet length, 12 feet beam, and 4½ feet draft. They are generally of about 12 to 13 tons full displacement and are frequently employed and rigged as trollers. As such, their tall outrigger poles give them a most rakish appearance.

A more modern, but still distinctive, boat type known as the Pacific "combination" fishing boat is engaged in the same independent employment in the West Coast fisheries as the Monterey boat. This type is characterized by trollers and purse seiners of similar and repetitive form, and can be found along much of the West Coast. The characteristics of the combination boat have not been entirely the result of the natural selective

Figure 6-61. A small West Coast dragger in 1965. (National Fisherman)

Figure 6-62. A double-ended combination boat from Port Angeles in 1965. This is a rugged seagoing fishing boat indigenous to the north Pacific coast of the United States.

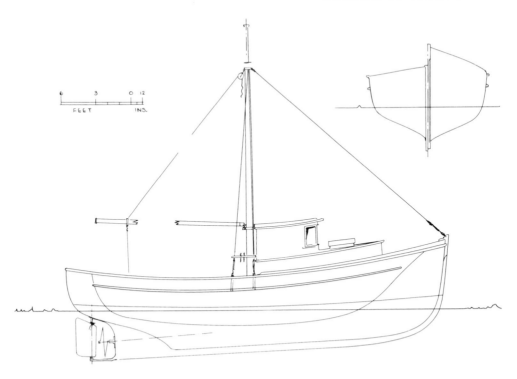

Figure 6-63. *The hull form of a small double-ended combination boat. This boat is most typical of the Puget Sound area in 1967.*

processes that normally produce other indigenous boats—professional designers have entered into the picture. This type, nevertheless, seems to be preferred by discriminating fishermen and is thus laying a strong claim to being a native American boat. This particular type has also acquired considerable popularity on the Pacific coast of South America.

There are many much larger combination boats, but Figure 6-63 shows the profile of a typical troller. This example is of a relatively small boat 36 feet long, 10½ feet in beam, and 4 feet in draft that has adopted the double-ended stern with the curved sternpost used on Monterey boats and the Maine sardine carrier, a feature

common in European boats. This, in conventional naval architectural terms, is normally called a canoe stern, but on fishing craft rather than yachts and larger vessels it seems more natural and less contrived. It is, thus, generally recognized as a trawler stern. (See Figure 6-62.)

The more common variation of this typical Pacific coast combination fishing boat may be seen in Figure 6-64. This example is 42½ feet long, 12 feet in beam, 5 feet in draft, and rigged as a seiner. The heavy construction and typical rounded-square tugboat-type stern is evident in this longitudinal section. This is a most practical and common stern used on West Coast boats that provides a broad and stable working platform. Figure 6-65 shows a boat of this type, but slightly larger with a slight variation in her deck profile and rail height.

In recent years welded steel construction has become increasingly popular. With welding skills and techniques improving, it is quite probable

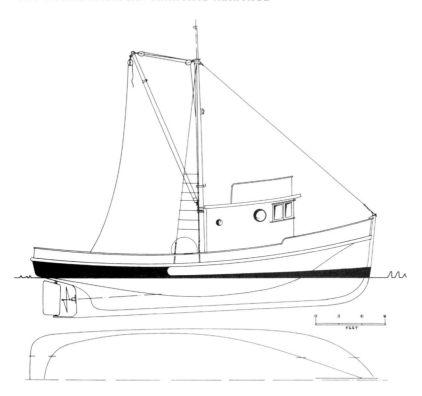

Figure 6-64. The profile of an old (1967) but serviceable combination boat of the northern California and Oregon coast. These boats engage in the sardine industry and are often rigged as seiners, but, as the name combination implies, they are easily adapted to other techniques of other fisheries.

that many more boats will be built this way. The external appearance of a steel boat in the same employment is very little different from that of a wooden boat.

I have been deliberately selective in describing American boats as well as those from other countries. Only healthy, functional types of working boats that exhibit strong regional characteristics have been discussed. It is interesting in retrospect to remark on the influence that many of these have had on the development of more universal boat designs. The character and style of the majority of the better pleasure craft have their origins in many of these regional types of working boats. Outstanding examples of this can be seen on both the East and West coasts of the United States.

The New England lobsterboats and the more beamy lapstrake New Jersey sea skiffs have contributed much to the configurations and styles of successful sportfishing boats as well as many power cruisers, pilot boats, and commercially designed tenders.

The V-bottom construction of the Chesapeake Bay craft has contributed heavily to the design of the smaller, more economical pleasure cruiser. V-section hull forms with their simplified construction and more easily molded shapes were not much used before the introduction of mechanical

propulsion. With increased speed and power demands, this characteristic shape became the base from which to develop the efficient chine hull with cleaner entrances, flatter runs, and broader sterns. Such hull forms provide optimum utilization of interior space. The demand for speed motivated this development. While they may reach high-speed planing operation more easily in protected water, these hull forms distinguish themselves in more rugged sea conditions as well with more modified deep V-sections, as do the modified round-bottom hulls mentioned previously.

The larger, heavier fishing craft of the Pacific coast, such as the trollers, seiners, and combination boats, have set a pattern for a healthy and popular type of yacht misnamed a "trawler" yacht. This sort of cruising yacht is being built in increasing numbers and represents a trend away from the high-sided, glassed-in, overpowered stock design cruisers of recent years. The term *trawler yacht*, however, is applied to almost any pleasure craft with a forward pilothouse and a stubby mast.

The tendency of naval architects, competent yacht designers, and discriminating builders and buyers to observe, refine, and promote the features of healthy working boats is most reassuring. This is not to imply or recommend that replication of working craft for pleasure use is the ultimate goal or even desirable. Direct conversions from working craft to pleasure craft are seldom successful. However, the recognition and employment of the basic features of seakindliness, simplicity, and performance where they are applicable are substantive evidence of the worth of indigenous working boats. There is always reassurance in working watercraft developed over centuries as successful and useful seagoing habitats and bases for humankind in an environment not dependable for hospitality.

INDEX